I Will Take
the Answer

I Will Take the Answer

Essays

ANDER MONSON

Graywolf Press

This publication is made possible, in part, by the voters of Minnesota through a
Minnesota State Arts Board Operating Support grant, thanks to a legislative ap-
propriation from the arts and cultural heritage fund. Significant support has also
been provided by Target, the McKnight Foundation, the Lannan Foundation,
the Amazon Literary Partnership, and other generous contributions from foun-
dations, corporations, and individuals. To these organizations and individuals we
offer our heartfelt thanks.

Published by Graywolf Press
250 Third Avenue North, Suite 600
Minneapolis, Minnesota 55401

www.graywolfpress.org

Published in the United States of America

ISBN 978-1-64445-011-6

2 4 6 8 9 7 5 3 1
First Graywolf Printing, 2020

Library of Congress Control Number: 2019933469

Cover design: Walter Green

For Megan and Athena

Songs to Learn and Sing

Talking Heads, "Take Me to the River"
Gilbert and Sullivan, "We Sail the Ocean Blue"
Woody Guthrie, "1913 Massacre"
Joy Division, "Atmosphere"
This Mortal Coil, "Song to the Siren"
Mexrrissey, "Every Day Is Like Sunday"
Dokken, "Into the Fire"
The Field, "Sequenced"
Concrete Blonde, "The Sky Is a Poisonous Garden"
Cinderella, "Don't Know What You Got Till It's Gone"
Gordon Lightfoot, "The Wreck of the Edmund Fitzgerald"
Belle and Sebastian, "Sweet Home Alabama"
Tom Waits, "Step Right Up"
White Town, "Your Woman"
Gene Autry, "Rudolph the Red-Nosed Reindeer"

Essays to Read and Enjoy

I Will Take
the Answer

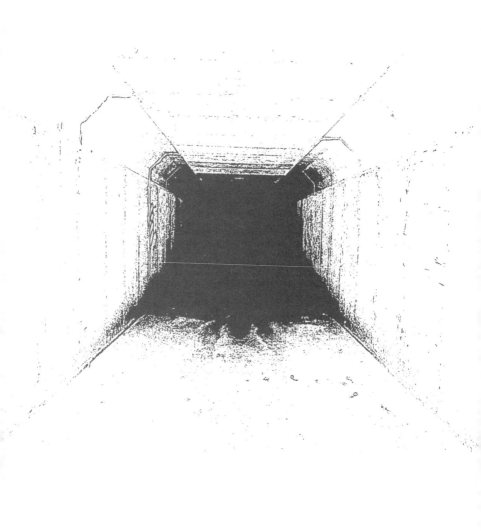

Five-Star Review of a Safeway

Let's begin this book with a hole, specifically a storm sewer that is designed to flush everything in its path from underneath Campbell Avenue into the Rillito River running along the northern boundary of Tucson, Arizona, where it will empty into the Santa Cruz. This space is manmade, concrete, and it's hard to forget that fact, that this is no cave, no hidden area carved out of the earth by a million years of limestone drip and white lives lived in silence, away from sunlight. A million people live in the Tucson metro area not counting the uncounted (not to say the uncountable), these white and not-so-white lives lived in sunlight or avoiding it. Of those million, maybe a couple of hundred have ever been more than a few feet inside this passage.

I'm not entirely sure why I was drawn to this here hole. It could be that I'm normed by having played thousands of hours of video games exploring passages that look an awful lot like this, or by coming from Upper Michigan's Copper Country where I'd regularly run across abandoned holes in the ground that I would fill with the requisite childhood wonder. It could also be that in this land of light I seek darkness and was just curious to see how far in it went and what secrets it keeps.

This particular storm sewer opens onto the long biking and running path called The Loop that runs underneath the Campbell bridge over the Rillito. From the path, it just looks like a tunnel, maybe six feet in diameter. Small bits of bric-a-brac are scattered by its opening where it enters the wash. The tunnel is dry. I don't know how long it is. There is no gate. Nothing locked or barred. Just a man-sized hole that retreats into darkness. It's not raining right now. I check in with my history of doing foolhardy things and head inside.

After a few minutes out of the sun, my eyes adjust, gradually, irritated, unused to so little contrast. The passage is almost tall enough for me to stand up straight in it. It is mostly clean.

By day Tucson is almost oppressively bright, but at night it is a dark city, so named because of laws forbidding excessive nighttime artificial light, so as not to disrupt the work of the astronomers at one of the many observatories outside or on the surrounding mountain ranges. And wanting to get away from civilization is in part why people come to Tucson and to the west, and having to be reminded that down the street there are five Bed Bath & Beyonds isn't all that helpful to this mythology. As such, night is dark once you get off the main roads. Few lights adorn residential streets. Even porch lights are often low wattage, if they are on at all.

Tucson is a city of roads and low buildings, a scrappy town that, despite itself, seems to believe it's still a Wild West cow town. Like most western cities, these days it sprawls wide and long and horizontal, a grid designed around the car, featuring Speedway Boulevard, the "ugliest street in America" according to *Life* magazine in 1970. To be fair, though it's still no beauty, Speedway has improved in the forty-something years since then, and has to be the only street in America that connects two mountain ranges, so that's something. What's underneath the street isn't something most of us think about a whole lot. That is, until something we took for granted fails: someone opens fire in a school or a crowded Safeway, like the one five miles away, or a sinkhole opens up.

A few years back and half a country away in Minneapolis, the I-35W bridge collapsed without warning, dumping cars one hundred and fifteen feet into the Mississippi River and killing thirteen people. I'd driven across the bridge many times on the way from Iowa, or Alabama, or Michigan, or Arizona, since my wife's family lived for many years in a northwestern suburb. Like you, I always take a bridge for granted: that it will support my weight, deliver me across the river to the other side without thought. The whole point of the interstate system is that it elides geographical features and provides a seamless, stop-free driving experience: without it we could be driving over moraine or over stamp sand, swampland, or tundra. Only sometimes when we are out over a long span of bridge surrounded by water and air do we pay attention, glance below, pick up a little vertigo, marvel at how far we are above the earth. It's one of many forms of contemporary magic that we ignore. I imagine being on that bridge that day as it buckled and collapsed, and, if I survived, wondering what else in my life I hadn't thought enough about.

My wife was in Minnesota when it collapsed, so the event felt even more alive to me. When I heard about it I called, as we do upon hearing of modern tragedies, to see if she was okay. It was possible, I knew, that she might have been on it. She was not; she and Sylvia, her mother, had driven a different route earlier that day, down to St. Charles, Minnesota, and were helping her grandmother move out of her longtime home, her husband having died the year before.

Cleaning out a house offers perspective on idiosyncrasies that have long gone hidden. (Why did she have ten one-gallon tubs of cake frosting, for instance, all having expired a decade ago, in the deep freeze? What kind of life do you have to buy frosting in gallon tubs?) Suddenly what you stashed away and forgot in darkness, or in the memory of the freezer half a life ago is exhumed, brought out to the light, questioned, analyzed as if by archaeologists or forensic anthropologists. Best not to argue about it. You live in a house and then it's gone. Your husband dies and your life goes seismic, shifts away. The bridge you drove across a thousand thoughtless times suddenly devolves into air.

Until he recently retired, my father-in-law was a civil engineer. He'd spent a lifetime thinking about structures so that the rest of us didn't have to. Like most experts in a subject, Steve was paid to know a lot about a little. Life offers us enough things to think about, more every year, our worries expanding outward toward the mountains like those western cities and their suburban rings. So having to think about building codes or maintenance schedules or concrete mixes and rebar configurations and geometries and calculations of physical stresses underlying anything gets exhausting very quickly. It's not possible to do, to keep all that in your head, for very long, unless that's all you think about, in which case we call that either pathology or a job.

His was a job. He mostly worked on water towers. It's a small fiefdom. I don't think of water towers except on the rare occasions when I'd wanted to climb one with a girl, or spray-paint my name and something awesome on the side of one, or when a high school friend's father hanged himself off the side of a water tower in the town where I grew up, sparking speculation. Then I think about it, choosing a public place for one's last breath and drop and struggle, what might that mean? Of course there were rumors, but it's hard to know for sure. I think about the structures of the family, its set of received gestures (here is what a father means, what a husband means), and then the unknowable secrets that exist underneath what we all thought of as something stable, impenetrable, and how quickly that unit can give way into something else if stressed enough. Steve told this story about getting called out to estimate a job: turns out a middle-aged guy crashed his car into the side of a water tower, trying to commit suicide . . . unwisely, in a Volvo, so he survived.

Consider the image of Jared Lee Loughner, the guy who shot my congresswoman Gabrielle Giffords and eighteen other people on a January day in that five-mile-away Safeway: he stares into the camera, his mouth somewhere between a smile and a grimace, his head shaved, and one eye just slightly in shadow. The eyes are the thing most of us remember, how he seems so *sure*. Sure of *what* is another question. The *New York Post*'s headline ("MAD EYES OF A KILLER: Leering Gunman in Ariz. Court" and caption "Evil emanates from the eyes of Jared Lee Loughner") gets right to it. Those eyes are why the mug shot kept getting circulated, sampled, clicked on, looked at: we are both horrified and compelled not just to look at the face of the murderer but to have him looking back at us, as if he knows or is tuned in to something we can't imagine. Like many psychotics, he was utterly convinced of the rightness of his usually incomprehensible ideas and observations. To cite two examples of his beliefs and commitment to them, he'd argued forcefully with his math instructor at Pima Community College about whether the number 6 could be the number 18 instead, and he had previously confronted Giffords during her visit to his high school and asked her, "If words could not be understood, then what does government mean?" (Though this statement doesn't quite resolve—or maybe *because* it doesn't easily resolve—I still think about it more than seven years later as we find ourselves yet again without an operating government.)

Loughner considered himself more wakeful, more in tune with the many subsurface resonances of the world, than the rest of us, than his classmates, his professors, his fellow Americans, nineteen of whom he subsequently shot. And though it's speculating to make this much of it, he certainly punctured the thin veneer of civil or intelligent discourse we felt we had going in this country, and that was in 2011, before our even more recent decline into wherever this essay finds you in the time line of our disintegrating political discourse. That is in part what acts of violence do, and where they get their power: they perforate our speech in ways beyond our capacity for grammar in the short term, where it feels like there's nothing we can say about these wounds that feels sufficient.

Acts of violence punctuate the sentences of our lives and divvy them up into before and after whatever feels most alive to you by proximity or awfulness, whether you think of your life as pre-9/11 or post-Columbine, where you were when you heard about Giffords, the *Challenger* explosion, the Boston Marathon bombing, Sandy Hook, Pulse, Vegas, before our childhood friend's murder and just after.

This essay is written on the occasion of the most recent American mass shooting you can think of. The questions I have about violence and darkness and structures and knowing largely remain the same, as they did in 2012, after the Giffords shooting, and without our having made much progress on them. I will hope to be proved wrong. In the meantime, because I don't even know what I can say about the mass shooting of grade school kids, I won't even try. I'll try to stick to the thing that most recently and closely wounded me.

A mile deep in the tunnel I freak out for a second—it's dark and close and smells vaguely of human refuse—and have to calm myself back down. Most of the time, this way is safe to traverse. But the monsoon, southern Arizona's strange, humid fifth season, just began, which means the possibility of sudden and powerful thunderstorms flooding Tucson's few storm sewers with thousands of cubic feet per second of runoff. I need to pay attention; I must be careful in the timing of my exploration. The good news is that there's no weather predicted. The bad news is that down here it's hard to feel any connection whatsoever to the outdoor world and its predictions, its petty concerns, and rainfall from a long way away can quickly flood the sewers.

Like living in Upper Michigan with its powerful and sudden blizzards, living in Tucson is a reminder of our precariousness. My beloved vintage Mondale-Ferraro election bumper sticker faded in the sun in less than a year. The wrong paint can fade in days. Most every desert plant harbors barbs or painful spines. Animals are poisonous or ornery. (A sign at one of the state parks begs: "Do not touch or taunt a rattlesnake. It is not a test of your strength or speed or skill." That's wrong: trying to pick up a rattlesnake is in fact a test, if an unwise one, but the teenage boys who receive ninety-five percent of snake bites, typically to the hands and face, need no encouragement.) Our gun laws are famously lax; no permit is required to carry, and you can find guns readily. I drive by half a dozen firing ranges or gun shops every day on my way to and from my job, not that this fact is unusual in much of America.

For long stretches of time this world appears not to change whatsoever, and then in an hour—in the monsoon season especially, July and August each year—it is submerged, deluged, swamped, many of the city's roads impassable. Every year the news runs stories of hikers trapped in box or slot canyons, flooded and killed. We all *tut tut tut* and mock the tourists. So being flooded in the storm sewer would be a tourist move, a really dumb way to die, even for me. I have a history of not thinking things through. I want not to be a tourist, even when I am one.

On the first day of my nonfiction workshops at the University of Arizona I ask my students to tell us about something dramatic that happened to them in the last year. We're going around in a circle sharing stories, when Lynda S. tells us that before she transferred here, she'd had a class with Jared Loughner at Pima Community College. She might be writing about it, she tells us. Trigger warning, she says. *Ha ha.* The laughter is less than comfortable. Before going back to school, she'd worked as a psychiatric nurse, she tells us, and when she saw him she could see the signs immediately. She told the professor, then the administration at the college that they had a problem. This guy was not safe, she said. I know, she said, he's nuts. Clinically. *Nuts* is the word. He belongs in an institution. But there's nothing they could do, they told her: he has every right to be in that class until he does something. So, she told us, she started sitting as close as she could to the door. She had her eye on it constantly. And when she heard about the shooting on the news, she thought to herself: *Oh God.*

The idea of the dungeon—which is to say the labyrinth—which is to say the mine—which is to say the sentence and the clicking tunneling we do online, burrowing from link to link to link, spectacle to spectacle—has occupied a significant chunk of my brainspace as of late, and not just because I'm literally down here traversing a tunnel. I haven't been this far underneath the surface of anything since I was last in one of the many mine shafts that punctuate Michigan's Upper Peninsula with danger and reminders of history, of the boom days of iron ore and copper that ended after World War II. It's a beautiful place when you're not down in a hole and it's not buried in snow. Actually it's a beautiful place when it is. But some of us just can't bear it.

The landscape up in Michigan has reclaimed much. Mine openings are overgrown and sometimes unmarked. Shafts collapse. Sinkholes appear. Warehouse windows smashed by teens reveal remnants of the economic history of the Copper Country, as it's called, and plants have grown through wall chinks, and are starting to split the walls in two. Animals nest and excrete in the corners and in the rafters. All as if to say the world is ours for only a moment, and only in our dreams.

In my dreams I explore tunnels, like those screensavers on older PCs that wander aimlessly through one corridor and then another. I don't know if my dreams are tunnels, or if they're dungeons, and if so, what's down there, or if it's just a convenient metaphor, or if what I do when I read a sentence is I basically go down a tunnel, so the brain has trained itself to keep moving forward into darkness following a passage even when my consciousness has relaxed its grip. Maybe it's that, as the Tohono O'odham suggest, the labyrinth is the life: the man in the maze is a powerful symbol of our progression through our lives.

In and just outside Tucson, too, there are ruins, abandoned mines, tunnels forgotten or ignored. Their presence reminds me of the ways the brain layers thought and memory atop thought and memory like a fattening, expanding, constantly reconfiguring cake: all those old electricities are still operating underneath the new if we can just peel the present back, see the pattern properly, if we can know that we are not just now, but that we are yesterday, and last week, and when we were eight and wanted to kiss that girl in the purple dress as the Marine Corps band played brass versions of Van Halen's "Jump" and Yes's "Owner of a Lonely Heart," which we'd only recognize as rock songs years later when we heard them on the radio. We contain our histories. We're built on them and of them: What are we if we're not our histories?

Flash-forward: half a world away in Athens, Greece, I walk the ruins of the Acropolis, the Parthenon, Hadrian's Gate, and other postcard places with a million other tourists who all resent the other tourists. The experience of being in Athens is one of constant reconstruction and consciousness of ruin. Our hotel is entered from within a busy fruit market about a mile from Syntagma Square where the demonstrations and the tear gas are happening as we walk up the pathway to the Acropolis, water bottles in hand. Even wandering the roads outside of Kokkini

Hani on the island of Crete a few days later, I run across a cordoned-off area that holds an ongoing excavation of one ruin or another with a plaque attached. It's locked down, not yet open for touring.

There are plenty of other, more contemporary ruins too: the old bar with the sunken patio and the overgrown tiki-themed veranda, probably from the 1970s. Dozens of half-erected concrete building skeletons, products of the housing boom and subsequent economic bust, remind me strongly of Arizona's own half-finished townhome graveyards, now collecting graffiti and methamphetamines. Perhaps, I think, this living in constant ruin and reconstruction is the norm, not the shiny sense of the new (our stainless steel! our glass and girders! our exclamation points! our press releases!) that suffuses American life. As a culture, after all, we're not so good at the past, though we are—or used to be anyway—outstanding at the future.

I'm jumping around, I know. It's almost as if I can't quite bear to look at this memory.

In Houghton, Michigan, home to Michigan Technological University (originally the Michigan College of Mines, though that history's grown distant since the college closed its mining engineering major), the whole industry of the region was built on mines, their networks of tunnels and excavations and disposal. Huge swaths of land along the Portage Canal are built on stamp sand, blackened mounds of perhaps toxic mine tailings, the material left after metal was extracted from the earth.

In the 1990s the Isle Royale Sands, a fifteen-square-mile wasteland of stamp sand, was made into a new and desirable development. Lots were sold. New lakeside homes were built to order. Canals were dredged to create more waterfront. Tons on tons of topsoil were brought in with enthusiasm and dreams of the future lives of those who'd live there. They dug great holes in the stamp sand and filled them in with that topsoil in order to plant trees that would only get to be so big before they'd run out of soil and their roots would terminate in the layers of mine tailings. Sod and marketing were laid a couple of inches deep, just enough to paper over everything. Sand was carted in to create the illusion of a sandy beach, the semblance of a semisuburban life for families along the waterfront. Chinese-made swing sets were erected, their swings creak-

ing in the summer breeze. Families were photographed frolicking on the
beach. Once-in-a-lifetime opportunities were available with little to no
money down with quantities of excess exclamation points that are free
to use because this type, like the lovely computer models of AutoCADded
future homes, is digital!

My parents bought a lot. They believed in it. They planned on building a house down there, among the other pretty properties. A couple of
years passed. My brother and I visited it. We were not impressed. This
did not seem to be a real place. My folks didn't build. They sold the lot.
I don't know why they sold the lot. (I don't know why they bought the lot
in the first place, though they do have a thing about buying property; I
suspect it's about the dreams that come with buying property, who they
might become in a different house, in a different place, in a different
life, or maybe they, like all of us, are running from something and find
it wise to look forward.) They bought another lot with an actual beach
on Lake Superior, not the simulated beach on the simulated lake. The
new cabin is about forty miles away in Gay, Michigan, home of the Gay
Fire Department, the Gay Bar (sample T-shirt slogan: "I Went Straight
at the Gay Bar"), the Fourth of July Gay Parade, and not a whole lot
else aside from the ruins of the Mohawk Mining Company's stamp mill.
The only obvious thing there to mark this site of once-vital industry is
the 265-foot ruin of a smokestack, an exhausted exclamation point that
juts into the sky like an obelisk, an upthrust fist, or an artillery cannon.
It can be seen from thirty miles away.

My eyes adjust to the darkness after the first turn, and everything becomes a little more visible. It's like the astronomer's technique of averted
vision: If you want to see a bright thing clearly, don't look at it directly.
Look just off to the side and let your peripheral vision do the work.

It's another 120 meters to the second junction, signaled by the loud
ring of occasional traffic clattering a manhole cover. I can stand up here
if I don't mind being separated from speeding traffic by just a piece of
metal. Standing is a relief. I'm a little bit too tall for the passage and I
keep bloodying my head, even wearing a hat conveniently already the
color of blood. The perspective from underneath reminds me of how
loud and fast traffic is.

Light filters down from the manhole gaps and the outlets to smaller
storm drains on either side. Here I find an open house sign from a local

real estate company that had been jammed down the sewer drain, perhaps in frustration. The city below the city is not for sale, even if the wall graffitiers stake their claims on top of one another. As cars pass above, dust and grit floats down, lovely in the sudden influx of light. The sound of my sneakers on the curved concrete is a slight and repeating sproinging. The storm sewer itself is quite clean, so much so that *sewer* feels like a misnomer, since there's no sewage coming through here. All that is processed through another station on Roger Road, about six miles away, and the resulting water is fed into the nearby Santa Cruz, a river that is mostly dry each year thanks to development and overuse, the increasingly dire levels of the aquifer as we, in our western way, don't think these things entirely through. Here in Tucson we console ourselves that we're better than Phoenix, where the lawns are ever present and inexpensive, the dream of the grassy oasis come alive in the desert, and you can tube down the Salt River in the summer, beers in hand, contemplating the fantasia of an unlimited ribbon of water.

I am increasingly aware that the space I am in is not meant for human occupation, though humans have left their marks all over it, mostly via occasional trash and the graffiti that adorns the walls in fragments. There is a great miscellany of spray-paint markings, their meanings only partly apparent and partly washed away by water or erased by other agents, or perhaps the inscriptions were intentionally obscure, or never finished at all.

Someone tagged the back wall on my property, and my neighbor tells me I need to get it taken care of, that it signifies gang activity. (I suspect it signifies bored suburban teens.) He says there's a number I should call to get it buffed away. The city does it free as part of its graffiti abatement program. I call. It takes a week and it is gone. Sometimes erasure's easy. The graffiti on the back wall of my yard meant something, and then it's gone. Down here in the storm sewer, though, the graffiti feels personal, since this thoroughfare is much more rarely traveled, and so it's like one person speaking to another, both of us celebrating in our way the act of being in a forbidden space.

I play video games more than I like to admit. I'm still working out why this is exactly, whether I'm looking for escape or elaborate, violent problems to solve, or whether I just like role-playing dark elf cheerleaders that I can dress up or undress as I like, or whether it's something relating to my childhood. Luckily it's impossible for me to be too sure. I don't think I'd like to know the answer, but I can't stop asking the question into the nighttime star fields that stretch beyond the game mountains. They're spectacularly rendered in high definition: the occasional rustle of wind through a creosote bush, the light haze from the city, and the motion of the skies with the changing months and seasons. These details are real enough that I begin to believe the rendered landscapes are real. Wait, maybe they are real. Wait, what are we talking about?

If I spend enough time playing video games, I start to dream in game. This also happens when I play a lot of chess, and when I play a lot of disc golf too. I'm finding that if I spend enough time underneath the city, I begin to forget the city and the tunnels populate my dreams. This is all there is, the skittering sound of a paper wrapper caught in a sudden gust and echo. Which is the life, and which the dream?

In the days following the Giffords shooting I am embarrassed to say I found quite a bit of comfort and surety in front of my television, not just watching the unfolding shock of coverage, which I did with my wife for much of the day of the shooting, but playing first-person shooter games. Some of us find comfort in Brian Williams, or in Nancy Grace, or in Anderson Cooper, Jon Stewart, Glenn Beck, Sarah Palin, name your anchor, name your avatar, name your open muppet mouth.

Me, I found my comfort and the answer to my recurring dreams roaming the virtual ruins of postapocalyptic Washington, DC, and shooting mutants in the head with a hunting rifle, or, if I missed, a combat shotgun with a twelve-shell clip similar to a gun I remember seeing in an issue of the *Shotgun News* when I was a teenager, the Striker-12 (also known, the internet tells me, as the Armsel Striker, the Sentinel Striker-12, the Protecta, Protecta Bulldog, and Cobray/SWD Street Sweeper), which had a tommy gun–style wheel of a clip and looked incredibly powerful, cartoonishly masculine, just past hard-core manly and approaching crazy. My friend Chris had a subscription to the *Shotgun News*, and we pored over the classified ads in the back: people in search of bounty hunters or hired killers and so on. It felt real, not like the fantasies of *Soldier of Fortune* or the ninja magazines another friend studied obsessively as he practiced his silent walk and threw throwing stars at the treehouse his father built. Chris had a lot of weapons, even before his sister was murdered, and after that his collection only increased. In Upper Michigan many of us had a lot of weapons. *Have* a lot of weapons. The inertia of weapons is immense: once you have them you don't get rid of them. It's the same in Arizona. You probably know about that. Sadly, this is one of the things Arizona is famous for. Do we feel safer with our stories erased? Do we feel more comfortable with our hands on our guns? Some of us clearly do. A gun feels solid in the hands, something to hold on to, a physical response to fear, a dream of agency, when someone has been in our house in the hours we were gone.

A friend relates this story: When his brother had his home in Tennessee broken into some years ago, the cops came, said, Well, to be honest, there's not a lot we can do. Why don't you just take care of it? So here's what you do: You get some huge boxes from Best Buy or Circuit City or wherever. Just the boxes. You leave them out by the curb. You buy a gun. You move the car around the block. You sit inside, lights out, quiet, and wait for them to come back. When they break in, you solve your own problem and call us afterward.

After someone broke into my house a couple of years ago, I began to understand that desire.

Some days this world feels only barely under control, except in our abilities to maximally explore our responses to our worst fears about what might just possibly happen. But in digital wildness as in video games, a chaos framed by the outline of the television screen, in shooting, in creeping, in tossing grenades and head shots, in leveling up and applying Stimpaks when shot or gnawed or chopped myself, in first-person shooter Xbox 360 games I find an easy and reliable comfort, a thoughtless, sort of zen space, though thinking that, I also think I probably misunderstand zen.

I know the irony is disturbing: head shot, simulated head shot, weapon, simulated weapons, reload, rewatch, rewatch myself reload; the unreality of reality, the reality of unreality: the visual is not all that far from the news footage. There's never a safety to click off in games, because that's not fun. The controller has a weight, but not like a gun. It's no surprise that after an event like a mass shooting we start to question what we thought we knew before: that the Safeway where I once heard a disturbingly catchy Muzak version of Joy Division's "Love Will Tear Us Apart" is a safe way to anywhere. That we are safe anywhere, even in a Safeway. That television news sometimes seems to get it right: the world is filled with danger, adorned with thousands of exclamation points, like a Christmas tree. That the well-built, solid world we thought we had isn't so stable.

That everything can be a threat. That if we can find the right angle, the correct psychological explanation for violence, or the proper YouTube clip, maybe we can make it all make sense. In games it makes a kind of sense, until we watch ourselves doing what we're doing, and then it suddenly doesn't at all. In games we are typically the actor, the agent, the perpetrator. We're good guy, bad guy, but we are we. We get shot, but we resume; we repair our armor; we don't feel shock or pain; we reload the game. From the math that allows us to appear to stand on digital ground we rise anew, reload again, take a different tactic, shoot faster, juke left and do a little dance, maybe teabag an opponent when they're down and chortle adolescently.

The question of whether the prevalence of guns might have something to do with mass shootings is hard to avoid. The statistics bear it out. It's not a complicated logic. Shortly after the Safeway shooting a bill was introduced into the House of Representatives by Democratic representative from New York Carolyn McCarthy (whose husband and son were victims of gun violence in 1993), proposing a ban on extended clips like the one Jared Lee Loughner used—the one that allowed him to reel off so many shots before reloading (at which point he was tackled by senior citizens). Other pro-gun laws were then proposed in Arizona, including one allowing anyone to bring guns onto campus, students, teachers, administrative staff, which threatens to change the tone of my nonfiction workshop. This law will not pass. Not this time anyhow.

The conversation about the defensive usefulness of guns—whether someone had had a gun and would have been able to shoot Loughner down, to stop the carnage—is beside the point. Several people present in fact *did* have guns, and in the chaos, they reported later, they weren't sure what was happening, and so couldn't and didn't use them.

I understand, though, where that idea comes from: having a gun sure makes you *feel* more capable. Sometimes you even *are* more capable. You hold a lot of power in that holster or that hand.

It changes you, the feeling that you can be in control: it's like a drug. It's like my SUV that I never take off-road, but better. That controlling feeling is among the most powerful feelings you can have—and one of the rarest. How often do you feel like you're in control of your body and your life? How much would you give or what would you do to get there?

Besides, everyone knows what a gun means, that if you see one in the first act it better go off by the third.

I take that pointless what-if conversation for what it is: a desire to assert control. It's a desire for do-over, for save-game replay, part of the appeal of the games we play.

That's what we did of course, replayed the shooting in our heads, even after the screens stopped replaying it, after the *New York Times* demoted it from the front page, which took a while. After a couple of days we were exhausted here in Tucson, used to our feeling of living on camera, used to film crews who might ambush us walking to work or whatever with questions about what it felt like to live here (making clear to us that *here* wasn't there, wherever the there was that these news crews were reporting from and back to); we became used to being the center of attention for the nation for all the wrong reasons. We got tired of responding to well-meaning messages from friends and family members wanting to be reassured we were okay. Were we okay? Did we know anyone who was there? What the fuck is happening down there where they filmed most of those shoot-'em-up Western films our parents and their parents watched? Is there really no relationship between Safeway and *Rio Bravo*?

That action replays in our hearts, in our dreams, like chess, like the simulations we run of our worst moments as we sleep, the virtual ways in which we're ruined or we've ruined something. You know it does. It always has, deep in the electric clouds of brain, as fantasy, as terror, as some subtle process running at an extremely low level, well beyond the boundaries of consciousness. These ruins that haunt us—that we haunt—change the calculus of living. I bet you'd do almost anything to stop it.

It's good that it's hard to pay attention to anything for long. Otherwise how could we bear it? I forget to keep my head bowed in the tunnel and so I ding it on the concrete ceiling, and I'm surprised when I put my hand to the site of pain and see the blood. I forget just how thin the skin is on the head, how much it bleeds, how long it takes to stop. I cringe and keep it down now, keep moving slowly. Under here, I get that ruined-ruin pleasure. It's like where I attended college, postindustrial Galesburg, Illinois, a town that had already passed its sell-by date as the Maytag plant closed down, and I'd spend nights wandering lonely through the manufacturing ruins that had not yet been overgrown. Not just the postboom cities of the iron belt and the gaping holes in the roofs of buildings easily seen from I-75 in Detroit as I drove by in my dad's 1987 Aerostar trying not to ruin the suspension on one of the hundreds of potholes swiss-cheesing the interstate (a video game sort of challenge, I thought then, even as I drove). Not the fucking *tarps* they covered the ruins of the city with in the weeks leading up to the staging of the Super Bowl in 2006, figuring nobody would be able to tell the difference.

Here's what I want to know: If no one can tell the difference, is there a difference?

I mean, really.

The appeal of a ruin in the age of digital sameness is that it feels unfakable, comfortably real.

Of course ruins are plenty fakable, and as our desire for them grows so does the incentive for fakery. Consider the remains of the Cretan labyrinth (the one with the minotaur and the red thread and everything). I visited them. These days it's a private site for tourists, and not one particularly easy to get to. What's there is entirely "reconstructed," meaning you probably shouldn't trust any of it.

But we want to believe in the ruin. We want to feel like we're seeing a real, true thing. It makes what we don't know or want to think about manifest. It brings the insides out, offers us a view of the skeletons and systems of buildings—of government specs and civil codes and building standards—as their results have failed into the stress of the future. We see what is underneath and inside our culture only after its collapse. We can understand what we had when it was going, when it was soon to be gone. Oh, those O-rings, an explosion in the sky. The Twin Towers, reduced to their component parts. Even the ruined interiors of the mortgage system post-bubble had a lovely stateliness to them, didn't they, their economic and emotional underpinnings obvious only in the past tense, once we passed the sweet spot, as we sorted through the causes and the corpses and the signage and the language.

At the third junction, 170 paces away, the tunnel's diameter shrinks half a foot so I have to stoop and scuttle to move forward. The pipe becomes more of a trapezoidal shape. In this section I will later install a dozen Billy Bass animatronic fish with their skins removed, reducing them to their robotic plastic parts, and coax them to sing. It will be a terror of a song: Bobby McFerrin's "Don't Worry Be Happy" sung in a sort of unison (a couple of the basses have flaws or their batteries are dying so they are off-key or make random clicks and buzzing sounds), echoing down the miles of storm sewer. Their encore is "Take Me to the River," unfortunately not the Talking Heads cover. The installation—these dozen plastic deconstructed fish in a storm sewer feeding into a dry river—is sort of meant to be a commentary on water issues in the Southwest but it's really a monument to interiority and its own strangeness. Very few will ever see it, but you can watch a video of it online.

A few junctions later, about three miles in, I reach the end of the human-accessible part of this storm sewer network at the center of a major intersection. I can't tell from here which one. I could emerge from the center of the intersection, rising up into the bath of sun again if I choose. For the moment, no one knows where I am. Not my family. Not my friends. Not my wife. It is a little freedom. Two tunnels go on from here but are too small for a human to traverse. Conditioned by games, perhaps, I had hoped the sewer would lead to some central passageway to the city's water stores, where I'd be able to shoot some dudes, take their gear, and enter the meaning of the city, maybe sneak in to the prison cell where Loughner is and exact revenge, end this quest with a spatter of simulated blood. I'm sure others have had this very same thought. I know my friend Chris did after his sister was murdered up in Michigan. He told me. I had it too.

I don't know the meaning of that event. I don't know the meaning of the city or its ruins, its infrastructure. I don't know the meaning of the shooting, of this place, of this people, of any people, of any place, of Loughner's blank slate of face. In that photo, in our minds, he is still there smirking, suggesting that he knows something we do not. Maybe we don't want to know what he knows. Or maybe we already do and we need not to think about it too directly. Look off to the side some and see if anything comes into focus.

And besides, Loughner's not imprisoned here in Tucson anyway. He's not even held in Arizona in one of our many prisons. He's jailed at the Federal Medical Center in Rochester, Minnesota, approximately eighty-eight miles from the I-35W bridge that collapsed in Minnesota. I can hear the game telling me: *Sorry, Mario, your princess is in another castle.*

Neither place nor people has meaning. Nor does the shooting, or any other tragedy, aside from that meaning or understanding we choose to give it. It's an unsatisfying end to a sad story in a strange, cramped place, I think, helplessly. I cough. It echoes down the tunnel. There is no do-over for the Giffords shooting, no saved game to load. Though Giffords survived, she is no longer the Giffords we knew or thought we knew before. America loves a comeback story complete with redemptive arc, but that's a fiction, not a fact. Narrativizing fact results in fudge, in game. What we have is history—context—subtext—our collected sexts and old failed dreams, chucked in the storm sewer under the city or whatever digital drain we can find for it. What we have is simulation, strangeness, a collecting. Anything else is a fake. The only redemption here is the one we make.

Okay. It's not the end. It's never the end until it is. January 8, 2012. I'm still here, a year after the shooting. I'm aboveground and outside the Safeway in question looking in at its lights. The city of Tucson, according to an article in the *Arizona Daily Star*, is "healing." I don't know what that means either. Maybe what it means is that this is all there is, to keep going on in spite of horror, and gradually it backs away from the fronts of our minds and we can believe in safety again, in stability again, kind of, enough to make it through the day. The sentiment is propagated across the newspapers that covered the story last year, and covered it again at the anniversary, our way of marking time, of remembering that things continue to happen year on year, the monsoon rains will wash away much of last year's discarded trash, and then they'll pass, and we'll be left again with the fact of sunlight, dry earth and short days and running our space heaters because we don't have central heat.

I may be heated but I don't feel healed.

What would it mean to feel healed?

Is it just a hope for covering over? To not be able to tell what happened here?

Is it just our willingness—not just our willingness but our need—to settle for the story, whatever story we've told ourselves?

It is true that time has passed. Those dozens of vigils and gatherings and remembrances marking the anniversary must mean something. If we haven't forgotten Loughner, we've locked him away, and we keep generating other horrors. Loughner no longer embodies our fear of the political other. It's embarrassing to remember how easy it was to believe he must have been unlike us politically, whatever unlike meant for us, right-wing gun nut on Benzedrine, socialist gun-toting extremist, how easily our brains fell into persecution mode, explained the murders to ourselves in the easiest, most reptilian, rote way: whatever he was and whatever we were, he was not *ours*. He wasn't *us*.

But it felt real, then, didn't it? It felt like we had been exposed to something true and fucked up and too hot to touch, much less to rationalize. For those of us who consider ourselves critical thinkers, this is a depressing reminder of how stable the self is in its echo chamber, how it girds itself against any news, how it immediately narrativizes terror in order to feel better about it, to file it safely away using whatever logic drives us. Even Loughner's corrupted logic, it was a sort of logic, you have to admit, and it's not difficult to imagine him feeling just as imprisoned by it, compelled by it. This doesn't excuse the act, of course: the distance from thought to act is an infinity we call civilization, we think, we hope—we must hope—or else we're lost. And you know this, the motion of the brain, how it sparks, but knowing it hardly stops the gears. How often in your life have you acted just as you feared you would, in spite of your belief in rationality and self-control? This strips the brain bare. Does this mean we are who we thought we were, or are we someone else?

I don't know. I do know the Safeway is a real place. It was one of seventeen in the Tucson metro area at the time of the shooting, though since then Safeway has been taken over by Albertsons and a bunch have closed. It's a simulation of a place, too, of course. Go on Google maps and type it in: Safeway, Tucson, Oracle. You can zoom around it using Google Earth. Maybe you can see me in the montage outside of it, waiting, thinking, listening, typing.

And like everything else on the web, this Safeway has reviews. One dated January 8, 2011, reads, "This is the location where the attempted assassination of Congresswoman Gabrielle Giffords occurred. Otherwise, I thought it was clean and the cashiers friendly." Another, by "Carl," dated January 9, reads, "The food is to die for!" He's given it five stars.

Just below, the usual rubric: "8 out of 48 people found this review helpful. Was this review helpful?" Perhaps. Yes, I think, it was, so I click "yes." If you click on "Carl's" name, his other Google reviews come up: eight Planned Parenthoods and women's clinics with jokes about abortion, and one in Casselberry, Florida, with a joke about another shooting. His image on the page is the blank silhouette avatar Google uses for anonymous reviews.

Well, fuck you, Carl.

"Carl" is an internet troll and an asshole. This is especially obvious since he posted the review just after the shooting, while the memorials were still being put up, all the flowers and balloons and cards assembled to perform just a tiny portion of our sadness. At first I experienced disbelief, then a kind of shock. It was funny in its way but pretty bad.

Returning to it a year later, though, I want to praise it for its exclamation point and the way it comes in at an unfamiliar angle on our sadness.

Well, it's been deleted now, no surprise, but I remember it. I documented it. I marked its passing. It's embedded itself in me: in my brain and now in this essay I pass it along to you.

Say it with me: fuck you, Carl.

That helps to expel it at least a little, to isolate it with some scar tissue.

If we are as healed as we all say, I should give it my grudging respect. Its trolling—maybe nihilism—is its own kind of spectacle, and a familiar one for those of us who spend time online (which is to say almost all of us these days). It feels like a particularly American response, a dark thread stitched into the culture that signifies some of my growing unease with online ratingness and the way the virtual sits atop the real, one more way we feel the need to pave the actual with fiction, how we try to organize just a little bit of our wild American muchness.

I mean, I have a complicated relationship with all of it: America, muchness, self-seriousness. I have to admire it even as I doubt it. Irreverence is built on reverence, and you can't have one without the other. Just *how* irreverent a joke can be is proportional to how deeply we have been hurt. The depth of our rage response to a joke like this is in proportion to how deeply we feel the subject. And I wonder if only in a breach of etiquette we can begin to understand the rules we all seem to agree to play by.

I should be clear: I don't think the review is funny, but I'm drawn to the act of posting it—and to the act of choosing to laugh at it—as resistance, one way of saying: fuck it, I'm alive.

I say that even as its context among his other "douche" reviews (to cite a metareview that comments on Carl's review) makes me pull away. "To die for" does engage, sort of. It engages me. It gives me something I can do. I can say fuck you, Carl, and I do. In the contemporary way, I can flag or dislike his review and maybe feel a bit empowered. I flag it. It is an action. I am a man of action. You can tell by the actions I am taking. I don't feel empowered, though. I unflag it. I'm not sure.

While the Safeway is tagged in Google with "shooting, gabrielle, star-bucks," the actual Safeway shows little evidence of this. It's amazing how resistant our culture is to showing the scars of our violence. It's like we could do almost anything to a building or a place or a group of people gathered there, and a Safeway or a Walmart or a Panera or a Mattress Firm or a Starbucks would come flooding back right in within a year, and there would be almost no mark at all.

We just have to dig a hole in our pain and fill it with enough dirt in order to plant and grow enough of a tree long enough to get it to bear fruit and give us a little shade from all of this debilitating sun.

I don't know what to make of this. I know that if we can't get our Unicorn Lattes, the psychopaths and the terrorists win. Or maybe get-ting the latte means I am too far gone to save. How much do I really want that latte? How much do we want to remember? How much do we want to change the way we do things? A lot (we're bored), not much, and not much it seems.

Fuck it. I get the latte. It is off-the-charts good.

In its honor I want to write an epic or an ode or at least a tweet.

Well, just outside the main entrance to the store, there is a small area with a tree and a couple of rocks, maybe twenty feet by twenty feet, cordoned off by metal parking barriers. Inside it is a stone the size of a man in the fetal position with a memorial plaque mounted to it. A few feet away, around the barriers, there are sixty-three bouquets of flowers, twenty-six candles, four glow sticks, four balloons, and a handful of local newspapers from January 9 a year ago. Does a place retain memories? Is there something here to be found or felt if I wait long enough?

Sitting outside the real place of Safeway, I'm reminded how much of everything else this place retains. It is, after all, a huge American super-market, run by an Idaho chain founded in 1919. The Safeway Corporation mounted this plaque so that we remember this place and the pain we planted in it, or the pain it planted in us. The bouquets are all Safeway branded, bought inside, thus commodified. There are quite a few shop-pers entering and leaving the store. (Many of us do our grocery shopping at night in Tucson.) Some are here for the memorial; others pay it no mind, if they notice it at all. There's a sign inside with information on anniversary events. I take a couple of photographs surreptitiously on my

cellular phone. I watch an older couple approach the site from the parking lot and stop there. The woman is blind and being led. After several
silent minutes they enter the store.

The strip mall containing the Safeway is typical of developed Tucson:
a Casas Adobe Flowers, a Great Clips, Sparkle Cleaners, Nails Art by
Tony, Pakmail, China Phoenix Restaurant, La Salsa, Honeybaked Ham &
Café, a Walgreens, and a Just Frames. The memorial is just another thing
to do. Or to walk by and have that momentary feeling that we live in a
place with a history.

I am parked less than fifteen feet away from where the first shots
took place. A teenager on his cell phone walks in and inspects the notes
left by those here before. He mutters something unintelligible, takes a
photograph, and walks away, says, "Okay, I'm sending it."

A younger woman walks to her SUV with an overflowing shopping
cart and glances over as she sideswipes the barrier. Irritated, she redirects
her cart to the vehicle, loads it, looks at me, and slowly drives away.

I get out of my car where I'm lurking and taking notes and I decide
to wander inside, not sure really what to do here. I purchase a box each
of two "new" flavors of Cheerios: Dulce de Leche and Multigrain Peanut
Butter. They are almost certain to be undelicious, but that does not stop
me, because they are new and I like to try new things. I restrain myself
from purchasing the Frosted Toast Crunch, also marked "new." I hesitate
in front of the "poetry in bloom" display inside above the wrapped bouquets, not sure what, if anything, to buy to mark the occasion and place
outside, whether buying a shitty commodified bouquet of "poetry" de-
natures me, poetry, tragedy, history, the Safeway, or this moment. Probably
all of us.

I've paused too long. I fear I'm looking creepy.

I pick out a bunch of baby's breath, thinking about the breath of
babies. A promotion tells me I can save three dollars with my Safeway
card. I check out with my three items, then place them all in a bag outside against the barrier, not reverently, exactly, but not irreverently either.
Then I drive away, not wanting to interfere if others want a moment in
this space undisturbed and unobserved. It's clear there's nothing here to
feel except what we bring in expectation and generate ourselves. That's
okay. We are okay, I think. We are probably okay.

I in

The channel at right surrounding—disappearing into—the spine of the book is the gutter. In the unlikely event of a water landing and your book acting as an impromptu flotation device, water would collect in the gutter. The pages would soak through and the spine would start to separate. The stitching, if any, would rot and pop like a long-submerged body in a river or a lake. Glue would dissolve, and you'd see the signatures reveal themselves. By this point in the water landing either you would have survived or you'd be falling apart. The binding would then fall into its component pieces, ruining the illusion of the artifact's wholeness. What is in your hands is just paper, collected, printed on. What you are holding is just ideas and language—the usual interlocking systems of signs—printed on paper. It is not engineered to channel or hold water, but it can do so in a pinch.

River

The Rillito River does not channel water through semiarid Tucson much of the year. It once did, and like many modern things—like the trains in Upper Michigan, my homeland; like Western Union's telegram service; like the pinching of my childhood cheek by tottering relatives; like the streetcars in Grand Rapids, Michigan, or most other American cities; like the increasingly anachronistic telephone cables strung all along our highways into the second-largest engineering project after the interstate system; like the blood through the bodies of our forebears, our betters, our mothers, our fathers, now dead; like the language recognition centers in my brain that fail now to bring the words I want to mind or tongue at awkward moments; like the awesome chugging rhetorical power of the periodic sentence that cannot go on forever even as it aspires to—the river channels water no longer, not year-round. But the channel's there, isn't it, plain as a wide June day, scrubbed clean in many parts and bristling with brush and trash in others, hundreds of feet across at points, hemmed in mostly by concrete culverts, effectively separating the city from the ritzier homes and restaurants that populate the foothills, whose owners pay no taxes to the city. It separates via space and threat

This year natural disasters have been everywhere, it seems. As I write this, "Tornadoes kill 6 in Oklahoma, Kansas" (CNN), and we're less than a week past the devastating tornado in Joplin, Missouri, not to mention the more obvious man-aided nuclear disasters occurring after the epic tsunami in Japan, the tornado system that leveled both of the places I lived in Tuscaloosa, Alabama, a couple of weeks back, then the crazy freeze this winter in Tucson that killed much of the saguaros though they won't keel over for some years, their death delayed, and then the massive floods in New Orleans, again, the Red River in North Dakota, the eruption of Grimsvotn, the Icelandic volcano whose ash cloud drift threatens to scuttle my summer travel. My mother-in-law is freaked out about the end-of-the-world prediction that didn't come to pass a couple of weeks ago on May 21, 2011, not to mention the Mayan apocalypse predicted for next year, just to name a few anxious highlights. I mean to say that the world's tribulations are present like weather in my mind, this month, going into the Tucson monsoon season.

I have a complicated relationship with weather spectacle. I get off the phone with my dad a day after Father's Day, and he's been driving around looking at the damage suffered from a once-a-century storm in which six inches of rain dropped on our hometown in a day. I watch drone footage of washed-out roads I used to drive on and marvel at the destruction. If I'm being honest about my experience, it's a little erotic, the way I'm both dazzled and horrified by the footage, and I can't seem to stop watching.

There's plenty to gawk at here during the monsoon anyhow, the one time a year when our weather is truly a spectacle.

of sudden flood surge, a reminder of the force of water when it's here, a reminder of the force we deploy in trying to contain it, a reminder of the risk we take in ignoring it.

And when the water's here in the monsoon months of July and August, it's everywhere: like nothing in the north except maybe a blizzard surge or avalanche. The Rillito runs high when it storms, meeting and joining the Santa Cruz and moving on north, bringing what benefits water brings to the arid bits of West that it reaches less and less each year.

It's incredible to look at damage like this, particularly to a place I know, and looking at it I know I'm looking from a distance. This isn't my landscape anymore. Even if I wanted to get up there to gawk or help it'd take a day.

Our spectacle is sublime, too, between the walls of clouds and lightning strikes and microbursts and transformative days of rain, rain, rain.

I'm not the only one to watch it from the highest point in town I can manage. We see each other on the fancy patios of foothills restaurants, our eyes cast up to the sky in wonder.

Of course the weather does not respond to my concerns. The rain goes on. I watch. The rain goes on.

I have recently started running much of the year myself. I do not run high like the river or cheerful, smelly Arizona stoners. I don't know what drives my spur to run: a fight against my own personal beltway westward expansion, perhaps. A connection to a fitter vision, finer version of myself. A bit of personal engineering: clawing some control away from age and the natural tendency of the body. Or perhaps it's a desire to court and better understand my capacity for pain.

Any individual one of the brain's channels—axon, neuron, dendrite—is idle much of the time, though not to say empty or dry, exactly. After injury or catastrophic change the channels reconfigure, find new ways to get the signal through the network. (As aficionados of weird brain injuries know, sometimes they don't redirect so successfully.) Perhaps like desert denizens they lie where it's cool and await the occasional electrical impulse, at which point they are signaled, woken and singing, alive.

The writers had to engineer a plot into which they could channel the songs.

I imagine most musical theater is built this way—songs first, plot second, with some backfill as necessary. One structure is built to accommodate—contain—control—another. That might account for the odd plots of Gilbert and Sullivan, for instance.

I wonder a bit at the ethics of this: How much pleasure should I take at a destructive, beautiful force?

So if one needed to, it is therefore possible to execute a water landing in Tucson a dozen or more monsoon days a year.

What else runs: my car (though not my old, sold, or crashed cars); my computer; my animals when playful or fearful; machines; programmed processes in machines; my nose in the dry air of the desert; coyotes, rabbits, dogs, humans, lizards, and rare javelina through the wash in the mornings when I run and spark their chase or flight; the blood through the veins; the thoughts through the brain late at night when they should be shutting down into easy, ecstatic dreams.

Trivia: The script for the movie musical *Singing in the Rain* (1952) was only written after the songs were already in place.

Back in Michigan, I'm seventeen and dancing jigs poorly as a sailor in *H.M.S. Pinafore*, Gilbert and Sullivan's sea-set piece of musical theater

It's fair to say that my life is suspended between two poles—the wet or snowbound landscapes of Michigan that still shape the way I think and dream and write, and the hazy desert loneliness of Arizona, where I now live and work.

It's fair to say I didn't think much about water before moving to Arizona, where water means absence, means scarcity, means need, means conservation, except when it monsoons, and the river runs high.

as it rains outside again: you can hear it on the roof. In Michigan water's abundance is an apparently incontrovertible fact. What is Michigan if not a wet state, a water state? Bordered by four of the five great lakes, Michigan's vision of itself as a vacationland is no less dependent on water than are the cities of the arid West. Fishing, boating, beaches, tourism, even skiing, hunting, and snowmobile riding—these are all built on water. Everything is lush, green, bushy, buggy, muggy, prickled, itchy, and wet except when the state is blanketed by the yearly onslaught of snow (still water, we're reminded, when our icy boots melt on return in the house). Michigan is all coast, two peninsulas separated and defined by water, settled by water, driven by water, separated from Canada by water.

Alternating landscapes like this, if done quickly enough, produces a double image, a composite of the two that compresses the space between them. The nineteenth century visualized it like this, as a thaumatrope, a disk with two distinct images on each side (empty cage and bird, for instance), twirled on a string. Spin the thing and it is not one thing or the other but both.

The channel through which the river occasionally runs high is partly natural and partly man-made. In the natural corner, the river's carved this space out from the earth over thousands of years. In the human-made corner, its course is constantly monitored and engineered, rejigged, tweaked, shunted, diverted, plotted, adjusted, and planned. In 2010 the city of Tucson dredged out and buttressed the channel walls of the Pantano Wash on the east side of the city where I run many mornings. The Pantano feeds into the Rillito, which feeds into the Santa Cruz, and its watershed stretches from the Ciénega Creek to the Colossal Cave out toward the Chiracahua Mountains.

Four years earlier the concrete bank protection along an executive park and a townhome development (our modern names as ugly as the structures they describe) was damaged in a 35-year flood event (a 35-year flood event happens roughly every 35 years, and has an approximately 3 percent chance of happening any given year), when upward of 15,900 cubic feet per second of floodwater passed under the Broadway Bridge.

For those who don't consider the Rillito or Santa Cruz to be rivers
because they don't run year-round, these occasional spectacular events
serve as useful and painful correctives to their notion of river.

Much human engineering works this way: we design our structures only
up to specific breaking points, knowing they'll be eventually exceeded.
The key is predicting when they fail and making them so they fail visibly
and—ideally—safely.

Admittedly the expense of anything engineered to be asymptotically
approaching permanence or perfect safety would be unfeasible.

The only flawless song is a funeral song, chosen to fit the form of
the funeral.

So which is the river, we ask: the channel or the water?

Some constraints aren't formed over time, but designed: a pagebreak

Farther northwest, the Cortaro Road Bridge over the Santa Cruz was destroyed completely in the flood of October 1983 and was rebuilt.

And when our structures fail, they fail big. Just last week a monsoon microburst ripped our entire carport off the house and flipped it onto the roof, launching a beam a hundred feet in the air and spearing it down through the roof into the bedroom. My wife was home to see it and described it as the unmistakable sound of part of the house breaking off and being blown away, and then another crash just after. A home is a thing you believe is stable—until it comes into contact with some really exceptional bit of weather.

In Tucson it freezes a few times a year, typically just for a few hours, but seven years ago, the temperatures dropped to 17 degrees and stayed there for eighteen hours. Incredibly, city building codes don't require insulation, so everyone's water main burst. All the pipes in the city froze—most spectacularly during the mayor's press conference designed to reassure the city that everything was under control. Behind him a pipe broke on camera and made a fountain into the air. No questions were taken after.

The only perfect safety is that of stasis, that of the virtual, that of math, that of death.

The upshot is that our engineered world is not built to last without constant intervention. So we monitor the river, tweak the river.

This isn't an idle line of thought. A great deal of money and development and, on the flipside, conservation effort depends on how we want to parse the definition of *river*. Definitions change over time. They're flexible, descriptive, liquid. Perhaps they're geographical too; they shift and mutate as we do.

is a designed absence, as is the gutter space. I don't think about inhabiting it often, unlike margins, which lend themselves to annotation, to notes on the marginal, aside from the text. Margins are for our fingers, so we don't obscure type with our hands, so our designed page can have a neat boundary in which it is contained. We like containment. We like order. Without order

there is no shape, no meaning, nothing to resist or push against

But as with any apparent absence, this preserve is soon inhabited.

You're not allowed to build in the preserve that cordons off (and protects (and contains (perhaps like parentheses))) whatever we define as the Rillito River.

(form)

or pull across an emptiness. The whitespace makes the text

an island.

Perhaps to conserve the imaginative, associative space around a text, principles of classical typography eschew using this space except as caesura.

In nights and early mornings wildlife fills this absent river, moving silently through the city. Much of that wildlife is now rare or missing, not seen for decades. The following species haven't been seen in the Pantano Wash since the dates in parentheses: Northern Goshawk (1999), Arizona Giant Skipper (1988), Poling's Giant Skipper (1967), Gila Longfin Dace (2004), Baird's Sparrow (2003), Felder's Orange Tip (1992), Sabino Canyon Damselfly (1988), Giant Spotted Whiptail (2005), Western Burrowing Owl (2004), Northern Gray Hawk (1994), Common Black Hawk (1977), Arizona Metalmark (1993), Mexican Long-Tongued Bat (2005), Western Yellow-Billed Cuckoo (2002), Pale Townsend's Big-Eared Bat (1986), Arizona Ridge-Nosed Rattlesnake (1999), Northern Buff-Breasted Flycatcher (2000), Greater Western Bonneted Bat (2005),

Is this list of absence an absence

A pause

It's hard not to be aware

It doesn't take much, though, to forget it again, since there is still so much world with which to contend daily. We're used to forgetting. We can't not forget. Our brains can't hold everything in memory, hence that whitespace around our ideas and our memories—how they're heightened in isolation, and anything could connect to anything, could be summoned by an image, redirected by a scent. So we internalize the absence of things as natural.

It's hard not to be aware of the absence of text through the gutter, okay, this page is done, so how do I get to the next? How often do you the gutter in the center of the spread and onto

Her gutter separates the verso from recto, west from the east, our space from another's, sunset from sunrise, the foothills from the city of Tucson, St. Louis from East St. Louis, the west side from the east side of Grand Rapids, Michigan; Iowa from Illinois; Missouri from Illinois; liquid from solid from vapor; the cold from the not; the haves from the nots; the

American Peregrine Falcon (2005), Gila Chub (2004), Cactus Ferruginous
Pygmy-Owl (1999), Sonoran Desert Tortoise (2004), Western Black
Kingsnake (2002), Western Red Bat (2005), Lesser Long-Nosed Bat
(2004), Obsolete Viceroy Butterfly (1966), California Leaf-Nosed Bat
(1986), Arizona Myotis (1992), Cave Myotis (2001), Pocketed Free-Tailed
Bat (2005), Big Free-Tailed Bat (2003), Texas Horned Lizard (1995), Gila
Topminnow (2004), Chiricahua Leopard Frog (2005), Lowland Leopard
Frog (2005), Yellow-Nosed Cotton Rat (2003), Mexican Spotted Owl
(2004), and the Northern Mexican Gartersnake (2003).

or a presence?

or a permanence?

of the absence once you see its extent, once you remember what was
here before.

though our brains forget it when reading. How often do you think oh,
think yes, left to right, top to bottom (in the Western world), jump across
the next block?

We learn that prose, like water, flows to accommodate whatever space
it's given. The brain's pathways accommodate this understanding. The
designer knows there is a visceral pleasure in reflowing prose blocks in
page design software like InDesign because she sets up channels and
adjusts the text box, watches the fluid dynamics work their magic. Today
she is an engineer. Today she is a small, beautiful god.

darker-skinned from the lighter; midwesterners from westerners; this list could go on as long as our culture. Rivers are easy geographical borders, shared features, not part of what they divide. Even when dry, those borders remain. The split between two contiguous spaces remains. The brain sees a line.

Keep this in mind for the quiz; we'll see what knowledge your spongebrain retains.

Thus the thalweg of an essay is where the deepest and most indelible remaining thought resides when the rest evaporates or is washed or erased or edited away.

And anyone who knows anything about rivers knows that, left to them-selves, rivers will often (if not always) meander

another curve. Or we think that's how it works. In an essay, "Meander," that appeared in the very first issue of the journal *Creative Nonfiction,* itself named for the recent American term to offer some form to contain the formless, Mary Paumier Jones suggests that, like the river, ocean currents also meander, as does the jet stream. That flow itself seems to be best modeled not as straight but as swerve under certain conditions. That the river's natural swerving is not

Flash Card 1: the path of greatest depth along a river channel is called the *thalweg*.

Flash Card 2: "The sinuosity of a channel [is] defined as the ratio between the thalweg length and the down-valley distance" (*Arizona Department of Water Resources Design Manual for Engineering Analysis of Fluvial Systems*, 1985).

So even if the riverbed isn't filled year-round, the thalweg is the most likely part to have water, whether runoff from precipitation on the mountains or from a sudden storm.

For the runner the thalweg will be slow going, the softest sand in the deepest channel if it's dry at all, the least firm surface you can run on, as I've come to understand, since it's the thing the water most often moves over.

in a series of sharp, snakelike, alliterative S-curves through the earth as the force of a turn eats further away at the bank; this increases until it's unsupportable, and it detaches into an oxbow or swings back over to

dissimilar to the way the brain cortex is bent and looped, folded up on itself so as to fit more brain in a small space. And that the essay—best simulation of the brain on the page we've got—its natural motion, like the river's, is meander.

Swerving has many advantages, one being that of what astronomers refer to as averted vision, in which you can only see certain astronomical phenomena by looking at their adjacent spaces.

Some information can be held within the thinking's momentum.

In the course of thinking the brain wanders, unguarded (but perhaps directed by subconscious flow, the thalweg underneath the surfaces we believe we're aware of).

Still when I see water running over the roadway I just want to gun my car and blast through it.

Minnesota recently enacted a similar law, billing stranded drivers who circumvent roadblocks to enter snow-closed highways for their rescue.

Still it's hard not to be suspicious of a prohibition.

It's a character flaw I'm sure my parents must have been aware of, even when I was a child.

And there are other gutters, of course, other abscesses, absences, holes in the ground, other ghosts that haunt these spaces.

Some events dent you so deeply that even to look at them directly brings pain.

Some detach, form pools of their own.

For instance, those caught in flooding washes are subject to rescue under Arizona's "Stupid Motorist Law," which maintains that anyone rescued after driving into a barricaded wash will be billed for the cost of the rescue. You'd be surprised how often this happens. The television news anchors are clearly thrilled by this footage. It takes only an inch of water, if moving quickly enough, to sweep away a vehicle.

How fast could it be going anyway? But then the wiser section of the brain asserts itself.

Some roadblocks and barriers, we understand—if sometimes only a little too late—are for our own protection.

I always wonder, Exactly what are they trying to keep us *from*? It would be in my best interest not to test the electric fence, and yet there I am reaching out to it, hoping to make contact.

I don't learn from instruction well or often or maybe ever.

The dead, for instance.
The shot, for instance.
The memorialized and descansoed, for instance.
The forgotten, for instance.

The voices recorded decades ago from now-dead television laugh
track audiences?

The (porn) actors or actresses remembered from your teenage years?

It's the mind. It goes where it goes.

For the hacker it's hard not to stray into the gutter, the deepest and
often weakest point in a system. For the graffiti artist the blank is a
provocation. For the oversharer. The awkward conversationalist who
fears silence. For the gossip. The linguist, who, at cocktail parties,
regales us with trivia: "gutter, a watercourse, natural or artificial; a small
brook or channel"—obsolete (*OED*). Be careful of linguists at parties.

Perhaps you're going to the wrong parties?

We take them for data. We take them for aesthetics. Found data can
be surprisingly beautiful as an aesthetic object, line on line of information spilling down the page; devoid of discernible content the form is
more apparent.

As is a line of thinking—

or your preferred infinity—

As is a well-oiled hinge placed so as to pivot from one thought
to another.

The lowest point where it all collects is often is the best source to
understand a culture.

They're fragments, suggestive of the whole.

Or how about the bodies in footage we conjure at night or in unguarded moments in erotic reverie that are impossible to stop?

The thought of dead lovers, gone lovers.

You sir, get your mind out of the gutter! You, too, miss.

It sounds like you're talking about river, or prose.

Archaeologists at parties tell me the gutter is where we dump our whatever.

The gutter is where telephone phreaks (I include myself) go through overflowing dumpsters out back of Michigan Bell buildings in search of technical papers, schematics, and streams of data uttered on paper forever.

The multimeter with its gleaming leads! The plastic caress of a lineman's handsets! Equipment is aesthetic too.

As is forever—

as is a river.

Pay attention to the absence. You can find a lot in the gutter, in the places where we dump what we disavow.

So those pornographic magazines you found down by the worksite in winter?

It's connected to the dungeon—

Whether it's the trunk systems of Michigan Bell tributarying into
abstract loops—

or maybe we're talking about a way to cross-section a culture and see
what is inside it, that inside that it prefers not to name except to itself.

Which is one good reason to keep your brain in the gutter: you can see
to the center.

An emptiness, a form waiting to be filled.

Waiting to be poured.

Pored over.

Or maybe just ignored and left alone

A gutter is a space

a snapped taboo, a margin

As you may have heard, Tucson is on the margin of the margin of the
country, within a finger's width of the border according to your map.
Living here you start to realize what it is to live up against another
country, living so far outside of the main tributary of the culture, what
it is to border.

or the modern dungeon, the prison—where we lock what we most hate about ourselves away, where we'll bury Jared Lee Loughner.

or the telephone lines looping my dorm room of a life ago to the telephone system so that others could dial in to my private digital meander and spend time there—

The movement at the center of anything—a culture, a community—is seen best from the margin.

That gutter: a blank. It stinks with potential.

Waiting to be born into.

Waiting to be porned.

Obsessed.

to sit in its silence.

elided, a kind of violence,

broken, wood suddenly unsplit.

That the border is porous is a commonplace, but it's an obvious one when you live here. Wall it up, man it up, dam it off—this accomplishes nothing. Like water, desire and imagination flow where they flow, and the people will follow.

Of course there's something on the other side of the border (and often inside our own border), but for much of the United States it might as well be nothing, a generality, other, ether, blank spot on the map and certainly on our tax returns and drug policies, until someone legislates something crazy and everyone freaks out.

I don't mean this entirely as critique: it's hard to pay attention to everything. Our lives are incredibly complicated, layered, looped, processed, remixed, and filtered in ways we're hardly aware of, and we can barely summon the energy to investigate some days, much less understand.

Odd to know the riverbed as a bed for the river, the sleeping anthropomorphized beast.

In northern climes I've gone through the ice several times in waking life, and nightly in dreams.

It can be breathtaking.

Which is a horror, because we rely on these things. If these too are hollow, of what are we made?

It can be nauseating as we rebalance, reconfigure the pathways of the brain, reckon with shock.

May their failure sustain us, renew our sense of wonder: the world is reconfigured and bright again. Meaning we are new. Meaning the meaning we're making can be too. Until we habituate and are old again, repeat, repeat, repeat.

Odd to think you can understand a country from the center, which is the real America, as pundits report. From the center a shape has no shape: it just looks like a field. Go instead to its wounds, where it bleeds and abuts and encounters its rivers, its edges.

Bodies are found in rivers all the time. In Winona, Minnesota, for instance, drunk college students fall into the river with surprising regularity. Sometimes they die. My friend Paul once nearly drowned in an Illinois river thinking that, like Jesus, he could walk on water because he did once on ice, in winter.

It's terrifying and exhilarating going through a surface, breaking what you formerly thought solid.

It suggests that the rules on which we base our understanding of the world—those givens, donnés, paradigms, unshakable foundational truths—the walls on which we built the space that channels the brain, which tells stories to the self about the self—might just be hollow.

And if these structures fail?

It's hard to ice over a dry river, though it's not hard to drown in one when it runs. Occasionally you might tube or kayak in one, but the fear here is flash flood and sudden rush, the quick filling-in of what you thought before was just a blank, the sudden reconfiguration of what you thought was your city, the roads suddenly water, the city no longer for driving, it's obvious.

And the best transport is—oddly, suddenly—the river. What was
formerly gap is now

What you find in the bed of the river is another world:

Ecosystem for the vanished and sometimes the present, home for
the homeless, where the landscape remembers what we did to it last.
The gutter is a place for the placeless teens in-between one world and
another (the word *teens* connotes this betweenness even as we deify
it in retrospect): of course they've found their way here and made their
marks on walls:

solid, and what was solid, now absence.

beer cans; a couple hundred types of plants, only a few of which I can
name; desert animals, confused or crafty; the supersonic clicks of migrat-
ing bats hanging under bridges and hunting by night; the occasional
runner; the bat-watchers; the kids; graffiti; horses; those walking their
pets. Shopping carts are my most obvious and frequent sighting—often
from the nearby Lowe's or the nearby Fry's or the nearby Albertsons or
the nearby Walmart or the nearby Costco or the nearby SuperTarget,
or the nearby whatever, abandoned here by teens, the homeless, or
homeless teens, then found with a sigh some days hence. Some of it's
pilfered by the river when it runs, but most of the human trash I find in
the riverbed is abandoned here or carted in by squatters who carve their
own spaces—campsites almost—out of the plants about midway up the
riverbed. These spaces are not visible from the street or the walkways
that run along the river. It's surprising when you run across one, which
can only be accessed via the river: world within world within world.

Gateway to Hell →
Get up off ya ass and wash it
Thank You Bitch: Heather Rose
Cream & Impulse, Lost Soul
Beware of Killer Frogs
Dan & Dalik, I Heart You, 5-28-91
Tom Died Here
Point of No Return
I live →
OK N 2 DEEP
Fuck Life

Most interesting to me are the absences in the absences: the darkened
tunnels that feed into the wash or the Rillito River. These storm sewers
are somewhat rare in Tucson, especially the big ones, seventy-two inches
wide and high, that I have been exploring, mapping, and annotating

You never answered the question: Is a river still a river if it's dry?

If we strip the river of river, if we de-wild the wild, if we fuck with—excuse me, engineer—the river enough, it will certainly find a different route when it needs to. Sure, pave it over. Develop its banks. It'll tear all that up. It'll take over Swan and Campbell, main thoroughfares, making your Bruegger's Bagels, your Bed Bath & Beyonds, your Chili's, sites of your future water landing. It will erase whatever is in the path of least resistance. The best you can do, the engineers say, is to try to control it, confine it.

Sometimes the river will do its river thing regardless. There's not much that can be done.

No *river* without *I.*

(where I found the graffiti above). They lead into the dark space underneath the city and into the metaphorical darkness underneath our
civilized, engineered lives. They too are colonized mostly by animals,
teens, and the homeless, judging from the graffiti and the trash.

In 2008 the Santa Cruz River (that the Pantano and Rillito feed into)
was ruled "navigable" by the Environmental Protection Agency, thus
making it eligible for protection under the federal Clean Water Act.
This followed the Army Corps of Engineers' second-guessing of their
own ruling of "navigable" the previous May, then withdrawn, in effect
punting to the EPA. *Navigable* is a tricky word, especially for the ninety
to ninety-five percent of Arizona rivers that are dry for part of the year.
Calling a river "navigable" means more roadblocks for developers
wanting to build along the river. Calling a river "navigable" enshrines it,
embodies it as a river deserving administrative, environmental protec-
tions. Calling a river "navigable" only if it runs year-round brands a
western river with the mark of the Midwest or the East. These notions
don't really apply here.

The riverbed is certainly navigable in the dry months, just not by boat,
by floating, by ogling the nonwet world from the center of the stream and
trying not to get caught on debris.

(I know it sounds crazy, but perhaps we could relinquish some of that
control?)

Sometimes the self will do its self thing regardless and spill into the
floodplain.

Well, that's self-centered, and we're already well into the margin. No
in either. No *either*. No *margin*, no *aquifer*, no *Pima*. No *Rillito*. And
certainly no *memoir*, no *creative nonfiction*, no *running*. *I* is central to

No *meander* without *ander.*

They mean if we make them mean.
Meaning will fill any space we can carve.

But if left unchecked it becomes a problem.

Meaninglessness and lawnlessness and selflessness do not stop my
neighbors from trying to involve me in their yearly competitive masculine
yard undertakings, but I am no longer a slave to the neighborhood
organization and the uncut lawn citations I dutifully composted.

the river linguistically, but also politically. It's easy to offload, subcontract
my concern, make it someone else's problem. And it is. It's not my river.
It's not just my river. Though I suck at proselytizing, at conserving, it's
obvious Arizona is not Michigan, though it might be the distant future of
Michigan once everything else is mined or sold. Given the water situation
in the West, I bought rain barrels to harvest rainwater. Got solar. I'm
lawnless, thank god, thank allergies, thank desert landscaping, thank the
culture of lawnlessness built on what was once the lawless west, like Girls,
gone Wild, gone Havasu, gone downloadable porno. Gone snowbird and
gunmad and darkness. Gone bagless, teabagless. Gone badlands. Gone
cholla, gone cactus, succulent, ocotillo. The fact of the desert is a sort of
purification by sunlight and drought, and to understand that is to start
to make a life here.

No *ander* without *other*. No *Duran Duran* without *ander ander* (say it
enough and you'll get it). It's easy to get obsessed with linguistic tics like
this. Do they mean or do they not? Do they make the world about us or
do they not?

We have no option but to apprehend the world through the lens of self,
the double heart of landscape we carry with us.

The problem of memoir. The problem of me. The problem of Facebook.
The problem of victim culture. Of Not in My Backyard, of apathy and
anger. The problem of no vision, of television, of unsupervised time with
teens we lust for but don't trust.

Living in Tucson means being reminded of lawlessness, of lawlessness,
of the edge of the culture past which we might drop off into nothingness.
Pointless national television commercials tempt me with discounted
riding lawnmowers offering tighter turning radii each spring. The lush,
trimmed lawn is still the culture in much of the country. Our yards
have been our cultures for centuries, probably since the earliest yard
got spruced up. That we can control our exteriors suggests the straight
cleanliness and orderliness of our souls, not to mention our manscaped
chests. It's obvious, isn't it, those Sunday afternoons spent mowing

To be lawless is to opt out of that one cultural norm. From the dusty
Tucson margin, ridiculous, lawned Phoenix and the faux-Venetian
Scottsdale are easy targets for critique or meandering rage—

And while I may be asymptotically approaching middle age, my running
in the river will beat back time, slow the growth of the blood plaque
in my arterial tributaries as I dream cold rushing something in the
Pantano, the Rillito, the Santa Cruz, as I map and annotate its storm
drain tributaries. It's a new interface with the ground below me that I've
found powerful and surprising and perhaps empowering, though it's
hard to say it that way these days; either I'm newer or it's newer, or both.
This is how I believe the I can feel, running along the Rillito on overcast
days just edging the darkness of self and of blindness and of nearly
infinite complication.

Does remembering?

Does writing?

I have to believe so: in tracing the lines that connect things
only having so much attention to pay, but now there's a slight
it will be obvious when it rains.

this sputtering gutter, making my mark when I can, dividing,
divining,
designing,
even though
slowly

after church, trimming the unruly, making a facade of control—the starch shaking out of our church shirts with every vibration, the clutch in the riding lawnmower getting looser by the day as we ride toward the future in the fading light, spitting gravel into the window when we hit it? We don't have that here and I'm thankful. Years of summers spent pointlessly mowing I'm thankful. Years of uselessly beating back wildness I'm thankful. Years of taming the rivers I'm thankful. Years of asthma attacks and allergy shots and shirtless underpaid work for older women for whom I may or may not have lusted I'm thankful.

but not today, I think. This is about the river and the I-shape that the gutter and margin make that separates the pages, that separates thought from action, self from subject, past from future.

Does thinking change anything? I wonder.

Does singing?

Does anything?

I loop them, even if just a little, and maybe you don't even notice, your depression that leads one to the next. It may mean nothing now, but

until then I'll wander—meander—the river, this river, this weather, connecting,
eliding.
diving,
I know I'm
dying.

Is That What's Behind the Dam?

If we are okay, if we feel buoyed by the light and cactus flowers and the lattes we drink, if we don't think about the dead, what does that mean for the grieving we felt? Do we still feel sadness if we don't feel it always? Where does it go when we are done with it, and what did it do to or for us when we felt it? What does being done with it mean? Are we even done with it? How long can we hold that sadness anyway, and what does holding it do to us? How long does it sustain or punish us? By what process is it metabolized or siphoned off into its component parts and released into the air or into song or into the ground? Into what is it transmuted or transformed? Where does that highway go to? Is the thing I hate the tool itself or the part of self that wants to wield the tool, to hold it in its fist and claim a space? Is what I critique in others the part of me I most desire? What is desire after all? What does it mean to aim a gun at a thing that can't shoot back?

I think of how, when my daughter gets angry at something or sad on another thing's account or too deep into a line of questioning I don't know how to handle, I redirect her attention. If I can get her to hold her attention elsewhere for long enough, meaning a minute or two, the inciting incident can typically be forgotten (the deeper the initial emotional impression, of course, the longer and more complete redirection it takes to overwrite the other), and her prodigious energies can push out in a different direction. So I wonder what separates one emotional response from another. I wonder how well and how deeply I've learned to navigate the world by displacement.

After Giffords's shooting it was easy enough to direct our anger at the culture of incivility, as our sheriff put it a little too rashly, which then President Obama doubled down on later when he came to Tucson. The spectacle of his visit helped to gather our energies from the remembered spectacle of the week before. Giving voice to a grief or an anger publicly and collectively is to gather it up, to take it from each one of us and give it to all of us. Redirection is perhaps the best thing we can do when confronted by an unimaginable thing. Look somewhere else. Look back.

Six years later, I sat down with Pam Simon, the third person shot by Loughner. The bullet had just missed her heart, and she survived, if barely. She's working on a memoir about that day and the years after, and we met to talk about it. She didn't want to be stuck in that day forever. None of us do. She wanted to focus on the recovery and everything after.

The business card she gave me reads, simply, *Pam Simon, Activist.* There has been a lot of everything after for her. Her energies have been redirected successfully into advocacy, and also into writing. Now she works for the Giffords Foundation and helps raise funds for the January 8th Memorial, and speaks compellingly and powerfully about gun violence.

When we met, it was just a few days after the Las Vegas shooting, which again raised the bar for America's Worst Mass Shooting, a reality show whose popularity apparently has not dimmed. For some reason we keep renewing it for another season, and I don't see that stopping.

It's easy to feel helpless in the face of this. Maybe that's part of what's behind the agency I get when playing games—onscreen and on the page. It's a false agency—it's just a game; it's not changing anything—but it feels like I can grab hold of something and move it, even if it's just on a screen. And maybe it's also me doing something counterintuitive to prove I'm in control of the violent part of myself. Which I am, mostly. These days. It wasn't always that way. My childhood was filled with violences and vandalism and wreckage, the sheer mass of which I can't really comprehend now. I think of the teenage kids who deface saguaro cacti, those iconic cacti of the desert Southwest that can take a century to grow big enough to sprout their characteristic arms. Kids spray-paint the things. They cut initials into them. They slice them in half or go at them with baseball bats (they say it feels a little like breaking a body). The plants are spiny, sure, and old, but they're easy to damage, too, one reason why you can't, for instance, build disc golf courses in parks with saguaros: they're legally protected, and they're easily bruised or cut or hurt once you get past those spines, which a golf disc will do. Even if it was allowed I couldn't swallow the price of my recreation. Living here you begin to learn a reverence toward saguaros in all their dorky lonely splendor: their bodies (those arms!)

remind us of us. If I had grown up here, as my daughter will, I might well have been one of those who'd deface saguaros, which may explain my revulsion seeing them cut in half now.

Those urges subside in time, or are countered as I see effects of what I did: when J— blew his hand off making homemade bombs, a thing we used to do together, or when I was eventually arrested for computer fraud, or when I saw one friend destroyed by drugs and another by revenge and grief and rage. That list could go on and does. But yet, there is still a story to tell. My own and the wrecked place where I am from. And there's Pam Simon, activist, smiling at me in my office and from her business card. She was shot through the heart (nearly), and we know or believe we know who was to blame, and yet she's here, arms raised, making a point to me. This, I think, is a song I'd dearly like to know how to sing.

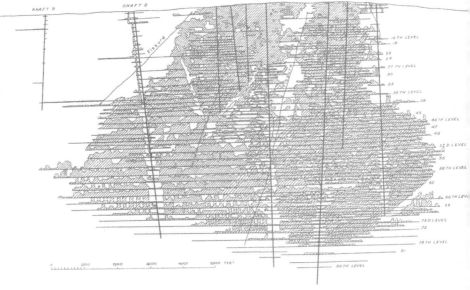

QUINCY MINE

Remainder

First Descent

The mine above is the Quincy, the mine I think of when I think of *mine*. I suppose that makes this mine mine, or makes me its; I'm not sure which. It's a copper mine in Hancock, Michigan, just up on the tall hill north of the Portage Canal that cuts the northern tip of the Upper Peninsula off from the rest, abutting the ski hill I used to think was huge until I moved out of the Midwest.

Though the mine is the Quincy, its lode is the Pewabic. The mine has had other names: the Pewabic, the Mesnard, the Pontiac, the Franklin. When I look at it, all I think is *down, down, down.*

Though we know it's true, somehow still it's hard to imagine that there is so much *earth* in the earth; that we've ever moved so much of it or gone so deep inside it. And that so much vastness there remains.

The town of Hancock has had other names. Claude Allouez, one of the first Europeans to show up in 1667, reported that it was a Chippewa (now Ojibwe) settlement but, though it surely had one, did not give its name. The Ojibwe didn't mine, though they still found copper from time to time, and directed missionaries to the sites those coming later would spectacularly exploit. Those who came before the Ojibwe mined: archae- ologists have found "shallow mine pits where Indians used huge rock hammers to beat copper nuggets from rock matrix. They were pounded into flat sheets, folded, heated and cooled to toughen them, pounded, refolded, and hammered again to produce useful objects" dating as far back as 5000 BCE.[1]

Second Descent

Right now the Quincy is a tourist mine, a mouth for gawkers. It's an at- traction. Come, they say, and see the remains. Here is evidence of how this land was once great and is no longer. The story goes that in 1847 a state law was nearly enacted to make Calumet, fifteen miles away, the capital of Michigan. It lost by one vote. In 2013 the population of Calumet was 710. Tourism is one of its only industries, not including ad hoc production of methamphetamines or an Upper Peninsula variant, methcathenone (cat), the commonly known slogan for which, when I was in high school, was "nine days high and then you die." Though I have never personally tried cat, I did later realize my friendship with G. was over when he was complaining how someone had spiked his crack with cat and ruined his weekend. He did not die after nine days, but I would not be surprised to hear he is no longer alive.

Here in Hancock you can ride the tram down the hill to the seventh level and walk into the mine about half a mile, plenty far enough to lose any trace of natural light and bewilder yourself entirely. It's rare to experience a dark as dark as this one is. I've never seen it outside of a mine. Probably you haven't either. It's a rare spectacle, this much of nothing. What we think of as dark—midnight without a moon with the curtains drawn—has no relation to it. It's a disorienting, terrifying dark, and worth coming just for this. Or come for the other tourist reasons: see why others once used to come to live and work and die here! Historical tourism is built around sites of pain, conflict, death, or decay. It says: Here's how we suffered, mattered; come and see our tragedy. How we matter now is as the site of story.

Or dial back the clock to 1945, which was when copper prices bottomed out and the Quincy ceased to be a working mine and became a wreck instead. The mine wouldn't have been as different as you'd think. All mines are wrecks, of course. They are built to last only as long as profit does, and then what they are is emptiness. They wreck the earth. There's no way around the fact of it. The only question is what the trade-off is for jobs and industry and growth and what it does to the history and the future of a place. Just look at the map. We drilled holes nearly two miles in the ground and excavated millions of tons of rock, refined some of its usable ore, and dumped what was left of our excavation in the lake or in mounds bordering the lake or in the country everywhere around us. Those mounds are not hard to find. You can see them from the road. Some of those mounds poisoned the lakes. By the time these consequences were known, the mines had closed and the companies gone defunct. There was no one left to sue. What's left for you is warning, we were told: Don't eat the fish in Torch Lake.

Dig a hole—or several—in the earth and in time it will fill. You've
made yourself a reservoir.

Dig a hole and you've made yourself a metaphor.

Third Descent

The map is from the US Geological Survey's 1929 professional paper 144, by B. S. Butler and W. S. Burbank, titled *The Copper Deposits of Michigan*. I love the plates in this document, though until I tracked down the whole document online, this one plate, this diagram of my mine, was the only one I'd seen.[2] And now to find so many others, similarly designed and executed! Consider the care evident in its precision, the way it's inked: the perfect 45-degree angles on the hash marks, the hand-lettering, human trace everywhere evident in its composition. This is only one way in which it matters.

Of course the image here is my scan of a copy. My stepmother or my father bought it at the Seaman Mineral Museum in Houghton and had it framed and sent to me. It's not the last cross section (the mine would operate for another sixteen years, eventually hitting level 97, and had at one point the longest shaft in the world), but it's the best cross section I've seen of the most productive mine in the area called the Copper Country.

There are other Copper Countries, of course. Tucson, Arizona, where I now live, isn't far from copper mining country. As such, until it closed in 2016, "Copper Country" was the name of a well-known antique store on Speedway Boulevard in front of which stood a forty-foot plaster buffalo.

I drive an hour and a half to visit Bisbee, a mining town built around the Copper Queen, a smaller mine of the same era as the Quincy, and encounter the familiar: the city has the same architecture as my hometown, and is similarly built into the crevice between two hills, though Bisbee's a bit smaller, and there's no canal running through the bottom to poison.

Here's the Carnegie library with the beautiful inlaid tile and the old oak card catalogs, the big buildings with the high ceilings and hammered copper or tin ceilings. Here's the bar that hasn't updated its look since the 1880s. Visiting Bisbee is visiting its past and my own. I fold a map of the city over one of Hancock and see what aligns. I could blast a shaft down through their superimposition and connect them: the Bisbee Grand and the Douglas Houghton House, for instance. The Franklin Square Inn and the Copper Queen Hotel. The Copper Queen Hotel is haunted, as is the Bisbee Grand, and not just by comparison with other former mining towns and their tragedies. I've stayed in both hotels and report no paranormal activity except once, in the middle of the night in my room in the Elizabethan Suite in the Bisbee Grand the ceiling fan just stopped working for no apparent reason: I could tell because I woke, no longer being cooled. I flipped the switch to no effect and scanned the room for ghosts. No luck. I watched for several hours to see if something happened before I fell back asleep. In the morning I woke to see it working again, but the doubling feeling stayed.

I'm unused to looking at vertical maps, largely because these days my life is conducted horizontally. Maybe I'd feel differently, live differently, if I lived in a major city where the vertical really matters. In Tucson you can't deny the horizontal is king; everything is flat, flattened out and widened, sunbaked, ranch styled, strip malled, and concreted. We don't have basements or second stories in our homes. We live in the wide basin between the mountain ranges, not on the sides of them, and not on top unless we are nuts or very rich. We live where the water collects, or used to until the water table began to drop.

The drive to Bisbee changes things, however: I find myself back in Michigan. Here, too, are hills and grades and tunnels through the sides of mountains. Homes are hidden beside hills where the sun barely hits them some days. The world is made of or in pursuit of copper, and now in pursuit of the story of that same pursuit: Bisbee's main business, too, is tourism. Here I am in search of what's underneath the world, flipping through a card catalog, contemplating darkness and obsolescence. Here I am tucked in a valley and every street seems to wind its way up into a hill. Here it snows sometimes, and the sun shines less than you'd expect, because so much of the sky is taken up by mountains on each side. And water, well, the water here is pretty rough. Though the government has decreed it's safe, it's hard not to think of Flint.

Fourth Descent

Four shafts (1, 3, 4, and 5) are unnumbered on this map, which means they're no longer operating. The only early shaft still in use when the map was made is number 2. I see how it ends at the eighty-fifth level and nothing's been found that far down, or maybe the excavation's barely started. How far down do you have to go before the lode bottoms out, or does it just become inefficient to mine it anymore?

I think of where an essay begins—a memory, maybe just a flash of one. I've been writing about mines for as long as I remember writing. But I don't know the Quincy mine, not really. I've been in approximately one percent of it. I trace its shafts with a fingertip but nothing is familiar. Is a mine a landscape or its removal?

I'm trying to understand what accounts for the way this map has remained with me—how it feels like it maps something personal but not yet knowable.

I read a student's MFA thesis and find myself writing toward it. It's about a dam but does not yet understand the metaphor. I want to ask her: What's the thing behind the dam you haven't opened yet? What's all this really about? It's hard to know how hard one should probe in moments like this, how big or hot or unnameable the thing is behind the dam (or the lode you imagine is just below you in the mine). Maybe what's behind the dam is only knowable from this side, by hands on its steel-and-concrete skin, by implication and echolocation. But who am I to say? It's her dam and what's behind is hers by birth or experience or refusal or choice. It's not even my metaphor.

Fifth Descent

Remove *mine* from *remained* and you get *read*, which is what I mean to do. I mean to read the remainder of the mine, what's left of it in earth or memory, what I take away from home (another kind of mining, this taking away): my reminder of where I'm from.

But how to read a map like this? I guess I assumed at first the darkened areas were the lode, but it seems more likely they indicate stopes (steplike open spaces left behind after mining: they follow the lode, which, if they knew exactly where the lode was, they probably wouldn't have so many false starts). The eye tracks to the diagonals, helpfully labeled "Fissure." The little one in the center isn't labeled so it might be a shaft they sank instead, but I would bet we're looking at a fissure here too.

As all maps do, this map flattens dimension, since shaft 2, the longest one, actually runs at about a 45-degree angle, in this case toward the viewer. Another one, shaft 7, runs—unusually—along a catenary curve, following the lode. And this map also flattens time: each shaft was a separate mine, operated by a different company, but purchased and consolidated later. And this map erases suffering: it takes no account of those who died down here, for instance, or later from complications from mine-related work, or as a result of the labor struggles, or as part of the 1913 Italian Hall Disaster, in which fifty-nine children and fourteen adults were killed at a Christmas party ten miles away.

Sixth Descent

I don't know what story I'm really looking at when I am looking at this map. I do know this is a story paid for by the government. What's left, I wonder, except for hole and scar, evidence of what was removed? There are stories, sure, but they've attenuated now through a couple of generations. I have my own. I've explored many other mines by breaking in or dreaming. If you spent any time outside where I'm from, you've stumbled on (hopefully not into) a mine shaft or two. There are hundreds sunk under everywhere. Maybe thousands. You begin to understand the whole landscape is riddled with holes. This is history, I know, but it's also mystery, and I'm drawn to it, the known unknown. Anything could be inside. Mostly the entrances are blocked off or filled in now. Some have been fenced with chicken wire so that bats can use them for homes. In an unintended consequence, what's used to keep kids out allows raccoons to roost and swat at bats as they fly out of the mine and through the chicken wire at dusk.

It's a cipher for me, a feature of geography, but what the mine represents is something else: the big hurt of the place, its most important myth. To grow up in a land like this is to know its best days are far behind. Everywhere there's evidence: the train tracks slowly getting overgrown, the mysterious ruins of buildings jutting up through trees seen from the highways through the snow. The whole Upper Peninsula of Michigan is like this now: once it was and is no longer, a song by Woody Guthrie or Gordon Lightfoot. Now the people come to see the wrecks, to tour the wrecks, to dive the wrecks of boats out in the Big Lake.

I don't suppose it's ever possible to feel that the best days of the place in which you live *are now*. What hubris that must be.

Or maybe these *are* the Copper Country's best days. After all, mine jobs were dangerous. Very many died from the work (cave-in, explosion, fire, or suffocation, in addition to the health problems miners brought

home from their time in darkness). The tourist jobs don't force you to
buy your own candles to keep the dark and chill away. You don't have
to deal with unexpected air blasts from shifting rocks loosed from an
explosion somewhere above you made for some reason you're not privy
to, a couple of columns that management averaged out and realized the
yield just might be worth the risk. You don't have to risk being trapped
there to perish in the dark when your BM-1447 Self Rescuer runs out
of its limited supply of air and those who own the mine determine that
a rescue would not be fiscally responsible or fair to the shareholders in
the company.

Now the jobs that pay are those shadowing these ghosts of jobs,
tracking their trails and the lives they made, the lives that left, where
all the copper and the iron ore went when it was taken from this place.
Another map might track the movement of the miners as they came
to work, what they did in the darkness, where their homes—company
owned, typically—were in relation to the holes, how long they spent in
each space. I wish I had that map. I doubt that map exists. Having this
one to gaze at just makes me want more maps, makes me want to go
down deeper and mine all this information. There are other maps, of
course. But it costs to make these maps. Now that there's no money
in the mine there's no need for maps. An industry begets an industry
to map it.

The map is a map of history. We drill down. Excavate the horizontal
until it becomes clear we've reached the structural limits or the end
of lode. Drill down again. Haul out rock and ore. Dump it in the lake.
Repeat.

Seventh Descent

What's the story with shaft 9? The map communicates one idea: though
it seems to connect to the 8 shaft, maybe it terminates in the fissure
instead; the angle is unclear. I don't know what a fissure does or what
exactly it disrupts. There's a value in not knowing everything. Here's
what mindat.org ("the world's most comprehensive mineral database
and mineralogical reference website") has to tell me: "Very little is known
of the Pontiac Mining Company. It was organized in 1859 to explore and
mine the Pewabic and Franklin Lodes between the Albany and Boston
and Mesnard Mine properties where ancient pits were discovered. It was

reported that good barrel copper and masses were found in the shaft, but the overall results were not promising. The company was bought by Quincy in 1897 and work was started on a new shaft in 1908 which was to become the Quincy No. 9 shaft; however, the great strike of 1913 forced Quincy to abandon sinking this shaft. A very small rock pile exists from this shaft sinking in 1908. Some copper can be found."

The strike led to the Italian Hall Disaster, also known as the Massacre of 1913. The story goes that on Christmas Eve, when the striking miners and their families were at a company party, someone (some claim a company man) screamed "Fire!" and the resulting panic turned into a stampede, killing seventy-three. The crowd pressed up against doors that only opened inward in the Italian Hall. Can you imagine it? Fifty-nine children crushed to death. I cannot bear to think about their bodies, but, for a moment anyway, we must. I know these tragedies occur—Sandy Hook, for instance—and yet they are for most of us easy to forget except in name. Perhaps the pain they spark is so great it cannot be borne for long and must be minimized in a name or song or metaphor, or buried somewhere deep inside ourselves, a lode we will hope never to find again.

Twenty-eight years later, Woody Guthrie wrote a song about the event, attributing all fault to mining management: "The gun thugs they laughed at their murderous joke / While the children were smothered on the stairs by the door."[3] There's no historical consensus on the facts (and what's known has become less and less clear as those who witnessed it died). While it's never been proved that the company engineered the tragedy to break the strike, the strike ended less than four months later.

The last shaft, the Quincy 9, leads nowhere now. Who knows how far down it really goes?

Eighth Descent

The Calumet near-capital story is apocryphal: a myth, recently debunked in a journal devoted to Upper Michigan Studies called *Upper Country*.[4] It was published for only three years (2013–2015) but serves as a kind of historical index to the place. It attests to our desire to assert ourselves in history. There was a vote to move the capital, but Calumet was not a city when that vote occurred. And as an article points out, no road existed in Calumet Village or Calumet Township then, so it's preposterous to imagine the legislature arguing for it as a possible capital. The heart of the story is true, though, in that the city's seen more prosperous days: its population peaked at 32,845 in 1910. At that point the population of Lansing, the present state capital, was 31,229.

I believed it when I first read it a few years ago. It had the ring of truth. It plays into the story we want to believe about where we're from: we mattered, once, it says, and so we listen and repeat. Caring about the facts takes mining, which means time and money and desire, sometimes explosives and pain. This story was dismantled easily enough that it embarrasses me to have ever believed it. Here was a wall I thought I knew, but it seems to have been paper-thin, and what's beyond it I'm not sure. Gas and rock and unknown passages. The more I look at the map on my wall the more it seems like it maps my own ignorance, vast and dark and bottomless. A map makes a pinprick in infinity, and illuminates nothing beyond its borders.

That there is a border to the knowable—or to the known—or maybe just to what I know or *can* know reassures me. It's not all light out there. Consider, for instance, the phenomenon of the Paulding Light, a little more than an hour away from this mine. The Paulding Light is a deeply freaky set of lights that emerge each evening and that, according to the lore, are spectral emanations—the ghosts of miners on the horizon trudging to their deaths. When you park at the end of the trail and watch the distance you can absolutely see lights in the distance, slowly rocking, moving closer, as if being carried from work to home after the sun has set. (Remember that their lives were often lived in darkness: in winter they went to work before the sun came up, and worked all day in darkness that they had to pay to light themselves, and walked home afterward in darkness.)

I didn't exactly believe the story, but what else could explain it? (*To resolve the mystery, turn to page 167.*) This, I was excited to think, was the most unexplainable thing I had yet encountered, and I dug the feeling of rubbing up against the unknowable. It felt important, mine-deep. So much of my world is rational and explainable. I felt more alive encountering a bit that was not.

But do I even know what I think I know? I start to figure out how little I know of my own place's history or even my own. I have a memory of belief: that my great-grandfather worked this mine, that he migrated here from Finland to work it. No idea if that's true or just another fiction I use to prop up the passage in my excavations. How much do I want to know about what holds up the passages in which I labor? Later, offering corrections on this essay, my dad tells me I'm right: my great-grandfather *did* work this mine. It's good to know, but I don't want to tell him it doesn't matter to me: my belief in the story is the thing that matters—*that's* the true thing. The story's truth is, for me, secondary. And I'm relieved there's so much about this place that most of us don't know. For instance, I only recently discovered that, until 2004, Upper Michigan and northern Wisconsin hosted Project ELF (also known as Project Sanguine and Project Austere ELF), massive, hardened, extremely low frequency (ELF) radio transmitters for broadcasting messages to submerged nuclear submarines all across the globe. That is not a story the government was eager to broadcast loudly. Now the transmitters themselves are gone, but the trails they cut into the pines remain. We still don't know the effects of those transmissions on ecosystems or on our stories or us.

Ninth Descent

I find myself wandering silently around my darkened house at night when everyone is asleep except the cats. My pleasure in doing this is not insubstantial. I believe I know everything in sight: this is the landscape I know best. This is my place, my home, my family's things, my teetering stacks of CDs and books and empty frames I've collected for the moment I find something to fill them, my thirty-four LED lights flickering on and off signaling devices that transmit and receive data and other signals throughout the house. These are our accumulations. I don't know what effect they have on me either.

Sometimes I fear being surprised by an anomaly in my habitat: blindsided by an intruder, toppled by an unexpected Lego underfoot, tripped into a window by a silent, passing pet. I remember a Kenneth Rexroth line: "The greater the mass of things, / The greater the insecurity." I carry the baby monitor in one hand and let it dangle from my index finger. It casts a little light, enough to illuminate just what's in front of me. When I turn the corner and see just the light rocking in the mirror down the hall, for a second I can't tell what it is. In that second I think of those bodies and the Paulding Light, a miner's lantern rocking in the distance.

Notes

1. Charles Cleland, *Rites of Conquest* (Ann Arbor: University of Michigan Press, 1992).

2. B. S. Butler and W. S. Burbank, *The Copper Deposits of Michigan* (Washington, DC: USGS, 1929), https://pubs.er.usgs.gov/publication/pp144.

3. Woody Guthrie, "1913 Massacre," released in 1941.

4. Emily Schmitz, "Place mats: Calumet, Michigan and the State Capital Myth," *Upper Country* 1 (2013). Available at http://commons.nmu.edu/upper_country/vol1/iss1/5.

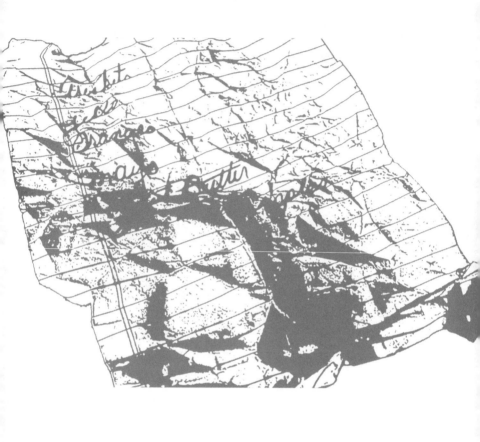

For Unknown Reasons

The Safeway keeps drawing me back. It's five years later now. How okay am I? Will I always be oriented to this violent site? In my absence the corner has developed quite a bit, now sprouting a Beyond Bread where I sit in the air-conditioning, watching America happen.

Now only two of the Safeway's fourteen reviews online mention the shooting. If the casual visitor didn't know it happened, she'd likely miss it. The complaints in the reviews are mostly about the poor customer service. "Carl"'s shitty review has been deleted for five years. How many others had read it in its brief lifetime?

I'm still saying it, though, and I encourage you to join me so that we remember:

Fuck you, Carl.

Your review is gone but we are still here.

And the memorial's still here and still well kept, but it seems smaller. Here's what's left: a fresh bouquet of red, white, and blue flowers that gets picked up and replaced while I am watching it; three metal roses wired into the shape of a heart; a green piece of hard candy and a striped mint candy; a picture of Christina Taylor-Green, the little girl born, amazingly, as you may know, on 9/11, who was killed here by Loughner with the others, and who is easily the most tragic face of that terrible day; a stuffed dog; a plastic rose; a couple of unreadable notes; a little certificate from Ben's Bells, a local organization promoting kindness; and a fabric necklace reminiscent of a rosary attached to a laminated plastic card of Saint Kateri Tekakwitha, "the first Native American to be recognized as a saint by the Catholic Church" (catholic.org tells me), who "contracted smallpox as a four-year-old child which scarred her skin. The scars were a source of humiliation in her youth. She was commonly seen wearing a blanket to hide her face. Worse, her entire family died during the outbreak." She refused to marry. To avoid persecution at the hands of her adopted family, she left for "a Christian native community south of Montreal. . . . Kateri was very devout and would put thorns on her sleeping mat. . . . She often fasted and when she would eat, she would taint her food to diminish its flavor. On at least one occasion, she burned herself. . . . She is the patroness of ecology and the environment, people in exile and Native Americans."

Right under that description you can purchase "St. Kateri Tekakwitha Gifts by Catholic Online Shopping" such as a pendant for $35.99, a 1 1/8-inch genuine pewter medal for $11.95, a sterling silver oval-shaped medal for $32.97, a 14 karat gold-filled pendant for $50.99, a 14 karat gold medal for $164.99, or a sterling silver medal for $43.97.

Next to the memorial—so close to it I'm unsure if it's part of the memorial or not, and so I'm unsure if I should pick it up—I find a balled-up piece of lined yellow paper. I do pick it up. I open it. It's a shopping list with six items: "triskets, jello, oranges, mayo, peanut butter, sm. eating apples." It's not a note or prayer. Sometimes it's not clear what the difference is between these kinds of documents.

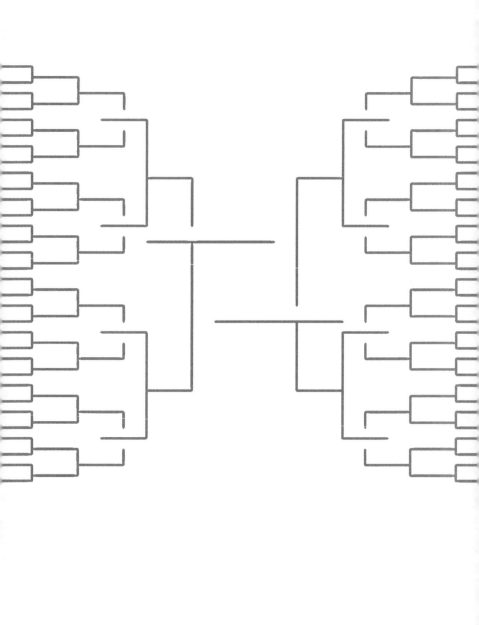

The Sadnesses
of March

I am caught off guard in my car outside the Goodwill on First Avenue when Morrissey comes on the radio and I'm thrown into a little torrent of torment. It is Sunday, so maybe that's why I'm more susceptible to "Every Day Is Like Sunday" especially only a few miles from the Safeway I'm still thinking of. I'm caught in the song's emotional tangle, and either the day is immediately transformed or I am. I'm pulled into an emotional state I thought I'd left behind, one I'd hardened myself to by time and the pleasures of consumption and pursuit of a stellar glass decanter I just bought to fit into one of my many collections. Listening, I feel suddenly transparent to myself: it's not so far to see through who I've become to who I used to be. The song makes me sad, but I'm happy for the weakening. It's a reawakening and a reminder of how it felt to feel exactly this way.

"Why listen to sad music if it makes one feel sad?" asks Stephen Davies, a professor of psychology at the University of Auckland, in 1997, ten years after that Morrissey song was recorded. I ask myself this not for the first time as the next day I'm neck-deep into the Joy Division discography on the way to a job I do not dread, mourn, or fear. Ian Curtis sings "Don't turn away, in silence" and I do not turn away, not as I drive past sun-blasted car dealerships, burrito shops, and the Tucson Upholstery Company. I turn away in song, if not in silence.

It's a good question, but for Davies, anyhow, it's not a real one. He suggests the *question* is false, because he doesn't believe music can carry any emotion at all. I'll take the answer, though, even if it's a counterintuitive one: Most of us don't like to think we seek out unpleasant experiences. Yet when it comes to music, many of us gravitate to tragedy, to lament, to elegy, breakup ode, cri de coeur. We seek out the funereal, the *fado*, the dirge. That is, we want to feel down. We pursue wrecked emotional states to the point of obsession, listening to a sad song over and over and over until it's done with us or we're done with it for today.

If you're listening to "Love Will Tear Us Apart," Elliott Smith, REM, Sinead O'Connor, Tom Waits, Kate Bush, Red House Painters, the Cure, Sarah McLachlan, or Neutral Milk Hotel this morning, then it's you I'm talking to. Or *Adagio for Strings*, Adele, woeful country, or even, I guess, "Every Rose Has Its Thorn": I say to you, I am your people. I know there are a lot of us out there getting our sad on today. Many of us lead very happy lives. And I like happy things too. I love pop music, too, though I'm drawn to the down moments in pop songs, the ones where you can hear the darkness in the daylight, as in Don Henley's 1984 single "Boys of Summer," which celebrates summer from the perspective of its end.

So what's up with us? Why am I built this way? I mean, why are we suckers for punishment? I want to know why I like sad songs, and why, though I'm not alone, I like feeling alone. And if a lot of us do, then what does that say about us, and should we come together and do or say something about it or play a game about it? Is there a machine we could make to process or disambiguate our lonelinesses, our sadnesses, or our grief?

In March 2016, I decided to try to build something to help me figure it out. It happened to be March, and though I'm no fan of college basketball, there's something about the elegance of the bracket the NCAA uses to determine its national championship that transfixes me. Consider it, if you would: sixty-four teams enter, and they each play a game, and then the winners play another game, and so on until only one team remains. And the genius of the tournament itself is that you don't even need to care about basketball to make a bracket. Just throw a couple of bucks into a pool your friends make and, presto, you have something to root for, and rooting for something feels good; competition feels good. It connects and fills me, even if I know it's stupid, and I feel part of something larger, if only for that month.

Arriving at a national champion is great—I mean, the tournament is designed to crown a champion—but it's always a letdown for me. The real excitement is, as fans know, in the first couple of rounds, when seemingly *anything* can happen: some upstart team that has never won a tournament game can beat a perennial favorite and blow up everyone's predictions. I'm sure I'm not the only one whose interest decreases as the NCAA tournament goes on, as the possibilities dwindle. So why not use this machine to disambiguate sadnesses? So I did. Or we did. My wife, Megan, and I thus constituted the Official March Sadness Selection Committee in 2016 and created a bracket, in which we selected sixty-four songs from the era of music we like best, being the era of college rock, loosely 1980–2001 with an emphasis on 1985–1995. We limited our selections to what we used to call "alternative," the sort you might find on MTV's *120 Minutes* or its outskirts and antecedents.

And so began March Sadness (see pages 80–81).

It's hard to imagine now, in the era of infinite availability and the ability to soundtrack every moment of our lives, that there was a time when, unless you lived in a really hip city or close to a cool college radio station, there was only the terrible Top 40 or country or Christian rock; there was only Loverboy and Foreigner and Asia and "The Piña Colada Song" and songs I do not believe will ever mean anything again. And even I find it hard to remember now how stumbling on a song on the radio that felt torn up and weird and confused and disturbed and not "pretty-girl sad" (to quote Megan Campbell, the other half of the Official March Sadness Selection Committee) felt like revelation, how it felt like salvation.

That's one of the appeals of the sad song: we recognize the sadness it describes. It articulates our own feelings better than we could ourselves. We project ourselves on it, and listening to it—*playing it,* which is, after all, an action—lets us feel our feels intensely and at will.

The committee limited itself to one song per band (with a couple of fudges: for example, we included a song by both Joy Division and the band that emerged from its ashes, New Order, since they're pretty different, though we resisted the urge to use the first New Order single, "Ceremony," still arguably their best or saddest, because it was pretty much a Joy Division song). We seeded these songs, sorted them into regions, in some cases set songs against each other in conference tournaments and play-in games, and then started up a single-elimination, March Madness/college basketball–style tournament that ran online in March 2016 and that you can still find and play online at http://marchsadness2016.blogspot.com. We annotated every song and matchup, disambiguated what we could of these sadnesses, and submitted the bracket to readers and listeners,

	1st Round	2nd Round	3rd Round	4th Round	5th Round	
	[3/5-12]	[3/13-16]	[3/17-20]	[3/22-25]	[3/27-28]	

1 — The Cure, Pictures of You
16 — Gear Daddies, Don't Look at Me
8 — Tom Waits, Downtown Train
9 — Pretenders, Back on the Chain Gang
5 — Swans, God Damn the Sun
12 — Pet Shop Boys, Rent
4 — Tori Amos, Silent All These Years
13 — Echo & the Bunnymen, All My Colours
6 — This Mortal Coil, Song to the Siren
11 — Yaz, Only You
3 — Indigo Girls, Romeo & Juliet
14 — Pavement, Gold Soundz
7 — Nine Inch Nails, Hurt
10 — Wilco, She's a Jar
2 — Radiohead, Fake Plastic Trees
15 — Liz Phair, Fuck and Run

1 — Neutral Milk Hotel, Two Headed Boy
16 — Violent Femmes, Add It Up
8 — Sarah McLachlan, I Will Not Forget You
9 — New Order, Regret
5 — James, Say Something
12 — Red House Painters, Katy Song
4 — Magnetic Fields, I Don't Believe in the Sun
13 — The Church, Under the Milky Way
6 — Peter Gabriel, Don't Give Up
11 — Ride, Vapour Trail
3 — Sinead O'Connor, Three Babies
14 — OMD, If You Leave
7 — Nick Cave & the Bad Seeds, The Ship Song
10 — Smashing Pumpkins, Disarm
2 — Jeff Buckley, Hallelujah
15 — Bjork, Unravel

FINAL FOUR

NATIO

5th Round	4th Round	3rd Round	2nd Round	1st Round
[3/27-28]	[3/22-25]	[3/17-20]	[3/13-16]	[3/5-12]

Elliott Smith, Waltz #2 — 1

10,000 Maniacs, Eat for Two — 16

Replacements, Here Comes a Regular — 8

Dream Academy, Life in a Northern Town — 9

Morphine, I'm Free Now — 5

Morrissey, Suedehead — 12

Gary Jules, Mad World — 4

Depeche Mode, Blasphemous Rumours — 13

Kate Bush, This Woman's Work — 6

Sisters of Mercy, Some Kind of Stranger — 11

Nirvana, All Apologies — 3

Slowdive, Alison — 14

Tracy Chapman, Fast Car — 7

Smiths, There Is a Light That Never Goes Out — 10

Eels, Dead of Winter — 2

Counting Crows, A Long December — 15

Joy Division, Atmosphere — 1

Erasure, Fingers & Thumbs (Cold Summer's Day) — 16

REM, So. Central Rain — 8

Mazzy Star, Fade into You — 9

PJ Harvey & Nick Cave, Henry Lee — 5

Midnight Oil, Blue Sky Mine — 12

Alphaville, Forever Young — 4

Dead Can Dance, American Dreaming — 13

Crowded House, Don't Dream It's Over — 6

Leonard Cohen, Closing Time — 11

U2, With or Without You — 3

Low, Words — 14

Bob Mould, I Can't Fight It — 7

Peter Murphy, I'll Fall with Your Knife — 10

Concrete Blonde, Joey — 2

Psychedelic Furs, Heartbreak Beat — 15

FINAL FOUR

ION

you who click through sites and magazines and social media and blogs, to see which songs you found the saddest, and, more importantly, why.

Why do we find this song sad? What makes it sadder than its opponent? Why do we seek out these particular sadnesses, and why are we still moved by them these many years later? Why do we court pain?

I don't know. It sounds like a dumb idea, doesn't it? Aren't all our sadnesses individual? Who wants to or believes they can judge and weigh and rate and rank another's pain? Well, we do. And we did. And no, as much as we'd like to believe it, our sadnesses aren't entirely individual. Time tells us that most of our heartbreaks follow a pretty conventional plot.

So we started with the obvious: the Smiths, Tom Waits, Kate Bush, Tori Amos, Magnetic Fields, before moving into deeper waters: Low, This Mortal Coil, Liz Phair, Eels, Neutral Milk Hotel, the Church, Indigo Girls, Swans, and Pet Shop Boys. Choosing songs was often easy: for the Cure, we selected "Pictures of You" and gave it a 1 seed, since they're one of the saddest bands of the era (as well as, oddly, one of the happiest: see also "Just Like Heaven"). The grandness of the way the song articulates its romantic loss and fixates on memory embodies a certain brand of sadness: beautiful, big, caked with makeup, dramatic, more than a little self-involved. It's easy to love a song like that, and many do.

It's trickier to love a song like Morrissey's "Suedehead," in which the situation of the song isn't particularly sad, nor is, if we're being honest, the speaker himself. If there's a sadness, it's at the speaker's expense, or at the expense of the you addressed in the song. Look at the lyrics ("It was a good lay, good lay, good lay"), which seem to describe an uncomfortable situation with an ex-lover or one-night stand, focused purely on the self-interested awkwardness of the speaker. It's sad, yes, but mostly for the lover, the you that comes here and hangs around. As delivered by Morrissey, though, it's a dramatic monologue in which we gradually understand that the speaker—possibly closeted—is an unlovable narcissist, perhaps the sort of person who demanded to publish his autobiography (not to say anything as banal as a memoir) under the aegis of the imprint Penguin Classics. But then that's how I read almost all of Morrissey's songs: they weaponize unappealing aspects of our personalities. One loves that about him, or not. As for me, I do love him and his songs for their layers and complications and many echoing ironies. Is it sad? Yes, but at angles.

So here's a related question: If a song has a sad affect, as "Suedehead" does, is it sad? On some level, yes, since affect is what most of us respond to. That is to say: Does it sound sad? That's partly because, unlike books or films, songs don't require so much of our attention: they easily background our lives and our dramas. So, for instance, I never felt I needed to look up the lyrics for "Suedehead" to understand what the song was about (all the "good lay" stuff was a revelation to me).

Consider REM's arpeggiated tearjerker ballad "Everybody Hurts": at first glance it's the most obvious inclusion, yet when the committee ran the REM regional play-in tournament, something became obvious to us that's probably already obvious to you: "Everybody Hurts" is a song not of sadness but of consolation. It's an antidote for sadness. So though we felt we needed an REM song on account of their being one of the mopier bands of the era, we had a hard time identifying a truly sad song, which probably speaks well of the complexity of their songwriting. We settled on (8) "So. Central Rain," a choice I've come to understand was wrong, and not just because (9) Mazzy Star's "Fade into You" defeated it soundly in the first round matchup. (Possibly we underestimated the appeal of Mazzy Star. And they, too, are not particularly sad.)

Any song that prominently features a plaintive "I'm sorry" in the lyrics would seem to be a good choice, and that's true, it was a fine choice: relatively well known, relatively old school, right in the middle of the bracket. We could have gone with "Country Feedback," the Serious Fan's definitive choice for sadness, but a much less known song. We talked ourselves out of "Man on the Moon" mainly because that campy "Andy are you tripping on Elvis' 'Hey Baby'" bit Stipe does spoils the pity party. We talked ourselves out of "Fall on Me" because of the political overtones that infuse a lot of REM songs, but I think that would now be my choice. Would it still have been bounced by "Fade into You," a song with a lot of resonance for a lot of people, even if to us it's more sexy and sunburned than sad?

Well, what is sadness anyway? It's not sex and sunburn. I talked with Mary-Frances O'Connor, a psychological researcher at the University of Arizona whose work specializes in a phenomenon called "Complicated Grief . . . a disorder following bereavement that is marked by intense, persistent and prolonged symptoms," as she describes it, particularly yearning, which is to say an intense desire for what's gone. In a coffee shop on the university campus, she talked me through some of the physiology of emotion as the radio warbled unidentifiable, Auto-Tuned pop that left no mark on me. This, I thought, was what alternative served to counter. There are physiological signs of sadness you can track, she told me: heart rate and sweat, for instance, so you could actually run an experiment in which you play sad songs for listeners and chart how they're physically affected. I perked up at the thought of this.

Plus, she said, almost all emotions have a third-party consequence. A communicative quality, she explained: because emotions are tied to facial expressions that are remarkably universal across cultures, we respond to them in different ways. We see someone crying and we want to comfort them. It's learned or wired—we're not totally sure which—that we have a need to give care. Caregiving is natural and enjoyable, as many parents would tell you. So, she told me, one feature of listening to a very sad song is that we perceive the artist in their moment of greatest vulnerability, and we're wired to want to love them.

This idea of yearning fascinated me: not just that the yearning can often persist far beyond the actual loss, but that yearning itself can be pleasurable in its way, that it can be self-reinforcing. O'Connor's studies have borne out what many of us have long known to be true. One of her articles, for instance, uses an epigraph by Aeschylus: "There is no pain so great as the memory of joy in present grief." As her work shows us (in slant anyhow), for some, the inverse is also true: there is no joy so great (or as persistent) as remembering pain. As she puts it in one article, "Although successful adaptation to the loss is the most frequent response . . . grief does not abate in a substantial minority; rather, it develops into Complicated Grief." Complicated Grief, I thought, sounds like something I could get interested in.

This is one reason why, though it should be objectively sadder, since it affects more people, for most of us, the political is less sad than the personal. That's because the political leverages its sadness toward another purpose. Songs with political content in the bracket didn't fare well when matched up with the tragically personal. Consider "Blue Sky Mine" by Midnight Oil, the most in-your-face political song in the tournament: the video for the song begins with a mashup of news headlines: "An Exxon oil tanker / CSR Company faced tough questioning at the company's annual / From Geelong / payouts to workers affected by asbestos," and the song gets right to it with lyrics like, "The company takes what the company wants / And nothing's as precious as a hole in the ground." The song goes from the macro to the micro: as you listen, you understand that the speaker is a mine worker, indentured, "caught at the junction / still waiting for medicine / The sweat of my brow keeps on feeding the engine." It was bounced from the tournament in the first round by PJ Harvey and Nick Cave's probably-more-grotesque-than-sad-but-totally-great murder ballad "Henry Lee."

Besides, political sadness wants us to be sad but then to move to understanding or action: it inflames to an end. It gives us an outlet for that feeling, so a political song can feel flatter and less complicated in its overtures (if surely no less so in its details). Peter Gabriel's "Biko" is meant not just to get us to cry or to feel empathy but to mobilize us, to make us aware.

For me, the really sad songs don't have that exit point: they're trapped in their emotion, unable to get out, to move past it to action, which sounds a lot like O'Connor's explanation of the pathology of complicated grief. The only action they can take is the singing of the song, like the Indigo Girls' version of Dire Straits' "Romeo & Juliet." Give it a listen. I'll wait. Pull the car over. Listen hard.

Okay. You're back? It's exceptionally anguished, isn't it? Amy Ray takes a doomed, star-crossed Dire Straits song that's riffing on one of the most famous pieces of literature of all time, and makes it utterly her own. Of all the songs in the bracket, this one surprised me the most. In fact, the committee selected it from memory (hey, you know what song was sad? oh, totally), and both committee members had it come on their radios while driving and were each—independently— overwhelmed and had to pull over and let it pass. It's a forceful song, probably the most impassioned, the angriest, the most desperate of all the songs in the bracket. Those other emotions are there, too, but in "Romeo & Juliet" they serve sadness, not the other way around. When was the last time you felt emotionally overwhelmed by a piece of music? When was the last time you went in search of just that feeling? What hurts you so good?

"Romeo & Juliet" does best what the dramatic monologue does: it exposes emotional and intellectual spaces beneath the speaker's ability to articulate that we the listeners are able to read; it also has its own narrative movement and rising action; it goes from sadness to anger to raw unfiltered rage to self-consciousness to desperation to resignation, as "A lovestruck Romeo . . . finds a streetlight, steps out of the shade" and sings this "love song that he made" and then disappears again into darkness and silence.

The song remains, evidence of that love and that betrayal (an echo we'd see picked up in a sequel tournament, 2018's March Shredness tournament of songs about hair metal). It's a ghost, a persistent yearning, spectral remnant that still floats out there—and it's out there even more literally in the era of *Every Song Ever . . . an Age of Musical Plenty*, to grab the title and part of the subtitle of *New York Times* music critic Ben Ratliff's 2016 book on strategies for listening in the age of the streaming service and the cloud: "We know all that music is there. Some of us know, roughly, how to encounter a lot of it. But once we hear it, how can we allow ourselves to make sense of it? We could use new ways to find points of connection and intersection with all that inventory."

Ratliff wasn't on our radar when we began the tournament, but when we stumbled on his book during the second round, we realized March Sadness is a machine made in part to root and sort through that old inventory. These songs are sad, we mean to say, and so were you. Remember. Not just the song but who you used to be.

One way to sort and root is to match up sadnesses against each other. The Indigo Girls have their political leanings, though the lyrical content of the song isn't particularly political. But sometimes the act of singing a song is political: Amy Ray voicing Romeo with such unstoppable passion in 1992 is a lot more potent than Jill Sobule's toothless 1995 song, "I Kissed a Girl" (sample lyrics: "I kissed a girl / her lips were sweet. / She was just like kissing me") or pop megastar Katy Perry's dull 2008 single of the same title.

It's not great science to generalize about sadness from just one game or even a nerdy online tournament, but in almost every early game between the apparently autobiographical (say, Sinead O'Connor's "Three Babies") and the more abstract (in this case Ride's shoegaze classic "Vapour Trail"), the autobiographical/confessional won. I guess that's not surprising. Our appetite in America these days is for our sadness to be personal, authentic, and autobiographical, perhaps in part because in our intensely consumer culture we feel less individual all the time: if we're treated as just a collection of likes and web searches and desires, it figures that we're hungry for evidence of others' individuality and realness.

So let's listen again to "Three Babies," a song O'Connor has described as being about her miscarriages: by so explaining, it's easy for us to assume the she who's speaking is the she who's singing. There's little to tell us otherwise, and that assumption makes it easier for us to enter into the song. Would it be less sad if she hadn't had miscarriages? It's a blunt question to ask but an important one. I think it would be, yes, because the object of the sadness becomes more distant. We wouldn't see Sinead but a character, or the idea or experience of a miscarriage, which we may or may not have any personal experience with. If we believe she has, it's easier for us to trust her: we add ethos to the song's already considerable pathos.

Plus, I don't know if she could or would have otherwise written the song—or performed it with the level of anguish and strangeness she wraps herself in, trying to console herself with her voice. In "Blue Sky Mine," if we knew the singer to actually *be* a downtrodden mine worker (and not a rock star and a future politician), we'd give it extra sadness credit.

Persona is an abstraction: it creates a distance the song or performance must bridge to be successful. So when Sinead's voice suddenly surges and nearly breaks the song in half in the lines "No longer mad like a horse / I'm still wild but not lost," it's thrilling: we feel the wildness. It sears us. We can't be anything but changed.

Compare that to (6) Kate Bush's "This Woman's Work," also a song about parenting. Bush is incapable of being untheatrical, and that theatricality—that is to say, the readable presence of artifice—creates a little bit of distance between the emotion of the song and us. As we learn not only that the song was written for the John Hughes film *She's Having a Baby* but also that it was written to score one particularly dramatic montage sequence in the film, we add more distance still. It went down to Tracy Chapman's more apparently sincere "Fast Car" in the Sweet Sixteen.

That readable presence of artifice is the gap Tori Amos crossed so effectively and powerfully with her very first single, (4) "Silent All These Years." At the time, the song almost singlehandedly seemed to shatter an unwritten code of pop and rock and alternative music that assured us songs, though they might be dramatic and disaffected, would still seem safe. These songs managed their emotion so as to move us but not to touch us, not really. I remember when I first heard "Silent All These Years": I was at my friend Graham's house, and one minute we were watching a Def Leppard video, and then all of a sudden here's this woman in a box and this piano and this voice. I don't know how else to describe it except to say it felt real.

That real feeling is partly the result of artifice: the greatest goal of a certain philosophy of production (the sort employed by Rick Rubin in putting together Johnny Cash's *American Recordings*, for instance) is to get the song to sound unproduced, to banish all the double-tracking and orchestration, to hide the studio, to make the song seem transparent, like what we're hearing is just a human voice and a piano. And it is, sure, but it's a made thing: it's not as if "Silent All These Years" or any other song is a first recording of a first draft, unmanipulated and recorded on the first take. That it feels like it could be is extremely effective artifice: it punctures some of the many defenses we build up against sentimentality and our own expectations of sad songs. When Tori lost in the Sweet Sixteen to the Cure's "Pictures of You" in a close game, we wept, appropriately.

Four months after the tournament had concluded, Rob, one of the few friends from high school I still am sort of in contact with, emailed me to complain about our choice of Tori Amos songs. He says, and I'm quoting him because I love the fervor of his emails:

"Marianne" [from *Boys for Pele*] is the song you crawl into a ditch and die to, or crawl out of and still fucking die to. [*Boys for Pele* is] a precious intersection of mad youth, voodoo, gospel, and rebellion against the father figures that had dominated her career till then. Her wildest and most free, uninhibited. The one I think she might admit that prolly shoulda killed her in just the writing and making of it. The one where she's suckling a suckling pig a la Mother Mary and Pieta.

Rob's an intense dude, and one of the two most obsessive Tori Amos fans I know. (Alison Stine's the other: she wrote the essay about Tori for the Sweet Sixteen; she was also the winner of the Tori Amos round of MTV's short-lived show called *Superfans* or something of the sort.) His email goes on to talk in a circumspect way about his love for Tori. I don't quite get it, to be honest, but I love hearing people talk about their obsessions, so I sent back an email asking for more. This March Sadness machine is powerful enough to keep eliciting some strong opinions.

Obsession is part of why we listen to sad songs: we listen to sad songs not just because the singer seems sad but because they allow us to be sad—and safely, insulated from the practical consequence of extreme emotion: the broken marriage, the miscarriage, the guilt at not anticipating the suicide of a friend; they open up spaces inside us that are otherwise inaccessible in our daily lives. Listening to a sad song punctures time and the lived experience of our moment-to-moment, which is to say it connects us to our own mortality. According to Ratliff, "When we listen we might think about the most vulnerable aspects of our own sensibilities, too—the irremediably blue parts, the hopeful parts, the shy or naïve parts. . . . Many of us are not only guarding ourselves against specific calamities, disappointments, or embarrassments, rites of passage that we will inevitably face, whoever we are—missed deadlines, bounced checks, the trials of school and money and love and work. We are guarding ourselves against death."

Art allows us to feel alive in ways we otherwise can't—or don't. This happens in at least three ways, according to a 2013 study of why exactly we enjoy sad songs by psychological researchers Ai Kawakami, Kiyoshi Furukawa, Kentaro Katahira, and Kazuo Okanoya. First, we experience empathy for the speaker or situation (this is familiar to all of us who read books). Second, when we connect music to personal memories, "such as a lost love or someone's death, the listener may experience a sad emotion that is accompanied with suffering," and that listening to sad songs can remind us of. Last, sad songs operate on us by allowing us to experience sadness vicariously—and safely: "Because the danger that is associated with listening to sad music does not pose a direct threat to us, listeners are able to trust and enjoy the listening process." The study concludes by suggesting one reason why we enjoy listening to sad songs is that we sense a sad song is going to be sad, and when it is, our brain rewards itself for its correct prediction.

The Kawakami study cites Jerrold Levinson's 1997 article "Music and Negative Emotion," which is included in the same book as the Stephen Davies question that began this essay. Levinson also identifies three benefits of listening to sad songs: "benefits of enjoyment, of understanding, and of self-assurance." We enjoy and take satisfaction in the feeling of feeling *itself*, no matter what that feeling is, and we enjoy feeling that feeling. We enjoy the ability to feel, particularly to feel sad things, but to feel them safely, without the "life consequences" of those feelings. And having experienced our own ability to feel things safely, we are pleased to have a sense of "mastery and control" over these emotions in part because the feeling of emotional mastery is otherwise rare in our lives.

Though Levinson's analysis isn't based on empirical research, Kawakami et al.'s is, and besides, these insights track well with my own listening habits. They feel right: listening to sad songs makes me feel like I can drop into sadness and leave it when I need to. I get to feel in control of my sadness, when it begins and when it ends. And when I encounter sadness in my everyday life it controls me, not the other way around.

As Levinson puts it:

> If one begins to regard music as the expression of one's own current emotional state, it will begin to seem as if it issues from oneself, as if it pours forth from one's innermost being. It is then very natural for one to receive an impression of expressive power, of freedom and ease in externalizing and embodying what one feels. The sense one has of the richness and spontaneity with which one's inner life is unfolding itself, even where the feelings involved are of the negative kind, is a source of undeniable joy. The unpleasant aspect of certain emotions we imagine ourselves to experience through music is balanced by the adequacy, grace, and splendor of the exposition we feel ourselves to be according that emotion.

Reread that while listening to "Pictures of You" and feel how well the splendor of the song—beginning with the tinkly synth sounds that cascade and chime into the first chord—leads to our ownership of it and sense of its—and our—majesty.

Grace is another matter. Now I'm listening to a cover of a cover: Robert Plant covering This Mortal Coil's version of Tim Buckley's "Song to the Siren" as an epitaph for Tim's son Jeff, who had recently died by drowning in the Mississippi River. I found it by watching the This Mortal Coil video on YouTube and following the trail to its covers, including versions by Sinead, George Michael, Bryan Ferry, Dead Can Dance, and very many more. It's a beautiful version Plant performs, indebted, as all the covers are, to This Mortal Coil's version, which found a song of timeless yearning in the slightly folky original, performed first (amazingly!) on the Monkees' TV show.

I know Plant's cover is not autobiographical, but when he sings it and dedicates it to Jeff, the situation makes it so. So I follow that trail to Jeff Buckley's (2) "Hallelujah," his spectacular take on a towering Leonard Cohen song. Here, too, there's no danger of our reading it as strict autobiography: instead, the experience of listening to both songs, each with just a guitar and a voice, is trying to parse out the feelings Buckley and

Elizabeth Fraser (of Cocteau Twins, moonlighting here as part of the 4AD label's This Mortal Coil covers project) are feeling, and letting those feelings run on whatever circuitry we've got. Ratliff calls this kind of self-effacing transparency: "Some singers . . . go transparent in their voice. They seem to become the property of other forces." I was crushed, then, when "Song to the Siren" was eliminated by Radiohead's (2) "Fake Plastic Trees" in the Sweet Sixteen. It took a while for me to understand how the voters could have chosen their beautiful, transparent song over mine.

The bracket is a machine for my humbling. I watched the sad songs I loved the best, the ones I felt defined me, go down one after another. And I tried to figure out why. Now I think Radiohead's "Fake Plastic Trees" defeated "Song to the Siren" because it goes anthemic, which means it allows us into it in a different way. Even though it's apparently personal (it becomes personal anyhow in the last minute when it moves from talking about the "her" ["it wears her out"] to "If I could be / what you wanted"), it's not specifically personal. That movement becomes narrative; it allows us into the song's sadness in a way "Song to the Siren" doesn't. "Song to the Siren" is like overhearing someone talking to a god or a myth. "Fake Plastic Trees" is like listening to someone speaking to us—and by the end we understand it's our voice we're hearing, like how some sung notes resonate in particular spaces that fit their frequencies: Thom Yorke is wearing us in that moment.

This happens in lesser songs, too, in clunkier ways. As one of our collaborators, Matt Vadnais, points out in his commentary on the first-round matchup between (2) Eels' "Dead of Winter" and (15) Counting Crows' "A Long December," when "December" makes its way to the re-peated "na na na na, na na na na na na na, yeah" outro at the end of the song, that's the invitation moment for us. Nothing could be less specific or autobiographical than "na na na na, na na na na na na na na, yeah," which is why it either rings right to you in the moment or perhaps as mawkish later.

If we were sort of inside the song before, well, now we've been ush-ered in entire. Our arms are around each other. And so what if the song was later adopted by fraternity bros across America? Don't they deserve to be included, to feel loved like that too?

Maybe, though, I'm projecting a personal memory of "Fake Plastic Trees" onto the song. In college I became friends with a guy I'll call Alex, and it quickly became obvious I was an obsession for him, a romantic fixation, as he revealed to me multiple times in increasingly awkward ways. I genuinely liked him but had no romantic interest in him. I've sometimes been oblivious to romantic or erotic undercurrents in my friendships, and I didn't understand at the time that what I needed to do was to push him away much more forcefully than I did, so as not to allow him to entertain his hopes. Anyhow, I drove several hours with him to his hometown to see a concert where Radiohead was opening for REM. He and many of my friends were Big Sad REM Fans. I liked REM fine and could shout obscure requests if I needed to ("Bury magnets! Swallow the rapture!"), but really I was going for Radiohead. Because he underestimated the travel time, we got there too late to see Radiohead. Pulling into the massive stadium parking lot with the windows rolled down I could just hear the end of "Fake Plastic Trees," their closing number, echoing over row after row of SUVs. I was, to put it mildly, pissed. I don't remember what I said, but it was probably needlessly hurtful. And while I remember moments from the rest of the concert (inexplicably I was wearing a fireman's jacket I had stolen from a Bible camp in Michigan the previous summer), the thing I mostly remember is missing Radiohead.

Alex's persistent pursuit of me went on for another several years (a decade, actually, in its way, more passively). I don't remember the last time we really hung out, but I do remember that a year after the Radiohead show we missed, he dedicated a cover of "Fake Plastic Trees" to me at an open mic (he was—and I'm sure still is—an outstanding singer and guitarist: he was more talented than me in most of the ways that mattered, I understood then), and I did not miss the feeling in that last minute of the song: "If I could be who you wanted." I'm sure we had a series of increasingly awkward interactions after that, largely on account of my failure to recognize that my attempts at kindness were too easily misinterpreted, but that's the moment I remember: a clear transmission, a good one, I think, to close a memory on.

I'm self-conscious about revealing these personal details to you here, but because we're talking about sad songs, they're important. They might even be crucial to how we experience these songs and why we keep coming back to painful memories: here's a song that showed us something about ourselves or about another or about the world, that articulated something we couldn't otherwise. Maybe we still can't articulate it properly.

It's difficult to write a truly good autobiographical song, professor of psychology Daniel Sullivan tells me in his office at the University of Arizona.

His research specializes in the intersections of culture and suffering, though not exactly sadness, as he explained to me in an email. Still, as an amateur songwriter, he had a vested interest in the question of why we love sad songs, so, sure, he'd love to meet. The emphasis on autobiography differs a lot across cultures and has evolved in America over time, so that our present obsession with autobiography is an anomaly and not by any means an international norm, and the songs that really stay with us, generation to generation, are the ones that tell all of our stories.

He explains that the songs that really get him are narrative but not necessarily autobiographical, like Richard Buckner's song "Elizabeth Childers," from his album *The Hill* based on Edgar Lee Masters's *Spoon River Anthology*, addressed to a dead child, and coincidentally recorded in Tucson. It's hard to compare any other grief to that: no parent wants to imagine how their child's death might extinguish them. But how autobiographical can sadness really be if it's physical and universal? The good songs feel autobiographical because they play in the background of our lives, so they soundtrack our sadnesses, and because we use them to prompt emotional experience.

Sullivan directed me to Sartre's 1939 theory of emotion, that emotions are "magical transformations of the world." That is, emotions are "experiential episodes that are prompted by the perception of difficulties. During these episodes the world is magically transformed . . . through the use of one's body," as glossed by Andreas Elpidorou in "Horror, Fear, and the Sartrean Account of Emotions." Emotional experiences are largely unreflective ones in which our consciousness of ourselves recedes to make space for an intensely physical experience. This is rare for most of us. And perhaps that's why the right sad song can be so powerful; perhaps that's why we feel so possessive of the songs that can induce them. Give Buckner's song a listen. It was released outside the years of our bracket, and wasn't on my radar until this conversation, but it—and the whole album—is exceptional. In connecting me with this song, I felt connected to some small part of Daniel Sullivan, and that feels real.

How do we connect with the emotional lives of others? For the Sweet Sixteen, I invited friends to write short essays introducing, advocating for, or analyzing the songs that made it that far. The thing I found fascinating about these introductions—each lovely, rangy essay in its way— was how personal they were, even the ones that didn't seem at first to be overly personal. It was obvious, reading what my friends had to say about the songs, that these were songs that Meant Something to them at important or impressionable points in their lives. This is what these songs meant to us then, each of us outsider, downtrodden, unformed in our ways. As poet and essayist Brian Blanchfield tells us, "The bigger mystery is whether and how This Mortal Coil anticipated that a boy in central-piedmont North Carolina needed to wail the elongated phonemes of this song of huge, free-floating desire, in the fathoms of its depths, even as he pivot-turned the lawnmower and paced parallel swaths, back and forth, back and forth, rewinding, starting again." Or as fiction writer Kate Bernheimer writes, "I first heard [Joy Division's (1) "Atmosphere"] in the 1980s, during an incomprehensibly fogged and hurtful awakening." She goes on to write the most personal prose she's ever written, she tells me, more evidence that the right sad song—or writing about the right sad song—can allow us to reveal and explore parts of ourselves that we otherwise conceal.

The comments section unearthed several more of these stories, as did informal conversations I had with everyone I bugged about the project, which was everyone I communicated with that month (sorry if you had the misfortune of running into me at a party or a reading that March). These sad songs are not just sad songs: they're modes of transport. They connect the past and present, and because there's so much more past for us, the older we get the more powerful that concoction feels.

In the case of Jeff Buckley's cover of Leonard Cohen's "Hallelujah," as March Sadness guest columnist Elena Passarello points out, referring to the very first vocal sound ("huhhhh") that begins his version, "Breath on a neck, a lover's last breath, or a dejected sigh—no matter what it signifies, that breath is like a reset button, blowing away all the sinister horniness of Cohen's original take and replacing it with high, earnest emotion." I think that's largely why his version is so successful for most of us: a song written by a fifty-year-old and performed by a twenty-eight-year-old is able to contain and sustain both experience and innocence—who we became and who we used to be. That rings true because it's also how we are: we are both those selves, shell on top of shell, accreting and distancing us from but never entirely burying our pasts.

I should say I was most sad to see "Song to the Siren" end its improbable tournament run, not just for its underdog quality and my attachment to it, but because it's not a song I attach to any autobiographical memory, so I feel like I'm experiencing whatever sadness it has to offer me in a purer, less self-serving way. Or maybe I just like to tell myself that. I was complaining about its loss on the blog, when Matthew Vadnais responded, referring to the relative ubiquity of "Fake Plastic Trees":

> More of us had an emotional experience with the song to begin with so that remembering the song (let alone listening to it) is remembering ourselves in a variety of moments, many of which either do or don't enhance the song's sadness. I, to my shame, have no history with This Mortal Coil (or the original song) so all it gets in terms of my sadness is what it has been able to generate in the five or six listens since the tournament began. While repetition can hurt songs too, for songs we still love, it makes it almost impossible for a new song to be sadder because our only compass is our own feelings. Without a history or a car trip in which someone I liked but wanted to love helped me figure out the lyrics and sing the thing, "Song of the Siren" is merely pretty and super forgettable, which is blasphemy I'm sure, but sadness will almost always privilege songs we've known forever because, when it comes to sadness, the real instrument being played is us.

This is true but it cuts both ways: for instance, it's possible I may have rooted (and voted) against Radiohead on account of my memories of Alex regarding the song. But in a contest pitting subjectivity against subjectivity, knowing my experience of "Song to the Siren" is not largely autobiographical, I craved these moments where I felt more able to trust that my assessment was not just autobiographical but aesthetic, when I felt I could see more clearly the song and the performance. Opposing that, though, I should also admit, is the considerable pleasure of (re)discovery: here was a song I didn't know I could love, but I did.

As a reward for our thought and our intense feeling and our sorting through the feelings these songs bring up, the tournament has offered us increasingly difficult choices: How could we choose "Song to the Siren" over "Romeo & Juliet"? How to pick Elliott Smith's brilliant "Waltz #2" over possibly the saddest song in the tournament, perpetual underdogs the Replacements offering us the sweet self-lacerating alcoholic haze of "Here Comes a Regular"? How can we possibly weigh Sarah McLachlan against New Order? How to hold the intensity of (14) "Words," an old song by Low, a band I've seen live more than any other band, against

(2) Concrete Blonde's "Joey," a song described by committee member and essayist Megan Campbell as "guttural and pleading . . . [un]attractively sad . . . [not] winsome or sexy or sweet . . . no cleavage and no pretty girl tears—just lead singer Johnette Napolitano looking fierce and unapproachable . . . backed by a band that was not good-looking or hip or even youthful"? That's a forceful read, one I find almost impossible to argue against.

I remember the song and the video well, and though I was secretly rooting for "Joey" to win it all, especially over some of the sad-boy rock bands I remain susceptible to, I wasn't voting my head on this one. I was voting with my heart, which is to say with Low, with whom I share more autobiography, and whose tournament continued past this point, improbably.

This was getting hard. At which point did the difficulty of these decisions become more excruciating than fun?

Low upset "Joey," then lost in the Elite 8 to Joy Division, who looked at that point frankly unstoppable. Tracy Chapman took down Elliott Smith and then did what seemed impossible and beat Joy Division to make it to the championship game. The Cure did upend Radiohead. Neutral Milk Hotel lost, perhaps unsurprisingly, to Jeff Buckley, who crushed the Cure to make the final game. I was surprised by how close it was not. This gave us, as one reader pointed out, the least edgy championship matchup you could have engineered from the original field. This was a North Carolina–Duke matchup we were looking at, one that "could have been played in a Starbucks in Overland Park, Kansas," as a listener tweeted. This is as unsurprising as it is true. It's not the final I would have argued for, but it's no shock that in a democratic contest we ended up with what the most people could agree on, which was this. And like March Madness, the tournament had become a bit of a letdown, with all the songs I felt most passionate about now eliminated.

What does this mean for the effectiveness of the March Sadness machine that we end up right in the middle, with all the idiosyncrasy of our sadnesses washed away? Does it mean we are not as individual as we thought? Or does it mean we ended up with what we could agree on?

Well, these are both great songs and performances, for starters. It's hard to argue with dead drowned romantic Jeff Buckley, the voice of innocence (about to be extinguished) channeling experience, the lyrical

complexity of a song written by Leonard Cohen, half a life his senior and
one of the best songwriters of the last century (and as we know, a year
after the tournament ended, Cohen also died). And it's hard to argue with
the narrative force of Tracy Chapman's "Fast Car." The song's got pathos,
pop, the movement between the doomed situation of the speaker and
the powerful memory of hope that sustains—or permanently imperils—
the speaker: "Remember when we were driving / Driving in your car /
Speed so fast felt like I was drunk." Chapman's alive, though a bit of a
recluse, and it's hard not to notice, too, that she is the only artist of color
in the bracket ('80s and '90s alternative rock was an incredibly white
genre), and a queer woman of color at that writing brilliantly back to a
John Mellencamp song ("Fast Car" echoes and is a riff on/response to
Mellencamp's "Jack and Diane"). Plus, Chapman's from Cleveland (as
a couple of Cleveland commenters pointed out). She's one of the city's
biggest success stories. Cleveland's a city of legendary disappointment.
At the time of our championship game, it hadn't won a national sporting
championship of any sort for more than fifty years.

Having said that, of all the songs in the bracket, "Fast Car" had the
most commercial success. It did so well, in fact, that that one year when
it was out you couldn't avoid it; it saturated everything, and no matter
how sad a song was, repeated exposure to its stimulus dulled response,
so much so that it was easy to forget just how sad and freaking flat-out
good that song is. The dulling feeling I felt circa "Fast Car" was the same
thing I felt listening to Buckley's "Hallelujah" for the fiftieth time in the
tournament: just dried out and wrung up, impermeable, reminded of
nothing beyond what I was doing: watching a video of a sad dead white
boy online.

We did some analytics at the halfway point. Of the fifteen women in
the original field of sixty-four, eight made it to the Sweet Sixteen. Of the
sixty-four songs, sixteen were by solo artists. Of those, seven made it to
the Sweet Sixteen. This means that women and solo artists punched
above their weight. Why is that? Is it that, as novelist, music critic, and
March Sadness contributor Rick Moody suggests, "The best instrument
for the music of loss, which is the best of all music, is a woman's voice"?
As it turns out, both solo artists (Buckley and Chapman) took down the
bands (the Cure and Joy Division) in the semifinals. So we were left with
just two people standing, their songs and their voices. Which prevailed?

Does it matter? Like every month, March 2016 got washed away, too,
with all its sadness and its memories of sadness. It's now July. I'm writing

this in 108-degree heat where the cool of March in Arizona feels pretty damn far away. And I don't think it really does matter whether Buckley or Chapman cut down the nets and hoisted the sadness cup. In a sad songs contest, losing's the better trophy.

If you really want to know, go to the website and see for yourself. Or—way better—take a month or a week or a night and run the tournament yourself from its beginning. The outcome of the games is secondary to the journey, since each of us will find and choose our own sadnesses: they will be the ones we desire, remember, and deserve. The bracket isn't a contest but a self-diagnostic tool. So turn it on and play it yourself or with someone you love or used to love. What does it feel like? Talk about it. A sad song is a door, or maybe a tunnel. Let me know where it leads you.

American Renaissance

America, having come to grips with 1776,
is devouring the Real Past.
—Umberto Eco, *Travels in Hyperreality*

As I drive the long road to the faire, I wonder how long it will take my companions to recognize the source material in Mexrrissey's "Cada Día Es Domingo." I suppose the name's a giveaway: these are Mexican adaptations of songs by Morrissey and the Smiths. When I moved to Arizona ten years ago, I had no idea how much Mexicans loved Morrissey, but the more I paid attention, the more inevitable it seemed. I asked my friend César, and he replied: Dude, seriously? How do you not know this? I'd just never had the thought before. So one reason I love Mexrrissey is because they actualize the devotion. They take the songs apart, singing them in Spanish, and by rendering them unfamiliar for a moment, they make them new. It's delightful, listening to it, getting to know a familiar thing again as if for the first time. There's even pleasure in that disorienting feeling before you figure it out. Damn, I should know this, I think, but it's a fun frustration. So when at last I figure it out, it's a physical rush. Is this really *relief* I'm feeling? It is. Clint starts laughing, and I know he gets it too.

We could take the interstate but instead we take Arizona State Route 79, the Pinal Pioneer Parkway, through Florence, Arizona, on our way up to Apache Junction, where the Arizona Renaissance Festival ("& Artisan Marketplace," the website reminds me) awaits. It's the last day of the twenty-fifth annual festival, concluding oddly—and surely arbitrarily—on Easter Sunday. This is the first free weekend in a month for me and my trusty companions Jon and Clint, so we have sallied forth into the sun.

Today I'm driving, one reason why we're taking the back roads through country filled with flowering chollas, and besides, as I'm informed, the wildflowers are also in what's called a superbloom after a relatively wet spring for us, so as we drive on this two-lane road, Clint points out a white desert lily, and Jon is murmuring something soft about lupine. These gents know a lot about plants.

A Chevy Aveo with a pennant on its antenna passes us at what must be a cool eighty-five mph. I mean, I'm not driving slow, but still . . . Maybe they are on their way to the faire? In 2011 *USA Today* named this road the fastest surface highway (not counting interstates) in the nation, having taken regular radar readings at what one presumes must be nearly every highway in America. Why they did this, I'm not sure, but I'm glad they did, and am glad also to know that another two of the top ten are here in Arizona. Well, that's one thing we got, I say, not out loud, because I'm quoting Deep Blue Something's crappy '90s song "Breakfast at Tiffany's," and it is too early to be mocked for my deep and terrible knowledge.

Jon and I first came to this, the Arizona Renaissance Festival, forty-five minutes east of the Phoenix sprawl, a couple of years ago. We were duly amused and pleased and turkey-legged, and so we meant to come again last year, this time with Jon's husband, Clint, who, in spite of living his entire life in Arizona nerding out to *Lord of the Rings*, has never been to the faire. We were a little too busy or forgetful, and for men like us, the Renaissance Festival is not quite the priority it is for some. That is, none of us is usually serious enough about it to undertake the two-hour drive from Tucson, in spite of a fairly encyclopedic collective knowledge of Tolkien, AD&D, Narnia, *Game of Thrones*, and applied linguistics, not even to get into the sci-fi domains that each of us may or may not be masters of.

I don't mean to suggest that we are not serious about anachronism, but we are not members of the Society for Creative Anachronism, those lovely geeks who faux-fight with swords on college campuses and in yearly "wars" (in their words, the SCA is "an international non-profit volunteer educational organization. The SCA is devoted to the research and re-creation of pre-seventeenth century skills, arts, combat, culture, and employing knowledge of history to enrich the lives of participants through events, demonstrations, and other educational presentations and activities").

Part of the reason I insisted we come today is that I've been reading Rachel Lee Rubin's epic cultural history, *Well Met: Renaissance Faires &*

the American Counterculture, which makes a strong case for the statement implicit in the title: that the history of the faire is deeply intertwined with the history of the American counterculture.

If you've been to a faire recently, its countercultural roots may not be particularly obvious. And while you're standing in line to pay your twenty-two dollars to get in, surrounded by a succession of fat kids, presunburned princesses, self-described redneck knights, teens in *Game of Thrones* shirts, and a group of hipsters dressed as Aquabats (I ask but still don't understand: I believe it might be a band), it may be hard to parse exactly what the point of this whole thing is.

According to Rubin, the point is not authenticity but primarily, historically, a shared sense of play: "In the fifth decade of Renaissance faires, historical authenticity characterizes them, and their participants, unevenly." This is one of many amusing understatements in Rubin's book. Ask the Aquabats, the Harry Potter kids, or the increased presence of Depped-out pirates what year their outfit harks back to and step back before you are spat upon or challenged to a duel. Well, what we mean by the Middle Ages is inclusive to begin with, spanning basically a millennium from the fifth through the fifteenth centuries. Since Americans didn't exactly participate in the Middle Ages that we deify in books and film, it's an odd choice for shared fantasy, except that, as Umberto Eco points out in his essay "Dreaming the Middle Ages," "all the problems of the Western world emerged in the Middle Ages: Modern languages, merchant cities, capitalistic economy (along with banks, checks, and prime rate) . . . modern armies . . . the modern concept of the national state . . . the struggle between the poor and the rich, the concept of heresy or ideological deviation, even our contemporary notion of love as a devastating unhappy happiness . . . the conflict between church and state, trade unions . . . the technological transformation of labor." We continue to contain the Middle Ages, then, even if we don't acknowledge them, so, like the subtexts of dreams, why be surprised that we're still working them out of our collective craw?

The faire and the SCA were both founded in California in the 1960s, the same years that gave rise to delicious and ubiquitous snack Doritos (also invented in California, in Disneyland, more precisely, in the Frontierland section, at Casa de Fritos, a Frito franchise). Perhaps it shouldn't be a surprise that these things go together: California, the faire, the SCA, Doritos: they are each artifices, entertainments, diversions, ways, perhaps, to forget about yourself for a little while. No one complains about Doritos' lack of authenticity: artificiality is what they're all about (see also Doritos Collisions Chicken Sizzler Zesty Salsa). There's nothing really to be authentic to, even if the Midnight Cheeseburger chips do contain beef tallow, traces of the beast they're meant to simulate. For the faire, Rubin says, "'authenticity' (and its complement, 'anachronism') is not a fixed or transparent thing-in-itself; rather, it is a tool wielded variously by the deft performer." Instead, she notes,

> The introduction of concrete historical reference added richness of detail to the faire; at the same time, it upped the intensity of the Renaissance faire's "functional paradox," in which attempts at historical authenticity act as commentary not on the past but on the present. This dynamic is evident in a "reminiscence" of the 1964 Pleasure Faire and May Market . . . an authentically attired "monk in full beard and hodded [sic] robes" hawking papal indulgences and calling to fairegoers: "Let me absolve you of the punishments and everlasting torments of commercialism!"

In practice, these definitions become fluid and subservient to the general feeling of play present at the faire. In fact, the idea is that you don't just *pay to attend* the faire: you *pay to play at* the faire. The term used to describe the most serious players, those who pay to attend in garb (period clothing, pegged to a very vaguely medieval style) is *playtron*. I've always suspected that attending the faire in garb would be an entirely different experience than showing up in the wicking golf shirt and cargo shorts that I have embarrassingly come to depend on.

Jon, Clint, and I had originally talked enthusiastically about coming in garb, possibly as badass wizards with glorious and contrasting gnarled, runed staves. In this way we would not just be here to gape, but we'd get to play harder, like the other dressed-up thousands here. Imagine what it might be like! Muscled vassals kneeling at our feet! Maidens and fair-haired princes blushing at our demonstrations of skill! Being lauded by our authentically costumed peers! I dream a thousand huzzahs on our behalf, but renting a costume seems like weak sauce, and, to my father's continual dismay, unlike the guy I went to grad school with who made his own set of chain mail for our Old English class, I have no crafting skills to mention, so what is a self-conscious playtron wannabe supposed to do?

Besides, this is the last day of the Faire, and it's ninety, the end of March, full sun in Arizona, and we are not small men. So if we choose convenience we would prefer not to be judged for it. Still, seeing some of the impressive costuming around us, I have to admit I feel weirdly unmanned.

Why do we even care about the past at all? What aspects of ourselves does it allow us to play out? And what might the past we choose reveal? We don't care about the details except as they serve us, but we do have a vague inkling that there was something there before us—before our family or before America, before all the Safeways and the Circle Ks we built. Remember: even the logo for Circle K is a mark for branding cattle. The corporation is based in Tucson, appropriately enough, though you'd be hard pressed to find anything inside that calls up a ranch. It's both anxiety about our ignorance of the past as well as curiosity about the lives our ancestors may have lived then, how they would have been bound or freed, in some combination, by the only world they ever knew.

The killer app is that by visiting the past—even in as half-assed a way as we do via the faire—we get to experience that doubleness: we're here and now and there and then at once. We don't get everything about it but we do just maybe start to realize some of the roles we play at work and at home and at the store and how they bind us without our knowledge.

In *Well Met*, Rubin's task is, through interviews with the many constituencies of the faire, present and past, to present a close cultural reading of the faire as it was and as it is, and, to some degree, to track the changes in the culture of the faire as it entered its fifth decade (making it a longer-running cultural monument than, say, the Super Bowl). *Well Met* is an excellent and comprehensive book. It's often academic but not prohibitively or unpleasantly so: if phrases like "to chalk the faire's impulse up to an anxious antimodernism is too reductive" are too much for you, then you'll likely want to skim to the good parts (of which there are many: see the chapter on sexuality at the faire, for instance). Her seriousness of purpose and straightforward tone serve her and her subject well. In devoting her unblinking attention to the potentially mockable faire, she deeply honors it and asks us to reconsider its cultural significance and what it might mean to us.

This particular faire may not be the most representative choice: there are few places less obviously countercultural than Phoenix, Arizona. That's not quite fair, I admit, to the many weirdos who have made the desert their home, but the overwhelming experience of Phoenix, a satellite campus of Southern California without the light from starlets, is one of endless consumer creep, blinding heat, inexplicable lawns, palm trees, Ikeas, casinos, gas stations, football, roads, malls, roads, malls, roads. Phoenix, like Las Vegas, like California, projects a powerful fantasy: that of unlimited possibility, *the future*, utterly disconnected from the environmental realities of the West's rapidly depleting water.

Arrive at this faire via the Phoenix interstate and you'll see exactly what I mean: it's spotless, lovely, white, weirdly green, sprawled, traffic-jammed, hot-asphalted, and spiritually bereft. But if you come the back route from Tucson, you'll get a different experience: one of great speeds, desert lilies, and cactus forest, a relative wildness modulated by the occasional development. Then you'll pass through Florence, Arizona, home to nine county, state, federal, and private prisons and host to the yearly Country Thunder festival. Florence is a town with an economy but without a fantasy.

Sometimes I like to tell people that Florence, Arizona, is the Florence of Arizona, but those who've been to Italy do not seem convinced.

Anyhow, you'll get through it, the disconnect between the city and its namesake, and then you'll be through the city itself. Hop on US 60, then out of nowhere from all this flatness and scrub grass the festival ariseth, and there is mucho parking to be had for free, courtesy, giant banners remind us, of local grocery chain Fry's. We park my Subaru in the Knave row by the exit.

If you've been to a faire in the past decade you pretty much know what it's like inside: plenty of stuff to buy including Frozen Princess Lattes and turkey legs and other meats on sticks; beer and "medieval" margaritas; probably too much mead to really be good for anyone; fairy princess regalia to fit all comers; plastic and pewter dragons; and, if you look a little more closely, plenty of leather BDSM regalia (a "Where There's a Whip, There's a Way" display just below the fur-lined handcuffs and so on) buried a little farther back in the leather shops. There are plenty of swords; a few improbable chain mail bikinis you might remember from schlock '80s films like *Red Sonja* or the overheated covers of fantasy novels (I cannot imagine the chafing you would experience wearing one of these bikinis); the Horn Shoppe ("Drinking, Blowing and Combination") and many other dirty double entendres, often of a homoerotic variety; scads of kids; underdressed teens; a large proportion of people dressed like pirates; jousting; funnel cakes; some kind of doubtfully medieval-themed

nachos; a couple dressed up, randomly, as garden gnomes; falconry;
rides; games; tests of skill; a mass of cleavage displayed by anyone with
half a boob to boost up and display; heraldry; courtliness; staves; knaves;
sad imprisoned hawks and owls; Huzzahs; and ATM after ATM to feed
your need for more of it, whatever it you're looking for more of here.
Though an amusing sign riffs "We accept Lady Visa and Master of the
Card," cash is preferred.

In America—and certainly in Phoenix—we do love a spectacle as
well as a Frozen Princess Latte. Clearly some of us are here just for
the spectacle—all these playtrons, all these people: if this many people
come, then we should come too. But the real appeal appears to be the
roleplaying. And maybe because we didn't have a Middle Age, exactly,
or quite as sexy a history as this, Americans love to role-play this historical dream.

For an afternoon you may choose to discard your regular life, put on
the garb, and play a role. Sure, it's stratified: you know your place, vassal!
Though we prefer to think otherwise, our lives are stratified too: How recently have you dined with royalty, with Hollywood, with Pulitzer Prize winners, with the president? Here you can, kind of, at the Pleasure Feast, twice
daily, at noon and 2:30 p.m., for $69.95 if you purchase tickets in advance.

A lot of us obviously like to play: if you count computer and video
games and tabletop RPGs, or if you look at what you do on your smartphone when in the post office line or driving, there are a whole lot of
us who like playing a character, even in casual ways. Reading is role-
playing too: for a couple of hundred pages, we're taken over by another.
Sure, we can't always control the plot, but good books involve us as
much as we're willing to give up control. And how else do sports work,
if not by way of a kind of identity transfer? It's not as if rooting for the
Green Knight is much different from cheering for the (also medievally
themed) expansion NHL franchise, the Las Vegas Golden Knights, or the
Alabama Crimson Tide. In each rooting we lose ourselves, if we're lucky,
for a moment, and in the clash we feel alive by proxy.

We enter through the gate. I startle on seeing a giant treant (a huge,
living, speaking tree, to use the D&D term—Tolkien calls them ents)
stretch out huge tree branch arms to encircle a teen. The costume's elaborate and fantastic. The sign tells us this is the Greenman.

There are also actual games to play inside. On the car ride up, I've been
talking about the ax throwing from two years ago that I remember I was

totally great at, though we don't see that yet. First there's the Dragon Climbing Wall, the High Stryker (the ring-a-bell-with-a-hammer deal), the darts you throw at balloons to win prizes. This isn't very interesting, we think, and hardly Middle Aged (you see how it is easy to slide into nitpicking an experience). There's a "medieval" version of the bar game shufflepuck (which I love) in which you slide a "medieval" beer stein down a sawdust-coated wooden lane and try to land it on a bull's-eye. It is called New World Slider Joust. It is real hard. Why do people even enjoy playing these games? I wonder. The odds are against you. You know this. But then there's Vegas, the lottery. Thank god the dream—the hope—is more powerful than the math.

Jon's face lights up when we find the archery range, which has no prizes, but you do get to rent arrows and shoot them into a giant purple octopus and a very large evil prince figure pinned to a backdrop of hay bales. This is surprisingly enjoyable. It is evident Jon has discovered a hidden talent that will be useful in the end days.

Actually quite a few skills demonstrated here—blacksmithing, glass-blowing, ax throwing, hypnotism, belly dance, falconry, insult giving, henna tattooing—may yet be useful when the zombie apocalypse arrives or after we all become Russian or Chinese vassals à la *Red Dawn* or its sort-of-recent remake. Rubin's got a long chapter on the history of craft presences at the faire. Jon and I agree that the "& Artisan Marketplace" here is more apparent on this visit, or maybe we're just noticing it more. Perhaps the recent resurgence of the handmade and DIY (*see also* Etsy) in the age of mechanical reproduction and digital explosion is partly responsible for its expanded appeal at the faire: here you can actually learn how to make a thing, preferably with a plastic cup of mead in hand and ready for the quaffing. You can buy things from humans crafted by human hands. Nothing here is delivered by drone from Amazon. Our parents taught us nothing, and we grew up educating ourselves on how to best microwave pot pies (bad idea: you want to pop that shit in the oven to brown the crust properly, even if it takes an hour), but here are people who can make things—who *have* made things—and there is an obvious power in it. They carry themselves with the swagger of the accomplished.

Still, there's no denying, what with the Monk's Bakery and Cappuccino Inn, and the ever-present signs that direct you to an ATM, that the faire is a commercial space (there's not much money to be made, one imagines, simply in the blacksmithing demonstrations). If Rubin demonstrates the faire's antiestablishment tendencies, she also finds it has had the edges sawed off it somewhat over the five decades of its practice. The term widely used by Rubin's interviewees (and thus Rubin herself) for this slow middling and settling is *Disneyfication*. This is widely lamented by faire workers, who, though they understand the commercial pressures of events of this size, still feel that an excessive level of rationalization and a policy of playing it safe so as not to alienate the "'lowest possible denominator . . . has had a high cost in terms of creative values and spontaneity and has turned some faires into 'shopping malls with entertainment,' a phrase that came up often enough to cause one to wonder how commonly, and through what media, it is circulating. [A performer] reminded me that a more anarchic, less regimented philosophy is what allowed the faire to develop into the financial success that brought mandates of increased regimentation to it."

What exactly are we experiencing, I wonder, watching Jon bury another arrow in the octopus? What does all this mean? If we're looking to understand the cultural significance of the faire, Rubin suggests, we should look to its detractors: "Indeed, as the faire itself has continuously evolved along with its historical content and changes in ownership, the terms on which it is commonly derided have been arguably the most steadfast expressions of the faire's social meaning." So she interviews some haters—both in person and online, where, as we know, the haters are particularly strong:

> Probing the reasons for this [hate] yields some useful insights about the way both the faire and ridiculing the faire function in tandem as collective social practice. Fascinatingly, if logically, the most frequent reasons for which the Renaissance faire [is] ridiculed are often the same reasons its fans find it so liberating. In the twenty-first century, contempt for the faire falls almost exclusively into three major categories. . . . "Well, like I said, they're weird. And then there is what they wear. I mean, they have the right to wear whatever they want, but people are going to laugh at a man wearing tights, you know? And look at them. They need to stop eating those turkey legs. Especially if they are going to dress like that" [from an interview with Michael K.]. Thus, in a tone hovering somewhere between belligerent and sheepish, Michael K. reels off several of what turn out to be the major ways in which

passionate faire hecklers mock the faire: nonconformity, clothing, and body size. . . .

The wearing of tights by men comes up in the majority of mocking accounts of the faire, the practice seemingly inspiring an outpouring of dread about what constitutes proper masculinity. The sheer frequency with which the specter of "men in tights" is invoked reveals that tights are operating as a sort of code or shorthand for transgressive male behavior, not unlike the wearing of long hair did in the 1960s and 1970s. . . . To put it more simply, anxious discussions of male tights-wearing vis-à-vis the faire are frequently tied to what we now call homophobia. . . . If "men in tights" operates as a kind of shorthand for gender disobedience in men, women at the Renaissance faire are most widely punished for departures from mainstream beauty culture in terms of body size.

While this analysis feels apt, it is perhaps odd that, in order to commit acts of contemporary gender disobedience, playtrons dress and conduct themselves according to a vague reading of an incredibly repressive feudal code, one with deeply rigid gender roles—and this is not even to get at the obvious questions of class or race, which for the most part Rubin does not address (in her defense, the book is plenty long already: while I'd love for it to be about everything, it cannot be about everything).

All this thinking is getting tiring. Clint is looking at me as if I am a tool as we eat our nut rolls. Damn, that's good. To reify some hegemony, I head into the Metal Shoppe to look at chain mail bikinis, which are gratifyingly real, if of dubious actual use. When I come out, Clint has taken up residence on a wooden bench. I go to join him, and we watch the sword swallower (his name is "Thom Sellectomy"; the tagline on the sign that abuts the stage reads "He can't help the way he is!"). Long wands of metal disappear into his mouth. There are a lot of jokes. Kids shriek. Jon can't handle this particular brand of entertainment, so he's wandered off into the shade. Clint and I get into it. It's hard not to appreciate a skill that seems almost like a form of magic.

Magic of course is part of the draw. Since after childhood we live in a mostly nonmagical world, we should be grateful for opportunities—like this—for wonder, for discarding the self for a brief moment and experiencing something totally baffling and new. Maybe we should not complain or feel obliged to nitpick our delight. Sure it's true that the "ye olde" is an error propagated from Early Modern English as Jon (did I mention he is a linguist?) informs me, based on a misunderstanding of how the letter þ (thorn) should be pronounced: not like a y but like a th—so it really ought to be *the olde*. But that doesn't mean you have to mansplain it to the wenches. While there's pleasure in a skeptical pose, which is to say a reluctance to participate in a ritual or a delusion, the greater pleasure for sure is belief.

I think of the sign adorning the Lutheran church near my home: "magic show this Sunday." I feel its pull. I assume they have actual fake magic and aren't referring to the act of transubstantiation. Actually I'm sure of it, since Lutherans do not believe in transubstantiation. But I see the appeal. Even I want to attend to see what happens, to marvel at what I just saw.

We finally happen on the ax throwing, and of course Clint goes to it immediately and starts dropping dollars on the bar. The skinny kid with the banter hands us three axes for three dollars. We're meant to throw the axes into another stack of hay bales like the fine examples of masculinity we surely are. There's a little painted heart that, if you hit it, you get a crappy prize. Kid has some advice for us on how to throw these axes—the secret is . . . whatever, sirrah, I say, I'm Nordic. This is my ancestral skill, handed down by my forefathers through the mists of time. I line up and launch, and . . . my first ax clatters weakly to the floor. Hmm. I look at Clint, and he buries one in the target, biceps flexing, like a golden, glowing god. His face fills with virility; my face just fills. Shit. I look back and Jon is helpfully taking video. Two axes later I do finally hit the target . . . with the handle. My three Nordic axes lie on the floor, just like prom night.

I tell myself that perhaps my ancestors bequeathed me another skill, like halitosis, that I will yet discover, but not this day. Clint has stuck all three in a nice pattern around the heart, like he's ready to cut it out and consume it to level up and double in strength and size. He receives his prize, which is a paper certificate. What does it contain? I can only guess and cannot know. This knowledge is only for the victor.

Tired from my demonstration of inadequacy, I grab another beer and immediately I feel better. Perhaps this is my skill. I played my role, and now am playing another role. (Interestingly, as Rubin points out, early faires had to specially import English ales, because they were not otherwise available in America, so for a decade most Americans' introductions to real English ales—another form of magic—were here at the faire. This is one way in which it's enriched my life.) I hear "Huzzah for the good tipper" as I disappear a buck into the elaborate wooden tip jar.

We're too early for the joust, but I've seen it before and it looks brutal. Jon says he's feeling a little ill and since he's an understated guy that means things are going south quickly for him and therefore us. A big dude feeling ill is a sad thing, so we decide to trundle toward the exit. And oh, here's the back of a woman in a corset adorned with fairy wings. That's kind of sexy, even if it's easy. Jon is not amused by this display.

A court processes by: we saw them earlier, at "The Princess Meets the Suitors, Scene 1." The last woman to pass has her breasts bustiered to the level of her face.

It's easy to mock this place—both for its play and for its lack of historical depth or fidelity: Where's the historically accurate dentistry? I wonder. But that's partly what's so amazing about the faire: of course it's easy to mock. It offers itself openly to haters, and in so doing, transcends them. Any group engaged in collective play—going this deeply, this often, on this scale—requires you to buy into its magic or be a chump. That's the counterculture right there: a collective opt-in hallucination, preferable for a day, to your job at the private prison in Florence, Arizona, named for the Italian city, but without its charm or cuisine. It's either that or you'll float above it, aloof, bored, incapable of wonder or losing yourself—and thereby finding yourself. Do you like what you find?

Of course it's hard to lose yourself. That's why we want it as badly as we do. Dressing up and playing harder would be a start.

I wonder at just who I could be if I freed myself through play like this. What if I came as an Aquabat, or got my knight on properly? These are worlds I could know if I wanted to, but don't. Something holds me back. I fear I'm poorer for not going harder.

One thing that holds us back is that Jon's getting greener as we evade the Greenman's bark arms again, pass through the gate and back into the reality of outer Phoenix, flat and dusty, unmagical, hot as ever, still ourselves. Now he says it's time to go, and I believe him. Maybe it was the turkey leg or a dirty tap of some crappy beer, or just the spectacle of so much of us all concentrated in one place as we congregate to prove something about our imaginations to ourselves.

Well, we talk again of dressing up next year. We're thinking: monks.

Or maybe death in robes. We can just silently point at people until they freak. We find our car still filed helpfully under *Knave*, and roll the windows down as we hit the road, going east then south, back through an infinity of cactus.

As I talk to Jon in hopes of distracting him from barfing in my car, I realize we will miss many scenes from the narrative of the faire, including "The Knighting Ceremony," "The Suitors Competing," and "The Royal Dating Game & Finale." But I think we all know that, unlike much of life, this story comes with a happy ending.

An Unburned Rose

I've always loved the off-season: the fogged beach, the cold shore of Lake Superior in winter, the Sonoran Desert in summer, hipster bars in the empty early afternoon. Admittedly, my home city's seasons are out of sync with most of the rest of the country: we have no perceptible fall. When classes at the university spin up again it's tech shirt weather until Halloween. Trees won't change colors except up the mountains. And by the time the official first day of summer arrives, it's been over a 100 degrees for a month and we are suitably beat down by weather and hoping to move into the monsoon season. So when everyone is Instagramming their white Christmases and the children's books are extolling the virtues of snowdrifts and bundling up, I'm trying to explain to my daughter what winter actually is, which is embarrassing for a Michigander.

From our perspective, just slightly out of sync, I like to think I can see some things more clearly, as they actually are, without their attendant mythologies.

When in mid-July I pull up to the front yard of Paul Weir, the technical director of Flam Chen, a fire-and-acrobatics troupe that burns a six-foot geodesic steel urn at the dramatic finale of Tucson's yearly All Souls Procession, I'm not sure whether I'll get the glitter or the grit, and which I'd rather have.

I'm here to see the ceremonial burning urn, which I've only seen on screens. Those in attendance at the procession write the names of the dead, remembrances of them and messages for them, and place them in the urn. A thousand or more walk along with their faces painted to look skeletal, mourning someone important to them. As the procession's official materials tell me, "At the culmination of the Finale, the Urn is burned, and our collective hopes, prayers, love, grief, memories, tributes, and remembrances are consumed by the flames and dissolve into the ether."

That sounds powerfully appealing, but today I know I won't be seeing anything burn.

I'm drawn to the urn though I know it holds no actual magic. It's just five hundred pounds of welded steel. But it looks magical. It's arty and geometric, and when hoisted fifty feet in the air and set afire, surely something happens.

The sign on Paul's front door says deliveries come to the back. I ring the doorbell but hear nothing. So I go around the back. It's quite a yard, with the Flam Chen school bus in it and all kinds of metal art and half-built projects. I ring that doorbell, too, and still hear nothing, but he comes around from the front to say hello. He has a large gauge in each earlobe. He shows me to the urn, which sits undramatically on a trailer, surrounded by metal scaffolding, next to a concrete block wall. I see some tarps, some wood, a bunch of pallets, a rain barrel, and an RV. Behind it is the old urn that was replaced in 2012.

The old urn resembles a huge, rusty cauldron. Plants grow up through its mesh sides, so it probably hasn't been moved in a year or two. The air conditioners on the roof of the house next door are going full bore, over which I can hear the buzzing cicadas in the oleander.

Paul tells me that the new urn is a stellated dodecahedron with twelve points, made up of sixty equilateral triangles. Not to be too nerdy about it, but looking it up online, it looks to me more like a pentakis dodecahedron, since each point is made by five triangular panels. Things get quickly very rigorous mathematically when talking about nonconvex polyhedra, though, so I decide to just take him at his word. What it mostly looks like to me is a twenty-sided die, the kind I used to roll a lot playing Dungeons & Dragons as a kid, so in my mind this shape has always been associated with magic. And as Paul points out, the new urn is a lot hardier than the old one, since it's solid steel.

I get closer to take a look.

In the bottom of the urn I can make out a plastic rose and a hundred or so handwritten notes. Paul says they were put in there at one of the yearly events in which the urn is made accessible to the public before the procession. These will be burned along with the thousands of other notes in a few months as part of the grand finale. For a moment I think about what it might be like to reach in and grab a few: I wonder if it would ruin their magic. It's only a brief temptation: I'd have to figure out which side of the thing opened, and first I'd probably have to battle Paul, the keeper of the urn, which seems unwise.

We're just a week or two past the big fire holiday, the Fourth of July, and this year I spent more money than I had in years buying fireworks because my friend Valyntina and I got each other pumped up talking about exploding things, and because I do want to carry some things forward from my childhood.

Plus, I wanted to give my daughter a show. She was thrilled to be part of the firework selection process, going to the pop-up tent that opens up in the empty lots next to the Church's chicken. In October this tent brings us pumpkins and in December Christmas trees. As you'd guess, all the fireworks have over-the-top names, but Athena didn't want the *really* scary-sounding ones like Kodiak Killers, featuring Open-Mouthed Salivating Bear Adorned with a Pentagram and either his comrade or his antagonist, Other Apeshit Bear Sporting an Eyepatch, Cigar, and an AK-47. Even I thought it was maybe a little too much, though I still suggested buying it, but she said no, I don't like bears, which was true, if beside the point. She also turned up her nose at the weirdly biblical 500 Gram Exodus and, my favorite, the relatively unscary but a little racist-looking Opera Face, with its vaguely Japanese art. Well, I said, you can have whichever one you want. Let's go nuts. She chose Bowl of Jelly Beans and Super Sno-Cone, both of which were the favorites of the woman at the register, she told us.

I hadn't bought more than some basic grocery store fireworks in the ten years I've lived here: ground blooming flowers, sparklers, of course, and a couple of fountains, meaning nothing that really gets one's blood going and the pets freaked out. In Arizona I can't buy firecrackers or anything aerial or explosive, which was surprising to me since I can walk into Diamondback Shooting Sports exactly a mile away and buy a Glock 19 semiautomatic handgun (the kind Loughner used to shoot up the Safeway) and wander around town with it concealed or unconcealed without a permit.

I imagine the rationale concerning fireworks restrictions is the risk of fire in an arid climate, and there's no right to blow yourself up or burn down a national forest written in the Constitution to justify this particular freedom. Just choosing today at random, a local news station tells me

"The U.S. Forest Service is mopping up the Salto Fire northeast of town," "A brush fire has forced the closure of Insterstate 40," "The Navajo Nation is tightening fire restrictions across the reservation because of ongoing drought," "Judd Fire 65 percent contained near Bisbee," "A second eastern Arizona highway closed earlier this week because of a wildfire," "Two homes were burned in a wildfire that broke out near Black Canyon City Saturday afternoon," "Three brush fires burning off Highway 83," and the list goes on.

This is why we can't have nice, explosive things, even on the reservations. In Michigan we'd buy fireworks, the illegal stuff, the sort that was actually dangerous, on the Ojibwe reservation, and we'd throw or fire them at each other and cause general havoc. I don't recommend it, but then I also never started a major fire with fireworks.

So this year was a significant upgrade for the family fire show, and the display did not disappoint. The neighbors came out to watch and my daughter was on the tailgate of my friend's truck doing her happy dance as our stuff made big sounds and burned, burned, burned. It was dark enough that I don't know whether anyone noticed Valyntina and I had also entered the state of frenzied, childlike glee.

Fireworks seem like a waste of money, and they are. They literally, ha ha, go up in smoke. We burned through a couple of hundred bucks in fifteen minutes of frenzied lighting and running, but it was sure fun to watch. I had forgotten how important a little spectacle can be.

Maybe this history of love for fire is why running my hands over the two urns means more to me than it does for some. These things have burned, spectacularly, for us. They mean something because we make them mean something, because watching them burn with our words inside changes us, or gives us the opportunity for change, should we be open to and ready for the task.

Ceremonial magic is still magic if we are willing to believe in it.

So I do. I place my hands on the old urn and then the new. The metal's hot from being out in the sun so I can't bear to touch either one for long. I feel nothing except for the heat. I don't know what I expected: right now the urn is just a metal contraption sitting in the sun. If there's magic here, it's situational.

If you watch video of it burning at the finale, as I have many times, it's a different story. One can't deny there's power in it. Thousands raise their eyes to watch. Its power is in part generated by the procession, in which thousands walk to celebrate and remember this year's dead.

There are so many. They keep coming. We keep coming. It's electric because we want it to be, because we need electricity. Because the charge
builds up and paralyzes us otherwise. We—or most of us mortals—can't
bear being surrounded all our lives by the dead and by our feelings for
them. We need a ceremony to set them free, we say. Or are we the ones
we're setting free? Is that selfishness or is it simply living?

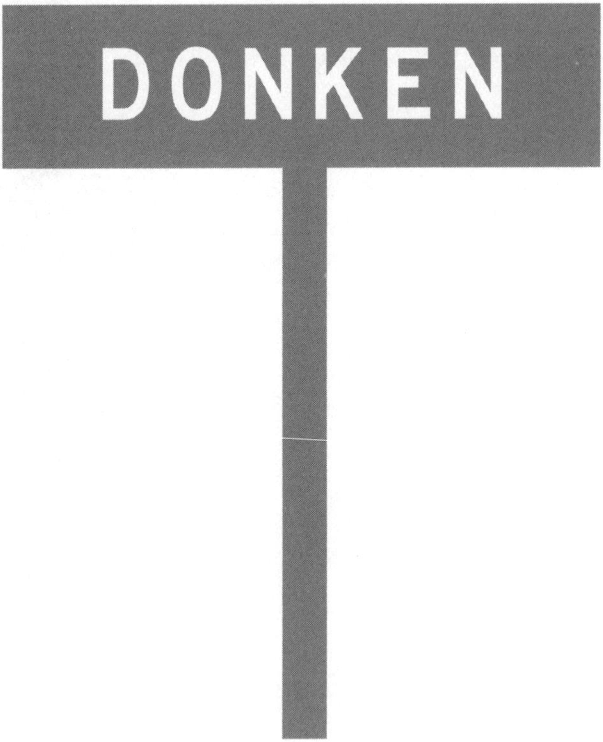
DONKEN

Uncharitable Thoughts on Dokken

Without Warning

It's probably a bad idea to begin an essay with Dokken, a 1980s metal band you would be forgiven for not knowing, particularly since I'm coming from a position of skepticism regarding their oeuvre, which, if you're aware of it at all, is likely due to the song they wrote (and the associated Freddy Krueger–featuring video) for *Nightmare on Elm Street 3: Dream Warriors*.

I'll take you down that road, but first, another, which begins with a sign for a town in northern Michigan not far from where I grew up that read *Donken*. Like many towns up there, it was once a town and now is not, and owed its existence in one way or another to its proximity to mines or trees or water. Every town in that area echoes something gone (I suppose most towns do), and driving through them as a kid, I don't think I understood what a town was for an embarrassingly long time: Did it really have to be more than a pair of signs and a number signifying population?

Don't bother looking Donken up: it's one of those nothings through which you drive and might wonder about long enough to find you've driven through the town and are on to more wilderness. It's unincorporated. Google Street View won't let you plow through it on your browser. Sometimes I think the only reason I remember Donken is because it sounds funny (like donkey) and more often than not when I drove through it someone had used spray paint to make the first *n* into a *k* so that it read not *Donken* but *Dokken*.

Felony

I wasn't offended at the defacing: I'd vandalized or defaced plenty myself, including for no real reason setting fire to a stop sign down the street from my house. I used gasoline I had stolen from the Boy Scouts, an organization for which I was inexplicably made Quartermaster. What annoyed me was not the act of defacing but its result. Dokken? Really? Fucking Dokken?

I was aware of them as one of the also-rans of the hair metal band era, and I'd seen a couple of videos on MTV, which aren't, let's be honest, all that great, but which inspired a visceral reaction in me at the time in ways I still don't entirely understand.

And it wasn't as if I was listening to cooler bands: I owned the entire Poison discography; I saw Warrant (opening for Poison) in Detroit. I saw Britny Fox live and I still know how to spell the band's name correctly. One of the first few CDs I owned—and loved—was the eponymous album by Wilson Phillips, which I'd bought along with Fifth Angel's *Time Will Tell*, Faith No More's *The Real Thing*, and Depeche Mode's *Violator*, which I will go down defending (actually I'd defend, to some extent, all of those albums). I owned at least one Grim Reaper CD, which I will not go down defending: I'm pretty sure I always knew they sucked, but one of my hacker friends told me I should check them out, which I did. I suppose I should have known that nobody good called themselves, unironically, Grim Reaper.

Where does taste come from anyway? What does it *do*—for us or for others? And where does it go? I mean, I had so many opinions that in recalling them I am once again filled with the feeling each one gave me, how it felt in the mind and the mouth, saying it, how good it felt to deride an early work or a later-era sellout, and to proclaim an allegiance to one band or another, and to feel better than and one with others who felt the same, and in doing so I am alive and fifteen once again.

But I also didn't get the memo that there was nothing inherently better about my preferences than anyone else's. By the time college rolled around I should have been smarter about it. The college I went to was a function of circumstance, not intention. I had been kicked out of the Fancy Boarding School I was attending just three months before graduation, and though I'd received full scholarships to two Good Colleges I would have loved to attend, both revoked their offers of financial aid on being informed by Fancy Boarding School that I had in fact not graduated, and instead I ended up having to go to the college where my dad taught. It was a fine school, and for some it's a destination, but for me it felt like failure. It felt a little like Dokken. Like Donken, it was less than half an hour from my house.

In retrospect, being from Houghton and having, largely through my own stupidity, to go to school in Houghton, drove me to attempt unsuccessfully to prove something to myself and anyone else I encountered. After all, I was the smart kid (if a little wayward on occasion). And at the school where my dad taught, a good engineering school, women were vastly outnumbered by men, which did not improve my prospects of affection. So by the time I found my way into my introduction to creative writing class, I was prepared to have to do some work to let everyone know I didn't really belong there. I wasn't going to end up here (like them, I didn't say). I didn't like the chumps that people from here liked or defaced road signs to represent their lame love for. So when my instructor asked everyone to introduce themselves by telling us their favorite band (having probably given up on asking new students to name their favorite writers), when that one kid said his favorite band was Dokken, I couldn't let that go. *Dokken? DOKKEN? You know Dokken sucks, right?* I went on like this for a while and made myself a spectacle. In college, I had assumed, I wouldn't have to deal with Dokken or with Donken or with people from or liking either. All I remember from it now is the feeling of satisfaction of having at last exhausted my opinions about the suckage of Dokken and only then noticing that my classmate was crying.

I wish I could say we later became friends. Maybe we did, but if so I don't remember. Probably not. I'm pretty sure in this story I remain the bully, unredeemed. This is in part why I am gentle with my students now when I ask them hey, who's your favorite writer, or your favorite band, and someone tries out somebody terrible. I too was a fool like you, I think, even if I do not say it as often as I could.

I'm pretty sure the band I would have named as my favorite in 1993 would have been the Sisters of Mercy, who had recently released their George H. W. Bush–trolling album *Vision Thing* featuring the single "More," cowritten and coproduced by Jim Steinman, best known for his collaborations with Meat Loaf. This would be the band's last proper album ever. It was received—correctly, I'd understand only later—as a shark-jumping of truly epic (Meat Loaf!) proportion. Then again, the signs all pointed to this. By this point the band had become a solo project of the excellently monikered Andrew Eldritch (né Andrew William Harvey Taylor), who had driven the rest of the founding members of the band away except for the staunch and always-credited (as a joke, I think—?) Doktor Avalanche, the drum machine.

And since I apparently feel like asserting another opinion, I would still defend the Sisters of Mercy and the album *Vision Thing* and even the song "More" (though not the 2016 Meat Loaf cover of it, which is terrible), but the intervening twenty-six years have led me to understand why their fans may have greeted the album's increasing pomp and ego trip with dismay. To that end, I would understand if you wanted to check out from this essay now, so I'll give you a space break in which to decide to do so politely.

Will the Sun Rise

I'm back and I'm reading a long poem by a friend and teacher, Sheryl St. Germain, from her book *The Small Door of Your Death*, written in part about her son, Gray, who died at age thirty. In it the two of them connect and reconnect over music: REM, Uncle Tupelo, New Order. Gray was a talented musician, part of the band Ghosthustler (you can find some of their stuff on Youtube), and while I met him only once or twice, his loss is still palpable. That's the echo good art makes (both his and hers), and even if I can't really register what it would be like to lose a child, the poems give me a little bit—as much as I can take—of the experience. I think that's partly why we connect so strongly over music, one reason why my wife and I run the yearly March Xness tournament of essays about songs: because thinking about music (however good or bad) is an opportunity for connection. So maybe even Dokken, too, can be an opportunity for connection.

Reading this poem and thinking about Sheryl and her son listening to New Order together I feel something opening.

In response to this opportunity I'm feeling for art, I cue up a couple of Dokken tracks. (I downloaded their entire discography so as to more exhaustively research this essay.) Listening to Dokken now, they don't seem any better or any worse than anything I listened to thirty years ago. They were fine. Better than fine actually. Some of their songs rock somewhat, and occasionally a lot. More than you'd expect. The videos don't help their cause, however: some bands chose their video directors wisely or found their own good ideas; for the most part Dokken was not one of these. Narrative helps, I want to tell them through elapsed time. Don't be too literal. Find hotter actresses if you're going to center the videos around them (see also "Breaking the Chains": look at the screenshot from the video on Youtube: it is just awesome/awful).

Dokken is named for the lead singer, Don Dokken, who reportedly years after the band peaked, required the smaller clubs that booked him to introduce him as "The Legendary Don Dokken" (a move Andrew Eldritch would respect) or he wouldn't play. Most bands named for the lead singer do not stay intact for long, and Dokken didn't either. After a few albums, George Lynch, the guitarist, left to pursue his own projects—Lynch Mob, if you're wondering: they're okay but they are, I am sad to say, no Dokken, but then neither was Don on his own. For sure, though, Don can sing. Or could sing. Judging from comments on YouTube in the past few years, his range has eroded, as happens to us all. After listening to Dokken for something like a hundred hours now, I can tell you he has a really quite melodic tone: there's a lightness to his vocals that's unusual for the genre. It feels like his voice is floating on the guitars.

Look at the video: Don was always a thin guy, but he was positively spectral by the time they recorded "Dream Warriors." One thinks: drugs. Unlike many of the hair metal guys, he hasn't released a book.

I Can't See You

So how do I follow this thread back to Donken? There's barely any Donken to get back to, I realize. Google Maps can show me its location, which is a kind of finding. I start wondering about how this place began and when it ceased. I find a cache of old photos, digitized in a collection at the Traverse Area District Library Local History Collection.

Donken was founded circa 1920 by Earl and Maude Case as a logging company town for Case's Lumber Mill and Camp. All the photographs I can find attest to its snow and bounty: "View of piles of logs covered with snow at Donken, (Mich.), 1919," "Tom Ridout with load of logs in Camp Donken near Donken, Mich., 1918," "Camp Donken's cook shanty in Donken, Mich., 1918," "Don and Ken Case, undated (sons of Earl and Maude)," "Ken Case standing in pile of logs in Donken, Mich, 1918." You get the idea.

In one photo I unearth ("Ken Case at Case Lumber Office at Donken camp in Donken, Michigan") Ken has become a ghost. A shower of what looks like sparks, scratches, snow, or ash, obscures him. Maybe someone scratched him out, or etched him into a flower. I don't mind saying I find it beautiful: he's indistinct, and the less I can see of him the more I can imagine in the photo. If it were clear, there would be little drama here. What he looks like doesn't matter. Rivets spell out "Office" on the outside wall above his head.

Into the Fire

Bill Morrison is a filmmaker best known for his collage film *Decasia* (2001), for which he cut bits of hundreds of old and poorly stored films that had degraded, their nitrate breaking down, into loops. Then he spliced them, overlaying each with music by the composer David Gordon, foregrounding the decay. Form and formlessness are its primary subject, and also time, and the slippage between recognizable images onscreen and their erasure creates an incredible tension for me, watching it. It's not often that I'm struck by something like this, but reading about Morrison in a Lawrence Weschler essay led me to a short Morrison film titled *Light Is Calling*, in the style of *Decasia* and with the same collaborator, and as I watched it on my computer I found myself silenced, my mouth haloed. Was I even breathing?

Here, I thought, was the sublime: the figure and its forgetting all at once, and more importantly, the slipping in between was both beautiful and strange in equal parts, and the balance of the two amped up the effect of both.

I've been thinking about the Tucson teenagers who take machetes or saws or axes to cut through the trunks of saguaro cacti, you know, the most recognizable kind of cactus, unique to the Sonoran Desert, the sort that grows arms only after a hundred years. Due to the extensive radius of their roots, they're often untransplantable, but people still dig them up to put them in their yards. They die, of course, only a couple of years in, with their root systems decimated from the transplanting. A terrible deep freeze, like the one-hundred-year weather event we experienced in 2011, also registers on these cacti, though it can take a decade to see just how badly the plant was injured. (Saguaros are in fact quite fragile in spite of their dramatic, spiny exteriors.)

Witnessing a hacked-up saguaro makes me want to vomit. It's a visceral, breathtaking act of vandalism, and it reminds me of the power of that kind of disfiguring. It seems to say fuck you to every scrim of social decency. To cut a cactus trunk or arm in half like that takes, what, just a couple of minutes, if that, of someone's stupid sixteen-year-old life, and its effect could echo for a hundred years or more. It's no accident that the terms we use for the bodies of cacti or plants—trunk, limb, skeleton, skin—are our analogues.

Vandalism, especially writ large like this, is a dizzying and adolescent power, as mute as it is stupid, as effective as it is brutal. I don't wish to ascribe to the vandals themselves any more meaning or intention than they deserve: I'm sure this is just assholes doing something assholey because they felt like it. I know these assholes. I've been these assholes. I know just how little I thought about what I did.

I wonder now: In what way can a defacement create and not just destroy?

In his films, Morrison is recovering and making something out of the things others throw away or give up on. Changing Donken to Dokken is as juvenile and meaningless as anything else, but the defaced signs stuck with me, and I believe they are also a revelation. Or I hope they can be. I ask a friend from home: Do you remember those Dokken signs? He does. They reach through both of us some thirty years.

That shot of Ken Case behind that spectral something at the Case Lumber Office: without its defacing marks, it wouldn't matter to me. If it were just Donken and not also Dokken (or the reverse), they would not mean as much to me as they seem to now. It's the doubling—and their elision—that resonates. It's as if I spin them, printed back-to-back, on a string or a stick or a sentence, and the resulting image is a third, the superimposition of both states. That the eye can perceive movement from still images led eventually to moving pictures, and that's still the illusion that movies are: just a bunch of static images. This is a fact we don't think about nearly as often as we should. Which leads in its way to Dokken's mediocre videos. And if poorly stored for long enough, those images, those illusions, also decay. But if found and used properly, these data can come back to life and be made to mean more than they once did.

Lost behind the Wall

I'm listening to a fifteen-minute song, "Sequenced," by Axel Willner, the artist better known by his DJ stage name, the Field. It's at the end of his 2009 album *Yesterday and Today*, and it, too, does something sublime to me. He works primarily by layering audio loops—some instrumental, some vocal; some found, some made—into songs. His work, unlike Dokken's, is pretty abstract. Listening to the Field is in part tracking how these loops accrete and build, how they wax and wane and converge. The vocal loops ghost in and out and are treated like all the other scraps on the album, and I'm reminded of how the human figures function in Morrison's decaying film loops: they're reminders of why we normally listen to music (or watch film). In this way the lead material is rendered background, and the art is made instead from scraps. This isn't normally the kind of thing I go for, but I've found it increasingly beautiful as an experience. Perhaps the most notable thing about this track—this album—is how long it's able to delay its resolution. The album is fifty-nine minutes long, and in this last track, around minute fifty-seven, after minor fall after minor fall after minor fall after minor fall, we eventually arrive, after all of this, at the major lift, with just two minutes left.

I picture it as an end of the nightclub track, the kind you play to bring a crowd slowly down from wherever they've been, however worked up and hopped up they've been on whatever substances and dancing and congregation and music and back to their individual lives. Like those on the dance floor, I close my eyes.

Stick to Your Guns

I remember seeing a lot of shotgun-blasted highway signs in Upper Michigan. It could be the Donken/Dokken sign I'm thinking of or another town's. We'd drive by and register its holes and wonder: What was the sign's offense? I'd wonder then—years before I understood the raw power of this kind of angry, helpless feeling—what would lead someone to do something like that? What would be the point?

That image of the shotgunned sign has also stuck with me. How many times did the Michigan Department of Transportation have to go back and replace that sign, and what did crew members think each time they had to do it? Do they track events like this?

I talked with Daniel Weingarten, an MDOT employee, who told me that "it is a serious problem. Unfortunately, its full scope is hard to assess accurately." They don't track data on sign theft or vandalism statewide across sixty-three counties. So he didn't have any data on Donken's sign, which, like the career of Dokken, has faded. I'm guessing it's probably not the hottest commodity in stolen Michigan roadside signs these days. Weingarten told me that the most-often recent recurring sign theft in Michigan is of M-22 route marker signs in the Lower Peninsula's northwest region. People steal about thirty of those a year, in spite of "theft-proof bolts" (they cut the whole post down) costing taxpayers something in the realm of $10,000 per year. To remedy that, the DOT is shifting signage to cold plastic markings embedded in the roads themselves. It will take determination to excise those.

Till the Livin' End

It's been a few years since I've been back to the road leading through the Donken part of Michigan, but I think about it often: it's like a landscape of a dream I keep having and that keeps powering me in ways I can't completely articulate.

So I have to rely on what I can dig up online. One of the few recent descriptions I find is on a website devoted to ghost towns, which I suppose Donken is now, written by Ryan J. Hill: "Although Donken had a post office in 1935, only two mailboxes remain at Donken nowadays (2004). Now Donken is a collection of quite obscene, dereclict [sic] wooden shacks on either sides [sic] of the road." I'm not sure what could render a wooden shack obscene, but I take his point. Is it the presence of ruin made so plain that offends?

I have no memory of anything being there except ruins, but most towns you drive through where I'm from are mostly ruins: a smokestack maybe or a wall housing a steam hoist, connected now to nothing. Donken maxed out around one hundred residents, and from what I can see these days it has none at all.

Don't Close Your Eyes

I don't know so many Dons. My wife's grandfather, now deceased. One of my workshop instructors, murdered. The guy who ran the all-night diner in the town where I went to college. I ate there a few times—slumming, sorta, I'm sure would've been the impression, another college guy with his half-past-drunk date, both of them wanting something fried, or just somewhere else to be for a little while. That's accurate enough: the town had a problem with the gown, as they say. Though it wasn't explicit all that often, you could feel the seams at times what with everyone trying to differentiate themselves or figure out who or what to blame when the Maytag plant closed down and what was left after that. What town isn't pulling itself apart? Donken, probably, since that's been done long ago. And even when I was in Don's Diner I bet Don was dead.

Oh: I forgot another Don I went to grad school with who somehow got his degree without ever writing more than one story and obsessively revising it: it was about a sexy lobster girl that turned out to be a metaphor. He kept rewriting it and turning it in for workshop, semester after semester. You had to admire his commitment to getting through the program without generating more than one actual story the entire time. I have a fondness for perversity in people, as in the case of another friend who wrote his entire graduate thesis the night before after having improvised it on the spot at the public reading that counted as a thesis defense. What did that spectacle serve? I wonder. It's a kind of defacement of the opportunity, given to few enough of us, to spend a couple of years really concentrating on producing something of meaning and note. But then I remember his story when I don't remember half the other people I went to school with, so that's a kind of achievement in itself.

I imagine Don of the lobster girl must have turned something in for his thesis to get out of there before his funding dried up. He could throw a party, though, and liked cocaine. I hear he's driving a cab in New Orleans these days. That makes four Dons I'm gathering and trying to hold here for a moment, these years gone. Maybe it's a lot of Dons. Enough for one essay anyhow. And then of course there's the Don of Dokken.

Don't Lie to Me

It's hard to even believe the stories I'm telling myself about my past now. That past is so scratched up that it skips when played, and it's hard to tell what's signal and what's scratch, what's original and what's artifact of my own obsessive working.

The past is etched up by pulling it out of its sleeve too often, I think, and fingering its grooves and reinscribing it and leaving it in the sun when our attention shifts to something shinier.

Dream Warriors

Time elapses. Dokken comes to Tucson. I have tickets and anticipation in spite of the comments I've read online about their recent shows. My wife and I will attend, maybe in search of some redemption, or, failing that, some reckoning.

Only two members of the original band are still part of the show. George Lynch, their then-often-shirtless guitarist, occasionally tours with them, but Don and George have a beef these days, in the tradition of eponymous lead singers and hypertalented lead guitarists. Or probably more accurately they just have different interests in or availabilities for touring their old songs. What must it be like to be in a band like that, still playing the songs you were famous for when you were younger and hotter and partied harder, but you're still striking the same rock poses at the same moments on some of the very same stages, probably to many of the same faces?

Of course I am hoping they play "Dream Warriors," which I'm assuming they'll have to. The chorus goes like this: "Dream warriors—don't want to dream no more." I use an em dash to punctuate because I am not sure what the relationship between these two things is. It's a line break in the lyric sheet, but it's indeterminate: Are Dokken the dream warriors? Am I? What relationship do the dream warriors have with the desire to dream no more?

If you haven't seen it, the plot of the *Nightmare on Elm Street* films is that Freddy Krueger, the villain, somehow can come into teenagers' dreams and torture and kill them there, probably because they are the progeny of those who tortured and killed him some years before. They didn't kill him permanently, apparently. So he visits the sins of the parents on their kids, except somehow the teenagers turn the tables and kill Krueger by the end, though of course, unlike Donken, when he's dead, he doesn't stay dead for long.

Why is an unkillable villain appealing? Is it because in these films the other characters aren't likable (at best they're clichés, a fact that films like *Cabin in the Woods* exploit), so the only option for us to love (or follow anyhow) turns out to be the killer? Or because the killer gets the most depth of character, by virtue of repetition? After all, we do need to find something new to say about a killer if he keeps coming back, movie after movie. Or is it because the other characters die and we get sick of loss and want to believe in something? Or are teenagers, these films' usual fodder, just dislikable? (I can't think of a horror killer who mows down those in middle age, which might tell us our fingers are on a seam.) Do we like to root for a repeat loser, prefer experience to innocence, or do we simply like that things come back?

Our parents' sins come back in our own actions. What, I wonder, in part, is the degree to which the sins I visited upon my father will be visited upon me by my daughter—or by Dokken or the kid who loved Dokken—in dreams? I could ask my dad to comment for this essay but probably won't because we're from Michigan and we don't talk about those kinds of things, at least not without a drink, and he's an alcoholic, so even I know it's a bad idea, even by my standards. No doubt I gave him and my stepmother more trouble than their share, which they like to remind me, only kind of fondly. If I concentrate on myself at sixteen, say, I can't really see.

Rewatching *A Nightmare on Elm Street 3*, I'm surprised by the quote that opens the film:

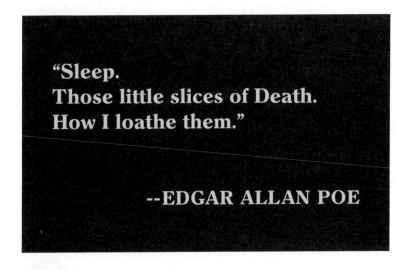

"Sleep.
Those little slices of Death.
How I loathe them."

--EDGAR ALLAN POE

Excited, I text it to my friend Paul, a Poe scholar. He texts back that Poe never wrote it as far as he can tell. Authorities on the internet concur: this is, for sure, faux Poe. It's true Poe was interested in what happens in the states beyond or on the other side of sleeplessness—the hypnagogic and hypnopompic states, those just before falling asleep or waking up, respectively. And most threads about the quotation trace its origins to the beginning of the film I'm watching. It appears that the quotation did appear in the screenplay for a 1959 adaptation of Jules Verne's *Journey to the Center of the Earth*, which is as far back as anyone has managed to track it.

I love the thought of Poe as a canvas on which we can project our dreams—quotations, whatever. It's fake news with just the right bit of truthiness. One might ask why we'd assume anything in a non-documentary movie is true. But to what end this fake, if fake it is? More likely it's an artifact of something someone said or wrote and thought they knew, and had an opinion on that they liked to talk about, and because they thought they knew it, they said it and said Poe said it and they wrote it and it went onscreen and now becomes the authority for its provenance. In sleep we reinscribe our failings and our erasings. Memories replay themselves on our television screens and we begin to remember them better than the events themselves. It takes work to get underneath the rational shell of mind we're saddled with most of our waking hours. No wonder Poe pursued the edge states just beyond or back from it.

In My Dreams

Alternate take: the level of kickassery and belief required for some teen-ager in god-abandoned Upper fucking Michigan to have defaced an MDOT road sign for the town Donken into the name of a metal band in 1987 is high. So high, in fact, that my expectations for said band should have been through the roof. And the commitment to claiming your favorite band as Dokken, well after they were remotely cool, deserves our praise and in fact our love: love what you want to love and claim it loud, my friend, I want to say! It's the cooler kids, those of us looking at each other as we're talking about something cool and thinking we're all cool, who've missed the opportunity. Kid, I mean to say, I hope you write about Dokken, but since I can't know, I'm writing about them for you.

Breaking the Chains

I've been thinking a lot about Jim Harrison, the novelist, essayist, and poet from Michigan who died in 2016. He was an acquaintance and a generous guy. On advice from my friend Sean, I've been reading Harrison's book *Letters to Yesenin*, poems of confession to a long-dead Russian poet who committed suicide at thirty, though the suspicion is that the KGB staged his death. Jim has a large reputation, mostly deserved, and I find myself often encountering people who knew one aspect of him. The mythology he built was so large, in fact, that I had a hard time getting to know him in life. We'd crossed paths a number of times, but I've only begun to spend real time—the kind of reading time that matters—with his work now that he's died. I'm not sure if this is a unique character flaw, or if it's shared among writers, to begin to approach writers we know only after they die. I'm not sure how I should feel about it, this feeling I have about the approachability of the dead or the mode they (being dead) put us in.

It's hard not to feel reverent—though I'm no believer in anything after this life—when encountering the dead or someone writing about or to the dead. Even so, I admit, that they are gone or are writing to one who is puts the work in a different class of communication. Probably it's because I don't believe in anything after this that these works of art take on new meaning, that I feel they're evidence of something.

Just Got Lucky

A 2017 headline in the *Arizona Daily Star* reads "Officials Seek Gunman Who Blasted Century-Old Saguaro near Tucson." The cactus was shot up to fourteen times with a shotgun, perhaps because the first thirteen times failed to satisfy. I try to imagine the scene, the sound, the damage, the disappointment. What might it do for or to you to unload on a huge, very old thing? The damage you'd do wouldn't be satisfying: just shot after shot into the cactus flesh, which would, I'd imagine, take whatever you gave it.

Defacing saguaros is a crime in Arizona, especially in a national park. Even cutting down one on your own property without a permit is illegal and could get you jail time.

I'm reminded, though, of another saguaro fact: though in some ways sensitive, these spectacular cacti can also be very resilient to damage. They survive pecking from birds and projectile impacts all the time, growing right around sites of damage and incorporating whatever's embedded in them permanently.

There is, however, a point at which damage may not be survivable. In the case of our shotgunned saguaro, park rangers did not expect it to survive, though they said they'd have to wait five years to know for sure.

It's Not Love

Would I like Dokken better dead? It's easier to admire an outline or a ghost than the person inside the lines. The inconvenient living can't hit the notes. They got fat or rude or old or tired of being who we wanted them to be, and they moved on, but the dead: the dead we can always own. I realize I'm having feelings of ownership toward Dokken, whom I've now listened to longer than my young self could have possibly imagined.

It's inevitable: the more we're exposed to things—however odd—the more they begin to make homes in our hearts and, like saguaros, we grow ourselves around those defacements, those injuries and embeddings.

Sleepless Night

I'm writing this as my father sleeps in the other room. His breathing, aided by the CPAP machine, soundtracks this very sentence. Hearing him strapped into the machine that feeds him breath, it's hard not to think about "Dream Warriors" again: Is it scary because it's sleep in which we feel so vulnerable? What is my father closer to at this moment than I am here awake?

Like all animals, we're vulnerable in our sleep. Because in sleep we're stripped of many of the conscious things that make us feel like us, we're left with something else, some stranger self. Like what happens if we remove all the likes and favorites and interests, all those prizes we pursue and adorn ourselves with, those things and feelings that feel like they fill us? What if we take the whole record collection and bookshelf and Netflix queue and erase those too? What if what you're interested in consciously just fades away? What are you left with? Your anxieties, your troubles, your weird dramatic miniplays. Is that dream you had with the circus freaks and the black stilt-walker who knocked on your door as racist as your morning mind suspects it was? It's a box he's in, even then, and he told you so in your dream. You'll be in your box, too, soon enough.

Sleep needs narrative less than waking life, which means it abuts something truer in us. Have you ever had a dream so shameful that you didn't and would never tell the ones you love about it? I'm guessing yes. So that selfishness makes the state my father's in even more inviolable to me, even less possible for me to write about and enter. Jesus: maybe I'm the parasite, I think, feeding on his dreams. I am, after all, listening to him breathe. Or maybe that's just intimacy I'm feeling and getting uncomfortable with.

Standing in the Shadows

Though the Dokken show starts late, and my wife and I are cranky because we're no longer seventeen, a metal show is a metal show, and this is, we are reminded, a metal show, now a redemption show for me, and it does rock. It feels good to feel that sound and to be among a crowd, even as I spend my time watching them watch the stage for news.

Watching old stars means coming to terms with their age—and ours. Don has put on some weight. (He asks: Haven't you?) He can't hit the high notes he used to hit, and maybe I can't either. What I'm realizing is what he's figured out and built the show around: a concert's not about him, but about us. Maybe it always was. This is, after all, my first time rockin' with Dokken. As usual I get to things everyone else knows a couple of decades too late.

When he can't hit those high notes he holds the mic out to us instead, imploring us to shout or sing it out, and we do, because we know the words, or most of us do, and if he's done his job right we'd rather hear ourselves, and he knows that well, and those who don't know the words or care to sing are happy to pretend and listen to our shitty chorus do our chorus thing, and it doesn't matter if he's singing.

At least he's here. At least we're here. That's what thirty years of playing to crowds teaches you about what it is you do: as virtuosic as your shreddy guitar solo is, we're not here for you. We're here for us, to be part of something, even something thirty years past its sell-by date. They play "Dream Warriors." They play "Breaking the Chains" and "In My Dreams." They play "Without Warning" and "Into the Fire." They play some later songs and solo songs I do not know. I don't believe anyone but the superfans, like my old classmate, knows these songs, but we play along, and I think of that kid. I hold my wife's hand. We are here together. When we're back in Dokken—I mean Donken—I will show her and my daughter where the sign is that, when spun, combined the two. And maybe the Dokken-defacing kids and shotgun-wielding weekend warriors are still playing their memories too—or their dreams. Or that workshop kid to whom I'd like to apologize, even if it's way too late: What's he dreaming of? What's his memory of Dokken? I'm sorry, you Dokken-loving dude. And maybe my dad's sleeping in the other room in his memories—or maybe in the two of ours converged, me tormenting him, him tormenting me, listening to Dokken, driving through Donken, over and over. What could be ever enough?

In the meantime, in the moment, in the encore, like Andrew Eldritch and Doktor Avalanche and the Sisters of Mercy, I want—we all want—more. What's more than memory? That's what we have when the music and the film stock and the road signs and the photographs fade. So I listen. My mouth's open. There's Don singing and gesturing at us to sing. You know I do. And doing, I play my memories. My wife plays hers. You play yours.

Long Live the Jart, Heavy and Pointed and Gleaming

Long live its long lines, thin fins, its lead head.

Long live its obvious danger, the way it arranged moments into living and hardly and summer.

Long live the jart, lawn dart with the aggressive, actionable name, banned in 1988 by the Consumer Product Safety Commission.

Long live the 3:1 ratio of boys to girls with "penetrating lawn dart injuries" that led to the ban.

Long live the box copy reading, mostly chronologically: "an outdoor game," "a missile game," "an exciting outdoor game of skill for the whole family," "fun for the entire family."

Long live the amended copy: "an outdoor skill game for adults," "a skillful sport for adults," or "a competition rated adult lawn dart game."

Long live the end of the jart.

Long live the end of childhood.

Long live the culture of protection.

Long live the name of the jart, javelin + dart, or jet + dart, or je + the heart, javelina + the art, Jeremiah + the shot through the heart, and you're to blame.

Long live the jart, modern family version of the plumbata, the lead-weighted military throwing dart used by Roman infantry from 300 to 700 CE.

Long live skull fracture and bone penetration.

Long live instruments of war packaged as a family game.

Long live convalescing in Spain.

Long live family, an arena of war.

Long live the jart, the backyard fléchette (projectile deployed from planes or balloons during the First World War).

Long live the dreams of those run through by fléchettes.

Long live the dreams of the four-chambered heart, about to be struck.

Long live *A Bell Is a Cup . . . Until It Is Struck* (album by Wire).

Long live the chambers of the nautilus.

Long live the heart, an organ, then not.

Long live the four percent casualty rate of children struck by jarts per a 1990 study published in *Journals of Diseases of Children.*

Long live air bubble and hemorrhage of left temporal region with surrounding edema as shown on CT scan in said study.

Long live "Male predominance . . . may be explained by sex difference in exposure to risks and/or behavior," quoted in said study.

Long live a corollary study, "Pediatric Injuries in the Back of Pickup Trucks," 1990, published in the *Journal of the American Medical Association.*

Long live trips in my father's or another's pickup truck as a child, taking jumps down steep hills, catching air into darkness forever.

Long live summer camp with its notions of archery and weird martial training.

Long live the marching band, remnant, reminder of that martial culture.

Long live Bill Millin, bagpiper at the D-day landings, who died on August 17, 2010.

Long live the bagpipe as a weapon of war, officially proclaimed by an English judge circa 1746, reasoning that his music was his weapon.

Long live Bill Millin, whom German snipers had in their sights and had not fired on.

Long live not firing on bagpipers: we know it is tempting.

Long live *Red Dawn* and the grossly simplified nuclear threat.

Long live the martial and survivalist action of Boy Scouts.

Long live the Webelos, the joint between cub and boy, we'll be loyal scouts, we'll be forever lost.

Long live the lawns of the dreams of the past, cleared out of pests.

Long live the idea of lawns, mostly absent from Arizona, like water.

Long live my heart in my mouth as I chucked the jart toward the ring on the ground where it gathered with others in thunder.

Long live the *shink* sound they make when they go deep in the earth.

Long live their banning, rendering them permanently amazing.

Long live our lives, soft, safe, servile, updating motherboards on servers, drinking coffee to feel alive.

Long live the last time you felt anything was possible.
Long live that must have included death from above. Long live that must include love.

Long live the decades of lawsuits.

Long live the legitimate lawsuit. Long live the spurious.

Long live the lawsuit of K—, who sued the city of Houghton, Michigan, for "not properly marking" the obvious speed bump he wrecked his bike on going thirty miles an hour like a fool down the hill, breaking his arm.

Long live the couple of hundred bucks he won or received as a settlement.

Long live his trajectory into Amway and fatherhood and irrelevance.

Long live screw that guy.

Long live my scorn, for it sustains me.

Long live Facebook for not reconnecting him and me with our shared, stupid memories.

Long live so far, long live yet.

Long live the pornography of memory.

Long live the scar on my forehead.

Long live the increasing expanse of my forehead, how like a lawn or a historical cat it creeps.

Long live the lies I told to girls about how I got that scar, my fake Australian accent.

Long live fooling no one.

Long live the kindness of girls.

Long live the stairways of memory, collapsing below me.

Long live the homemade bomb.

Long live my friend J— whose homemade bomb blew up while he made it.

Long live the static that triggered it, that triggered our hearts, that redirected our circulations and ambitions.

Long live our many other bombs before that.

Long live cannon fuse, saltpeter, Vaseline, improvised nitroglycerin.

Long live the crazy heart of *The Anarchist's Cookbook*.

Long live the surgeon who attached his big toe to his hand in place of a thumb. Long live the millimeters by which the fragments missed his vas deferens.

Long live his succession of long-suffering hot girlfriends.

Long live my collection of teenage pornography.

Long live the Upper Peninsula, where his name is inscribed.

Long days were ours, those summers of incredible Eastern Standard Time. Long live the air stretching out toward the irreducible evening, and our forgetting.

Long live the arc of the jart, parabolic in air, sometimes in hair and in tears. (More rarely in sweating glasses of tea.)

Long live the *shink* sound of it hitting the earth, of it splitting the earth, of spitting on wounds from things stuck in the earth.

Long live the jart's long flight on my grandmother's lawn.

Long live the exact width of the sky above my grandmother's cabin on Pelican Lake, Minnesota, pontoon boats trolling through the summer evenings, my family lining the shore.

Long live my teenage collection of pornography.

Long live demography.

Long live invincibility.

Long live you not noticing it ending.

Long live the summer of selling stamps door-to-door to neighbors for some reason lost in memory.

Long live the later summer of failed grassroots organizing in Madison, Wisconsin. Grass roots for what? Organizing for what? Gone now, like minnows, like moaning, like each new morning.

Long live my grandfather dying of emphysema just up the road, sucking air.

Long live my grandfather, Heinz salesman, buyer, deployer of jarts on the lawn, in the shed, in the air.

Long live the loss of his hair, for I feel you now, America.

Long live remembering minnows nibbling my legs, though I have not waded in that or any lake with minnows for years. Long live my dulling senses, my hardened skin so that I could not even feel them if theoretically I were to wade in the water, that water, those minnows, my marrow, tomorrow.

Long live the feeling of power in weapons and jarts.

Long live the power of art.

Long live its weight in my hand.

Long live its barrel, how like a gun.

Long live the sound of my brother tracing circles on the lawn.

Long live blindfolds over eyes.

Long live the rocks I threw at my brother while swimming.

Long live what this means to our continuing relationship, never just dust in the past.

Long live the dumb men in our family, who mostly die younger, from bodily neglect rather than guns.

Long live our dwindling numbers.

Long live the elegy, geology's long thought, the brains of those struck by jarts and hospitalized, their names redacted from the record.

Long live Elkhart, Indiana, home of the last boy who suffered a brain injury due to lawn darts before the ban.

Long live we bumblers, stumbling through summers.

Long live the humming of mummers and their plays, their plays on words.

Long live the absence of birds.

Long live any of us surviving Michigan men. Long live either luck or timidness.

Long live fire, fir trees, the disfigurement of our friends. Long live Safeway and Starbucks and other American shrapnel.

Long live Misery Bay and the dredge.

Long live Torch Lake, poisoned by mine tailings.

Long live its phalanx of swarming, cancerous fish.

Long live my childhood and the disguises it takes even now.

Long live the swears I learned, when to deploy them, and not.

Long live actually never really figuring this out.

Long live this pornography of teenage collection.

Love live the collection of weapons, the blowguns, the crossbows, bottle rockets, shotguns, air rifles, shuriken, katanas, morning stars, pistols, throwing knives, kidney knives, bowie knives, butterfly knives, carving knives, hatchets, gasoline.

Long live our desperation to be able to affect something, anything.

Long live remembering sensation, a powerful urge growing stronger each year that I age. Long live the inevitability that it will be the only thing remaining in memory as I expect to dream out my last, institutionalized decade on the IV television drip in my Craftmatic, nothing and no one so close as to possibly harm me ever again.

Long live my heart, the machine of my thinking. Long may it not burst.

Long live the earth. Long live the jart stuck in its heart.

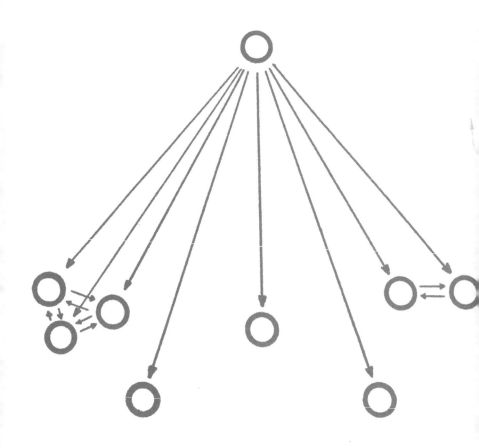

Exchange Rate

*The closer you get to a mystery, the more
important it is to be realistic. Radios in cars,
coded messages, short-wave signals and
power cuts are all familiar to everybody and
allow me to keep my feet on the ground.*
—Jean Cocteau

I remember the radio in my 1987 Nissan Maxima, a car I bought in 1998,
in Des Moines, Iowa, after my stepmother's Camry finally died for the
last time: it was brushed steel, with a volume and a fader knob up top,
accompanied by a tape deck with some logos: Stereo, Dolby System,
something next to some text reading "CK 145." Some buttons I never
figured out what they meant: PLAY/PRO meant play and something
else; REW and FF were easy enough, but both also read APS, whatever
that was. What MTL did I never learned. The radio itself came accompanied by an impressive-looking seven-band graphic equalizer ("CU115")
in which you could manually adjust the sound at 60 Hz, 125 Hz, 250 Hz,
500 Hz, 1 kHz, 3 kHz, and 10 kHz by sliding metal bars up and down.
I fiddled with it constantly, trying to come up with the ideal sound that
fit perfectly whatever jam I was listening to then.

The Maxima was not a great car: the cruise control was wonky, it had
a burned-looking mark on its hood where the paint was starting to flake
off, and the sunroof had some damage and leaked when it rained, which
was often, this being Iowa. Later I would find out that it had quite possibly been through a flood, which may have been why I could afford a car
with a V6 and such an impressive-seeming radio at that point in my life.
I mean, it had an impressive stereo. The radio itself just did what it did:
it picked up signals broadcast from towers I could see and wonder at as

they jutted high above field after field of corn, vertical reminders of just how flat everything else was. The internet tells me now it was a Clarion Model Pn-9130, and I can buy one, disambiguated from its Maxima, from eBay for $124.99 + $24.99 shipping.

I couldn't tell you what the stereo on the car I drive now looks like. It's way more advanced, I sense, and I use it all the time, but more often than not I'm scrolling on my phone through a playlist or a podcast, or just hitting Scan and hoping for something magical. And when a song that I like arrives, I rarely think that since what I'm listening to is old, the singer may well be dead. The band's almost certainly broken up. Maybe someone else hijacked their brand and is doing casino-nostalgia tours. It's old news that arrives, that makes me feel like I felt when I was new.

Besides, old news is what radio *is*: *news* and *past*, the result of a transmission sent just before I receive it. So when the not-quite-classic rock of 98.1 supersedes 98.3's bleeped-out hip-hop stream I recognize the song: Cinderella's 1988 power ballad, "Don't Know What You Got Till It's Gone." If you don't know or remember this song, here's its calculus: while what you used to have is now gone, now you know what you had, and more to the point, you know what you *have*: it's just this song, and though it's sure as hell not enough, it's not nothing either. The beloved has vanished, but the shape she made remains in the form of this very song of longing, if longing is what it is, and though we might not wish it, the song is the enduring thing, and anyone who listens to it takes possession anew.

A sad song may be an artifact, but it's also a memorial and a spectacle. If some songs are inspired by spectacles ("The Wreck of the Edmund Fitzgerald"—surely one of the more funerary songs you may have heard a lot), some songs inspire actual spectacles: in 2016, Winslow, Arizona, erected a statue of recently deceased former Eagle Glenn Frey standin' on a corner in Standin' on the Corner Park as tribute to the Eagles lyric, and to remind tourists that Winslow, Arizona, once a mainstay on historic US Route 66, mattered, and maybe still does, even if it's been bypassed entirely by I-40 since the interstate was completed in the late 1970s. And our sadness is a spectacle, too, even if unmemorialized or made into a song. How often have I made a wide berth around an adult just flat-out weeping in public? I'm so well wired to expect a "doing fine" or a "great" or an "aight" in response to my polite inquiries that I don't know what to do when occasionally presented with a real answer. Even a brief encounter with someone in the throes of deep emotion—grief or frustration—can rewire me in the same way a brush with a brush fire as I drive by it on the interstate does. My day is punctuated into before and after the fire or the weeping.

I'm almost weeping now, listening to Cinderella, which is a sentence I never thought I would end up saying or writing. How is this dumb song the thing that stays? I think, too, of how rarely works of art (if you don't mind me calling "Don't Know What You Got" art) overtly acknowledge their being works of art, and what that means for the emotion or situation that motivated the making of the art. I mean, I know it's a shitty power ballad from a genre of music that got rightly extinguished by grunge, yet it registered with me—and it keeps registering. Now I know what I got, and it's this song, and that takes me back, but it's not so easy, and it takes so long. It's almost as if all I have is the glass slipper that so seared me but no memory of the foot it once fit.

I pull the car off to the side of the road to let the song finish. It's held up well over the years, if not quite as spectacularly as Sappho's odes, and I wonder about how we register and aestheticize and process sadness. It hurts, the memory of pain and the sadness it invokes, and when we write about pain (or loss, which prompts pain, or sadness, which often comes after), as we necessarily memorialize it, are we also insulating ourselves in aesthetic or affect? I mean: In writing sadness or pain do we separate ourselves from the experience of it? Is writing *feeling*, or is it *processing*? I remember an essay I once read about writing love poems that suggested that in order to write a truly great love poem the poet must love the poem more than the beloved.

I don't remember the author, but I see her point, even if it's still hard for me to swallow: if you love the poem more than the beloved, then I can see how it might be a better poem, but it may not be a better love poem. (I doubt it's a better love.) And that I remember the sentiment but not the author makes its own point well enough.

I mean, I know it's probably necessary—it is, right?—to separate an experience into artifact so as to get some distance from it, but is it okay? Is that the same effect that dulls us to the shock of gunfire and how easily we go back to our regular lives even though much of the territory in which we live is stained with blood, and to the extent it is "ours" that also means it's not (it used to be) someone else's? How many years does it take us to shop again at that Safeway, or to bring those jarts back out of the shed after they punched a hole in your brother's foot? Would it be quicker if we could leach those feelings out into a song? Is that even desirable?

At the Eckstrom-Columbus Branch of the Tucson Public Library I find an archive of condolence cards written by schoolchildren to those hurt or killed in the January 8th attack. On one, Zevi Shane Bloomfield writes: "Pain does't [sic] just wash away like the sea. Pain covers your body until it melts beneath your heart . . . until you can't bear it any longer. Pain stays there forever until you talk about pain. It washes away and never comes back until sorrow."

That's a hell of a formulation, and not one I could have come up with: talking about pain is the only way to wash it away, but sorrow (perhaps pain's echo?) brings it back. Bloomfield may or may not know that, in English, sorrow is a deeper and longer state than sadness. The *OED* glosses *sorrow* as "deep sadness." The 1947 edition of *Funk & Wagnalls Standard Handbook of Synonyms, Antonyms & Prepositions* tells us that "grief is more acute and less enduring than sorrow; sorrow and grief are for definite cause; sadness and melancholy may arise from a vague sense of want or loss." S. I. Hayakawa's *Choose the Right Word* (1968) tells us that sorrow combines sadness with regret. Pain may be "washed away" by talking about it, but sorrow is a deepened state, perhaps the sort of state that memorials touch and are meant to externalize.

My Tucson, my desert city, has more memorials than most, even if they're often unofficial, contingent, only semipermanent. Descansos ("resting places"; from the Spanish, literally: "to rest"), makeshift memorials for those who died at the site, litter our roadsides and are found on many roads in the Southwest. I saw one at a park I took my daughter to along the wash just today. She and I have been discussing death in the context of our recently deceased favorite cat, Napoleon, so it's not an uncomplicated subject to arise from the walk back from the jungle gym to the parking lot. Some descansos slant a little political, like the white-painted ghost bikes that remind us to be cognizant of those with whom we share the roads, but more often they're personal, and those are the ones that penetrate: the fresh Arby's meal left by a cross, still sun-warm in a bag. The pictures and the notes. When I pass one on foot I stop and gawk. I take a picture, but it's complicated. I don't want to seem irreverent, and I'm not, but they rivet me: to mourn so openly, so publicly: it's wonderful and raw.

At first I was a little shocked by these installations: I never saw these in the Midwest growing up, and not just because of the snow that covers most of everything for long stretches of the year. They come from the cultural traditions and iconography of Mexican Catholicism and have been spreading slowly outward into the rest of the country. I appreciate that in a place like this one they stay and keep on marking. This region's more honest than most about how we exist among the dead. For instance, Tucson hosts the yearly All Souls Procession (not to be confused with a parade), an Americanized, Tucson-specific version of Día de los Muertos: one night a year you can attend a procession in memory and celebration of the dead and how we want to remember them. And it's not a comfortable spectacle either: it doesn't minimize. It's often silent, somber, spectral, and mostly it's a potent combination of the beautiful, alarming, reverent, and truly upsetting: I remember my friends Erik and Nicole coming down from Flagstaff to attend it with their daughter, Zoe, then three years old, and the succession of emotions that played across her as thousands of painted skeletal faces passed, often in silence or accompanied by the beating of huge drums. This, you could tell, was something she was not prepared for. Who is? Its solemnity is hard to take. Perhaps this buildup of emotion is why the procession ends with a huge bonfire, in which the names of the dead are burned.

For the rest of the year the city has decreed that descansos can usually stay where they are placed. The City of Tucson Department of Transportation Policy 30.35 on Roadside Memorials indicates:

[They] may be left in place within the City of Tucson's [right-of-way] as long as they are well maintained by others and do not pose a safety hazard or sight visibility issue. Memorials that do pose an issue should be moved to accommodate visibility and safe passage, but not removed.

It's not just my weird city either. Arizona Department of Transportation guidelines (which apply to state highways and the interstate) indicate that markers

—may be no more than 30 inches high and no wider than 18 inches;
—may have a foundation no more than 12 inches deep, and that foundation shall not involve concrete or metal footings;
—may be fabricated from wood or plastic/composite material;
—may include components no larger than 2 inches thick and 4 inches wide;

—may include a plaque up to 4 inches by 4 inches and 1/16 inch thick listing the victim's name, date of birth, and date of death; —may not include a photograph.

Words and iconography are allowed, but likenesses are not. It's odd that they find it necessary to note that "only one marker is allowed per victim." And why no photographs? (And I've seen a lot of photographs, so this must be more a guideline than a strict prohibition.) Is a photograph too personal and less of an emblem, or is it technical: photographs fade quickly in this here sun?

You'd have to overlook these remainders intentionally to miss them here, though after a while it's true that you do norm to them, and they begin to become just scenery as parsed from a passing car. That's what happens to all the dead and all the debts we owe them; we can't think about everything all the time.

It's when I'm running that I pay the most attention, in part because I'm most in my body then; I'm more my body than I am otherwise, and to stop short and short of breath at the site of someone's death is no small reminder that there's less to separate us than I'd like to think, and all it would take is one lapse of attention or the wrong blood vessel's bursting to add another cross and photograph and beef-and-cheddar to the sidewalk spot. If I die here, I tell my wife, remember me with a lot of Doritos, like as many as you can buy. Just pile them up. *When you die,* my daughter tells me, *I'll remember you with your photograph.*

There is no official limit to how long descansos may remain, but the city notes that they may be moved with sixty days' notice if construction is planned. Mostly they seem to stay, as long as they're maintained, which means in part as long as they continue to serve the purpose they once did to the living. What will it be like, I wonder, when every block in the whole city is finally adorned with one? When we are only too aware that everywhere we are people have died—often *been killed,* and *by us,* even, or people a whole lot like us. That's an uncomfortable thought, so I hold it as long as I can, which I know isn't really long enough, but what could be long enough to properly pay back all I've been given? And at what point do those thoughts become too much, an unparsable mass, and fade into background noise? I mean, if they haven't already?

My bookshelves, like yours I'm sure, are filled with the dead, which I don't like to think about too much. For instance, I pull down Jake Adam

York's last book of elegies, *Abide*, posthumously published. Reading it, I'm filled with something I can't quite name: a combination of reverence for the dead poet whom I knew and a palpable feeling of heaviness, the knowledge that there will be no more Jake Adam York poems, or no more poems *by* Jake Adam York at any rate. (Let this little moment pass without our calling it a poem, as it is not one.) Because I didn't know him well enough to generate the kind of lasting sorrow that occurs when a loved one dies, the idea of him is a little hazy, so it's easier for me to miss not the man but the idea of the man, or his kindnesses and the ways in which his poems construct a Jake Adam York of words, which, as any writer knows, is no substitute for the real self, even as it is for most of us the only thing we'll leave. And so I take a couple of steps back.

From here the book becomes an epitaph, a descanso on my shelf, marking *that* he died if not *where* exactly (his driveway is what I remember—and suddenly and young, roughly my age, surely one thing that drives the nail of his death into me a little further, and I too stand in the driveway and look up into the pressing dark). There he is, upright and stacked, not far now from other dead poets I knew personally, if only in passing, but whose work I obsessed over: Reginald Shepherd, Brigit Pegeen Kelly. And here's *Unbidden Angel*, the only published book by Robin Metz, the best teacher I ever had, who died yesterday.

Consider the elegy, delivered after a passing: like a funeral, it's the living's custom, not the dead's, a rite for us, not them. I can't imagine York thought of his book as a self-elegy, and this sure isn't an elegy for him or any of them, but I do want to register their passing and mark it in the way I know best: on the page.

Maybe I'm thinking of this because the small press I edit is publishing *An Exchange for Fire: The Lonely Poet Guide to Volcanoes*, the last unfinished work by Craig Arnold, a poet who disappeared in 2009, having presumably fallen into a volcano on Japan's Kuchinoerabu Island. I knew Craig a little when he was alive—he stayed the night with me in Tuscaloosa, Alabama, some years ago, as a favor to a friend, and we'd crossed paths a few times after—but since his death he's begun multiplying. A colleague tells me she used to date him. A former student dated Craig's then girlfriend after he had disappeared, and could always feel his echo in the relationship, and maybe that's what fucked the relationship up (or maybe not: it's hard to accurately assess the work of ghosts). And though Craig has faded to me as a person, his work's begun to mean more to me.

Rebecca Lindenberg, his partner and literary executor, is working with us to make his unfinished manuscript as well as a series of posts from his blog *Volcano Pilgrim* into a book. We're trying to figure out how best to present the intentions and the shape of this last work, and how much to edit his work, if at all. I wonder what these conversations must take out of her, whether doing this is any different from making a descanso of his work, but I don't ask, not wanting to open a seam that I know must be hard.

Craig titled the book after a quotation from Heraclitus:

> This world, which is the same for all, no one of gods or men has made. But it always was, is, and will be: an ever-living fire, with measures of it kindling, and measures going out. . . . All things are an exchange for fire, and fire for all things, just like goods for gold and gold for goods.

The quote—and the book—asks: What fire do we exchange when we devote our lives to art, even at the expense of our lives (literally or metaphorically)? And what knowledge or whatever else do we get back in that exchange? Or, once removed, what do we exchange when we make the things we make? Are they diminished versions of emotion? Are they things that prompt or contain emotion? It would be foolish to believe nothing is consumed in the chemical reaction of the making of a power ballad or a poem.

Or consider a more troubling equation: What do we as listeners or readers exchange for the fire we take away from an essay or a song and the way it burns in us thereafter?

I have to believe the flip side's true too: something must be gained in the exchange: the making as well as the reading or the listening. We bring something flaming back with us when we go there, and the process is additive as well as transactional. If we're seared and want to sear another with what we learned, then we're also a little bigger than we were before. Otherwise why would we go at all?

A few miles away, there's a wall at the back of El Tiradito, "the only shrine in the United States dedicated to the soul of a sinner buried in unconsecrated ground." According to the plaque on that wall, "The many legends about its origin all involve a tragic triangle love affair in the early 1870s." The person to whom the shrine is dedicated is Juan Oliveras, a man who "falls in love with his mother-in-law and is murdered by her husband in a jealous rage," according to Tucson magazine *Zócalo*. Or, I should say, it's dedicated to his story—legend, really, since accounts naturally differ—and to the power of desire and memory itself. If you're in town, you can find it on Main, just south of the Tucson Convention Center. Like the best shrines, it's kind of half-assed and you come upon it with a minimum of fanfare and you wonder just what it is you've stumbled into. There, in the lot right next to what's now El Minuto Café and right up the street from Castillo Middle School, where "attendance is important," the sign reminds me, I find handwritten notes stuffed in hundreds of cubbies and the wax from countless candles burned in hope of making contact with the dead or in pursuit of wishes that might be granted to the supplicant. No music presents itself but I think each of these notes, rolled up, looks like an antenna jutting out into the super-heated summer air.

Zócalo tells us that "El Tiradito invites anyone wanting to make a petition to Juan's ghost to bring a candle; it's said that if one's candle remains lit throughout the night their wish will come true." The shrine is prefaced by an iron frame with spaces for 157 candles, none occupied at the moment I am there. Behind it I find a wall with many fake flowers, some real ones, quite a few handmade angels, a rusted bicycle wheel, several faded photographs in frames, graffiti (samples: "I Love You Momma" and "In Meamory [sic] of Michael Olivas," "Obey," "Let God Touch You") written on and scratched into a concrete alcove, and a cigarette butt and a penny seemingly placed as offerings atop a stone.

If this is what we offer the dead, besides our songs and our poems and our assorted other words, what should we ask of them? Anesthesia? Analgesia? Relief from pain is one common request I see on the notes stuffed in the cubbies (yes, I read a few, even at the risk of canceling their magic). We ask for forgiveness and to be reunited with the ones we loved and lost. We ask that our sons be accepted, and for the strength for us to carry on. One asks simply, "Please bring my family & I peace & happiness and to let go and move forward." I wonder: Do we wish for them to let go or to let go ourselves?

Granting wishes has got to be pretty low down on the dead's list of tasks. If tasks they have, perhaps chief among them is remembering us, running their hands along their memories of loss, that somehow have a mossy smell, accentuated as they've been left alone too long and have become a little gross, eventually overpowering every other scent: that is, if the dead could smell. They might sing of their memories, or stage their own parade opposite the All Souls Procession in which they remember us, we who remember them and are seared by them, even in a crappy song on 98.1 that briefly interrupts the hip-hop of 98.3 before it disappears. There isn't signal everywhere for them, and sometimes they have to punctuate ours to make a point.

To note the dead is to pick up their signal again, if just for a minute. Cocteau was right in having his Orpheus listen closely to the car radio. I've always been enamored of those scenes in that movie, and of the essential mystery of the radio: it's there and it's not; with the right equipment we can pick it up and it can mean: it can split a day in half with just a fragment of a song, and remind me of what I felt so long ago. It cross-fades back into beats I don't recognize, and I shut the whole thing off.

I'm always surprised to see the Radio Society of Tucson's Fall Hamfest (hams are amateur radio operators) out back of the Old Spanish Trail Target I shop at some weekends. Just beyond the three-foot red concrete balls that separate the parking lot from the entrance to the store, the north half of the parking lot is mobbed with trucks license-plated with their call signs and old vans bristling with antennas. Old guys in vests and Boy Scouts in vests mill around, excitedly brandishing obscure-looking equipment and discussing the finer points of their usage or construction. These guys spend their nights in pursuit of signals that most of the rest of us aren't even aware are out there, and they love to accumulate or build equipment that extends their reach.

Who could blame them? The nights here are cold and dark and open, and the overwhelming sensation is one of space, and then of loneliness, and then maybe you look up to Mount Lemmon and its cavalcade of transmitters winking red lights down on us and wonder what signals they carry through the sky.

It's worth remembering now, in the age of the supernew, that the technology of radio remains both magical and undersung. It seems like radio came and went within my lifetime, but I'm reminded that it's still ever present. Even if I'm not listening to it, I know others are. It's refreshing to be able to tune something in and get a transmission. And as a technology, it's old but not that old: in 1941 Hadley Cantril and Gordon Allport felt the need to argue for the unique qualities that differentiated radio from live performance in their book *The Psychology of Radio*. The image that begins this essay was taken from that book, particularly the

chapter "Radio: A Psychological Novelty." Its caption reads: "The social
situation *in radio,* showing the linear relationship between the speaker
and his auditors, and, excepting where listeners are grouped in their
own homes, a complete absence of social facilitation in the audience."
By *auditor* they mean *hearer,* and commercial radio has this quality, it's
true: the same stimulus gets transmitted, and we each receive it differently. If we're in the same room with someone else, making out or on
our way to making out, for instance, it soundtracks our shared pleasure
and desire, or perhaps it reminds each of us of former griefs or lovers:
even though we listen to it together, we listen to it alone. If we hear it by
ourselves in a car, it soundtracks our thoughts or our loneliness or the
dull natures of our drives.

My friend Leonard and I had a radio show in college from 1 to 2 a.m.
on Saturday nights, a time slot we wouldn't have chosen but one that allowed for a substantial amount of freedom. We had the sense that really
no one was listening, not even our girlfriends or friends, and we could
do whatever we wanted. So we'd play a whole album by the Dick Nixons
(a Nixon-themed punk band that shockingly never achieved mainstream
success) and cross-fade it into This Mortal Coil. We'd only occasionally
be reminded of the communicative nature of what we were doing, that
we were actually sending a signal into the world. When someone called
in with a request or a complaint, it would come as a great shock.

It's not just the disconnect between the chunky metal kit the Hamfest
guys are obsessed with and the China-made slick digital plastic junk
sold at the Target that interests me but the particular quality of their
tech-frenzy that's on display when you get a bunch of members of the
Amateur Radio Relay League together. Maybe it's just the glee of kin-
ship, knowing everyone else in this parking lot knows Morse as well
as you and can tell you on which of the following bands (160 meters,
30 meters, 17 meters, or 12 meters) is phone operation prohibited. Or
maybe it's that the look in their eyes reminds me of dark nights spent
in my youth trying to dial out from Upper Michigan and in to Bulletin
Board Systems in California before the internet connected all of us so
we could all be chirping at each other all the time online. Many of the
hackers and pirates I spent time with in those days doubled as hams,
collecting broadcasts and signals from the night and posting inexplicable
messages about them on the discussion boards. These two kinds of nerdi-
ness often spilled over into one another, and while I admired their project,
it felt outdated even then, thirty years ago. To be in love with *radio* of all

things seemed incomprehensible, but that was before I took incomprehensibility as a challenge. There was the telephone to be enamored of, for starters, and the modem that connected the computer to the telephone, and the networks of computers connected together through the telephone and through hardwired lines in rich or university towns, and even from here I can imagine lines connecting networks to networks and whole arteries lighting up throughout the country, and then the phone would ring and I'd hear the garbled handshake tone, and all of a sudden I was somewhere else. I even felt like some one else. *That* was what excited me, and still gets my signals firing, these years later. So I get it. Both of these constituencies have in common a romantic confidence in connection as a central and unrivaled good, a way in which the more nodes you can light up and write down the better your world becomes. *Only connect* goes the Forster quote that seems to have been his most memorable data chunk, and it's easy to see why these, of all his words, remain. But it's no "Don't Know What You Got . . ."

In 1936 early radio theorist and critic Rudolf Arnheim tried to get at what was essential about radio in his book *Radio*:

> The sound of mourning, more directly than the word of mourning, transmits sorrow to the hearer. And all natural and artificial sounds of mourning which are soft and long-drawn-out and in a minor mode, are appropriate for increasing the effect of the mourning-chorus. To add such sounds skilfully, without constraint or redundance, to reinforce the expression and to purify it, is the task of the artist in radio drama.

He continues:

> The rediscovery of the musical note in sound and speech, the welding of music, sound, and speech into a single material, is one of the greatest artistic tasks of the wireless. But what we mean is not the cultivation of the sung word for instance. That has been cultivated quite enough; the wireless, too, cultivates it quite sufficiently. The new possibility is quite different. Novalis says: "Our speech was at first far more musical, but it has gradually become prosaic and lost its note; it is now a noise or a 'loudness'; it must become song again."

That's what I think I'm after here, trying to reclaim some fragment of Cinderella, or listening to Cinderella after a shooting in Tucson, by quot-

ing Arnheim quoting Novalis (that was just his call sign; he was born
Georg Philipp Friedrich Freiherr von Hardenberg).

I mean, that bit of Cinderella somehow playing on the radio seems to me proof of the beyond better than anything else I can think of. Not just Cinderella but the radio that converts it from energy in air to a thing that means in my car's interior. Radio, you may be an unsexy technology these days but you still know how to cut me and show me what's on the other side.

That other side is where the songs come from, and probably where they disappear to afterward, leaving only our memories of our own loss and pain and what prompted all those feels in us wherever we were listening in from after all these years.

I think of Arnold and his volcano, of York and elegies and hot concrete, and of the descanso just up Pantano toward the wash: all these places are marked by death. What place worth anything isn't? Like you, probably, I live in a place of death. I sing to thee of Cynthia, the woman from whom my wife and I bought our current house: her husband had died (too young) of mesothelioma after a career as an electrician working in asbestos-insulated attics in England. When we walked through it for the first time, I had the sense that the house was only half-inhabited: it was too big for her, and was filled, I'm sure, with memories of him and the two of them together. How could she get any separation from the past while still living in it? Now they're both gone, and the house is ours, and we play our songs and dance to them, and we think we understand, as we always do.

Our own deaths will cut the cord that connects those we remember best to the places we knew together, and after that we will be alone. That is, unless someone else leaves a mark or writes a poem or sings a song or calls in a long-distance dedication to tell us who was here, and for how long, and how and for whom their Os moaned in a minor mode, and who they loved and were seared by, and who they were made by, and what they became after, and what we are meant to make of it.

The Exhibit Will Be So Marked (Treemix 12" Remix with Fade-Out)

Rarely do mysteries of any sort in life resolve satisfyingly. More rarely do they suspend satisfyingly and stay there, interestingly dangling, on the edge of memory, light just visible and twinkling through a stand of pines. This one starts with paper pulp, pressed, the US mail, an unmarked envelope.

I asked friends and family to make me mix CDs for my thirty-third birthday, hoping to get one for each year I'd lived. I also put out the call to friends to pass it to anyone they thought might be interested in sending a mix CD. I got fifty-nine, including some, pleasingly, from strangers. Somewhat predictably, though not unpleasantly, there were a number of Jesus Year–themed mixes, though fewer Jesus-themed songs. I made it a project to listen actively to each of these mix CDs and to acknowledge them by annotating, riffing on, and responding to the selections, and sending notes with my responses to the mixmakers, or I suppose we should call them the arrangers, since therein is the art of the mix.

The idea I had was that the collective mix CDs would somehow represent my network of friends and family. I thought I'd be able to divine something about myself from how others viewed me, what they thought the best approach was to making the mix, whether they used the mix as an opportunity to impress, to educate, to colonize, to woo, to irritate, to posture, to stake out some emotional territory between us. I'd done all these things in the past, usually with an emphasis on woo. I'd made hundreds, I'd guess, maybe a thousand, though I'm not obsessive enough to have kept track of all of them, their recipients, the occasion for the mix, the strategies I employed, if any, and the tracklists over the years. Whether an individual mix meant anything was hard to say, but it would be tough to avoid making some conclusions about the first third (I hope) of my life from the aggregate information contained on these compact discs.

One disc arrived partly cracked, but incredibly the first few tracks were playable. Another mix, this one pie-themed, arrived so broken that only the tracklist was readable. Another was virtual, a ghost mix, a list of the worst thirty-three songs in her iTunes library, without any actual music to inflict said songs on me. One was all songs written and recorded when the artist in question was thirty-three. One, also impressively, was all songs released in 1933. The length of one disc added up to exactly thirty-three minutes and thirty-three seconds. My brother sent me, in lieu of a mix, a box set of Americana from Rhino, which says quite a bit about our relationship. Another mix consisted of songs I had never heard before. One, maybe the most meaningful in the way mixes can be, collected songs by bands the mixer and I had seen in concert together. Perhaps in a bid to piss me off, several featured "Sweet Home Alabama." More than one included a Bon Jovi song. I am not sure why.

One mix CD was not a CD at all. It was a microcassette without a case that arrived broken. I filed it on my shelf with the others. It did not fit in the box with the others because the box was designed for CDs. The envelope it arrived in was a plain, unpadded business envelope, you know the sort, designed for folding a letter-sized sheet of paper in three parts. It had no return address. Addressed to me with a barely readable postmark from Nebraska City, Nebraska, the tape was an enigma. Did it have anything to do with the mix CD project? I did not know. It was broken and unplayable. As I listened to the other mix CDs and wrote about them, or in response to them, I thought more about what might be on the broken tape. I filled the room with thought. I paid attention to the songs on the listenable discs and tried to correlate them with my relationship with the person who made the mix. My head was elsewhere as I contemplated the moonlit limbs of the sumacs visible from my office window, the invisible network of roots converging at the base of the trees, and waited for snow to come.

«

Nebraska City, Nebraska, is the official home of Arbor Day, the last Friday in April (in most states—sometimes differing climates lead to different dates), a "day to celebrate trees," according to the Arbor Day Foundation website. You've heard of it. Maybe you've celebrated it. I'd guess that only a few of us, though, have revered it. Founded in 1872 by Julius Sterling Morton, a journalist and politician originally from Michigan, Arbor Day is surely the least sexy national holiday. (It is a postal holiday, but only in Nebraska.) While it's odd to think about the burnt, windswept prairie of Nebraska as the birth of the day of tree celebration, Nebraska Citians are pretty serious about Arbor Day.

From what I can see of it (which, thanks to the internet and Google Earth, is extensive in a way that would not have been possible even a decade ago), Nebraska City, Nebraska, appears undistinguished. Just south of I-29's intersection with I-80, it has the usual stuff of American towns: golf courses, churches, monuments, Super 8 motels, a hospital, townhomes, Buick LeSabres, football fields, insurance agents, a sewing store, a mostly abandoned downtown, quilts, sadness, pretty girls, fields and fields, a factory outlet store, one or two Chinese restaurants, a Mexican restaurant with wack burritos, the smell of farms, a Friends of Faith thrift store, scattered signs of both doom and joy. When you start to look at what distinguishes cities from each other, particularly in the American Midwest, it's pretty easy to despair of our culture for its portability, its replicability, its easy genericism.

Nebraska City, Nebraska, is one of those State Name City cities that feel peculiarly American and complicate schoolchildren's memorization of the states and their capitals: Oklahoma City, Oklahoma, may be the capital of Oklahoma, but Iowa City is no longer the capital of Iowa (as of 1857), and schoolchildren know that New York City is oddly not the capital of New York. You've probably never even heard of Ohio City, Ohio, or Minnesota City, Minnesota, for good reason. I'd reckon about half the states have a State Name City, and a few have cities named after other states, often straddling state lines. As such, Nebraska City, Nebraska, could be—though it is not, except maybe in a few lonely dreams—the center of the center of the country.

The Midwest is an odd place when you look at it closely enough, though it gets caricatured as Norman Rockwellville, a place of the safe and boring, hard work, religion, football, "family values," whatever they are. My experience with the Midwest belies these broad brushstrokes: most of the Midwest is much stranger, darker, more hollow, anger- and treasure-filled. You find serious evidence of weirdness in the abandoned factory steam towers and knockoff Dairy Queen called Kastle Kreme in Galesburg, Illinois (they'll make a blizzard out of anything you bring in, including salt pork), or the closed Blue Bird school bus assembly plant in Mount Pleasant, Iowa. You find the World's Biggest Ball of Twine in a small town: Darwin, Minnesota. Another contender for the twine-ball crown is in Cawker City, Kansas, with one more in Wisconsin and inevitably one in the weirdest town in the greater Midwest: Branson, Missouri. Looking closer at Nebraska City you learn that it is the oldest incorporated city in Nebraska, and has the only Underground Railroad site in the state. Then there's the legacy of Morton's Arbor Day—thousands of trees lining the streets of Nebraska City, thousands of saplings in kids' hands about to be planted, or maybe those are metaphors: the hands, the kids, the trees, Nebraska city.

Strange enough on the ground, then, but from the air it must seem like the least identifiable city in one of the least identifiable states, identifiable only in its display of absence, the sort of place where someone mysterious might hide and send out strange microcassettes or bombs.

«

Every move across the country, and every visit, if it's a good one, if you pay attention: these force you to recalibrate your sense of place and what you thought the place might be or mean. When I moved to Tucson, Arizona, I was surprised by just how green it was, belying the broad brushstrokes that "Tucson, Arizona," brings to mind. My vision/version of the place was of the flat, swaled infinity that you might see in Riyadh, Saudi Arabia, where I lived briefly as a teenager, or in the Sahara, where much of my consciousness of what desert means was born. Not much grew in the desert around Riyadh. But the part of the Sonoran Desert surrounding Tucson (a valley city, surrounded by mountain ranges) is comparatively speaking a celebration of the tree, particularly the Martian green-skinned palo verde, Arizona's unreal and prickly state tree, and Tucson isn't technically in a desert at all: the area gets enough rain (twelve inches a year most years, though a little less in the past decade's ongoing drought) to be considered only semiarid. Landscapes here are filled with the iconic saguaro cacti that only grow in the Sonora, the green spray of blooming ocotillos, a dozen different palms, yucca, mesquites, and thousands of fruit trees bushing out of backyards throughout the city, to say nothing of the hundreds of other succulents and varieties of cacti, though like many of Tucson's denizens, both flora and fauna, many are hardly native to the region.

I found the fruit trees particularly fascinating, since orange trees spectacularly line the Third Street bike path that dead-ends into the campus of the university where I teach. Being from Michigan, and spending much of my life in the cold realms, I fetishized fruit trees, fetishized cacti, images from vacation postcards, television, and deep winter dreams. Fruit trees especially were tied directly to the myths of California and Florida, Disneyland and Walt Disney World, twin visions of escape from the endless snowbound heart of Upper Michigan.

Like many orange trees planted on public property, the Third Street trees produce oranges that are incredibly bitter. They offer only visual sustenance—glossy nests of leaves cradle orange orbs. When they fruit, they become more of a nuisance than anything else, dropping inedible oranges that rot in the street and taunt hungry students and passersby who fetishize fruit globes.

I have a problem with inedible things—particularly soaps and bath products, though the sour oranges qualify—that smell or look like something edible. If sufficiently hungry, I will disregard sense and eat them, or try to, and spit out a mouthful of soapy chemical mess or too-sour fruit. I am no smarter with age. Biking down that street I've been tempted. Too often desire is a more powerful force than restraint.

«

At the request of a pair of Alabama sorority girls, Scottish indie rock band Belle and Sebastian once covered "Sweet Home Alabama" at a concert I attended in Atlanta. It was a glorious, if ill-fated, collision, the sort you look for in a cover situation. After all, Belle and Sebastian was a famously shy and media-elusive band in its youth, so the prospect of their inviting requests for covers was a funny surprise. I was shocked that the guitarist knew the riff at all, though the band didn't know all the lyrics. Said sorority girls were pulled up onstage to sing.

University of Alabama alums know that the proper way to sing the song is with "Roll, Tide, Roll" inserted like a virus in the chorus. As a northerner in the South, you understand quickly that this song is important to southerners, particularly Alabamans, partly for its famous fuck-off to the Canadian Neil Young: "Southern man don't need him around."

By the time I heard it covered in Atlanta, the song had lost whatever meaning it might have once had for me as a result of sheer oversaturation. But in listening hard to all the mix CDs, I listened hard to "Sweet Home Alabama," which is a sentence I never thought I'd write. When I actually *listened* to "Sweet Home Alabama" I was surprised to find it's actually a catchy song. This raises uncomfortable questions about "taste" in music or in any other thing, but I can't think about that too hard, too often, if I want to maintain any sense of what self means.

Fast-forward a few years, and tornadoes destroyed much of Tuscaloosa, including both of the places I lived in when I was in grad school: an apartment complex named, in an attempt to ape the patrician South, Charleston Square, and a house situated about five miles away on a street called Cedar Crest, though there were no cedars anywhere in sight. I remember seeing the damage on television, trying to reckon the images in the media with my memory of the place. What corner is that, I asked myself, only to realize, holy shit, that was the street on which I lived: and it was entirely wiped out in a mile-wide stripe, just erased, like magnetic tape. You could tell it was Cedar Crest by the railroad tracks, the decimated Krispy Kreme, and the few remaining individual trees.

A couple of months before the tornado, an Alabama football fan was arrested for poisoning a stand of 130-year-old oak trees 160 miles away in Auburn, Alabama, commonly called Toomer's Corner. These oaks are among the oldest of Auburn's trees. There are 8,236 trees on the campus. According to tradition, fans would festoon the oaks in Toomer's Corner with toilet paper (a tree product, notably, though I wonder if anyone thinks about this) after important football victories.

Alabama and Auburn have a long-standing and especially bitter rivalry, but the poisoning of the trees by sixty-two-year-old former state trooper Harvey A. Updyke Jr. is certainly a new low. Evidently he had problems with mental illness, though you could argue that the degree of obsession hard-core Alabama fans often exhibit borders on crazy. Rarely do you get a sense of restraint overriding desire when it comes to Alabama football.

Updyke used a powerful herbicide called Spike 80DF ("80 percent tebuthiuron [the active ingredient] and 20 percent inert ingredients," according to a *Huffington Post* news article on the subject, farmed certainly from some other website in the way of modern aggregated media). The same article suggests that the herbicide "kills from the roots up." As a result, it might take years for the stand of oaks to die as they shed, regrow, and re-shed their leaves like past lives, past iterations of selves suggested by mixtape tracklists and embarrassing letters written to girls we yearned for. It's not yet fully certain whether they will live or die, but the prognosis for the trees is not good.

The prognosis for my old neighborhood is worse: it's since been

bulldozed, the rubble and uprooted parts of trees removed along with
the few remaining halves of houses and the graves of the many stray cats
my wife and I fed and tried to save. You can only do so much. The roots
of my memories there are now erased entirely, along with the house
next door to ours that (we were informed by an obsessive football fan
who came to our house to take photographs) once housed football star
Joe Namath.

«

According to the July 7, 1936, issue of the *Toledo News*, comedian Hugh
Herbert was the first inventor of a particular mixtape of a tree, the "fruit
salad tree": "[He] is developing a horticultural marvel to be known as
a fruit-salad tree, or Herbert's Folly. On a grapefruit tree his [*sic*] has
grafted oranges, avocados, peaches, apples, plums, and walnuts." Two
months later, the *Christian Science Monitor* ran an article about McKee
Jungle Gardens, almost two hours southeast of Orlando, in Vero Beach,
Florida (now McKee Botanical Garden), that had a fruit salad tree of
its own ("the Mexican salad fruit tree . . . pineapple, strawberries and
bananas combined").

These Frankentrees are made by grafting parts of different trees
onto one trunk in order to maximize the variety of fruit grown on the
one tree, and also for novelty or entertainment. Contrary to the *Toledo
News*, these fruit salad trees, also called fruit cocktail trees, probably
predate 1936, since the technique of grafting branches tree-on-tree has
been around since antiquity, and someone surely had the idea before
1936. Circa 300 BCE, for instance, amateur botanist Theophrastus
writes, in *De causis plantarum*, that "it is also reasonable that trees so
grafted should bear finer fruit." He goes on to explain the technique
of grafting in detail. Much of his discourse in "Propagation in Another
Tree: Grafting" could more or less be copied and pasted directly into
any contemporary manual on the subject, since the techniques have
not changed much. It's hard to believe that, as an experimental botanist, he or his contemporaries wouldn't have mixed multiple fruits on
one tree.

By this time pretty much all our domesticated trees, particularly
citrus, are hybrids, only reliably reproducible via grafting. All fruit trees
are Frankentrees. So it shouldn't be surprising that the fruit salad tree
would later be developed by the University of California at Riverside, and
more recently commercially popularized by the Fruit Salad Tree Company

out of Emmasville, Australia, which distributes four fruit salad tree varieties (Stone Fruit, Citrus Fruit, Multi-Apples, and Multi-Nashis—Japanese pears) that are ready to plant, tend, and fruit.

«

A mysterious and unmarked tape arrives . . . straight out of a noir novel. Was it a message? Was it from a stalker? A crazy Alabama football fan? A former lover? A family member? I asked the most likely suspects. Then I asked everyone I knew. No one claimed responsibility. The actual magnetic tape was not broken, though its casing was. I headed to Radio Shack to procure some new microcassettes in hopes of nerdily dismantling the broken casing and rethreading the old tape through an unbroken case. None of them turned out to be openable without some mystic wizard moves.

A couple of months went by. I thought about other things, worked on other things, as I do. Watched the trees out my window lose their leaves and wind down, spectral, for winter. I thought more about it. The hacker in me said I had to fix the tape myself. The reasonable person just said, eh, forget it. But I couldn't just forget it. Eventually I sent it out to a specialty audio restoration company that fixed the tape, burned it to a CD, and mailed it back.

It sat in its package on my desk. Should I listen to it? I wondered. What if the mystery disappointed me, and it was just some heavy breathing? (Actually I'd take heavy breathing. It could connote anything.)

«

The best mystery I know is that of the Paulding Light, Upper Michigan's most famous unexplained phenomenon. At one point, *Ripley's Believe it or Not* offered a $100,000 reward for anyone who could definitively explain the light. It was even featured on an episode of Robert Stack's redundantly named television show, *Unsolved Mysteries*, as well as a more recent Syfy network show.

The Paulding Light can be seen in the Ottawa National Forest, south of Bruce Crossing, a bit more than an hour from the town where I grew up and in which my parents live. Driving south, it's off an old mining road on the right of US-45, a couple of miles before you get to Watersmeet. You drive in at night and park where the other cars are, among millions of towering pines. Most nights there will be a dozen or more people sitting on the hoods of their cars, often with binoculars or telescopes looking north at a series of lights that emerge, slowly move down a hill, and disappear. The locals have stories of these balls of light getting within a hundred feet of the viewers, floating, moving, changing colors, spinning, and splitting up. The official US Forest Service sign (adorned helpfully, surely unofficially, with an illustration of Casper the Friendly Ghost) reads as follows:

> This is the location from which the famous Paulding Light can be observed. Legend explains its presence as a railroad brakeman's ghost, destined to remain forever at the sight [sic] of his untimely death. He continually waves his signal lantern as a warning to all who come to visit.

> To observe the phenomenon, park along this forest road facing north. The light will appear each evening in the distance along the power line right-of-way.

> Remember, other people will be visiting this location.

> Please do not litter.

In a place adorned with a long history of suffering (the miners, mostly, and the families of miners, many of whom died in the mines or in related accidents, or in the Italian Mining Hall disaster, and the Ojibwe before them, who suffered in ways all too familiar to students of American history), the Paulding Light is a cryptic and appealing experience with a speculative and storied past. There have been several scientific explanations offered for the light, including excess energy from high-voltage power lines, swamp gas, headlights on a highway, pranksters, and so on. Though several other television shows and paranormal investigators and experts have investigated the light, most have concluded that the phenomenon remains unexplained. In 2010 a group of Michigan Tech University optics students claimed (with a good claim to fact) to have proved that the light was a result of headlights in the distance. I have my doubts. It's not just that I love the mystery of it, but that, after having experienced the light myself on several occasions, the optics explanation doesn't fully track, or maybe I don't want it to. Whether debunked or not, I still call it *unsolved*. *Ripley's* has not yet paid out its bounty.

Was it worth forty dollars to get the broken microcassette fixed? It turns out the answer is yes, if only to know. It is always worth forty dollars to know. That's what makes me a crap poker player. I want to see everyone's cards, to see the flop, the turn, the river, to see how it turns out. And in poker you have to pay to find out. And I almost always pay to find out. Now you know. No, I will not play with you.

So. I popped it in and gave it a listen. It appeared to be a recording from the judge's microphone in a murder trial taking place in Upper Michigan. There is no real identifying information beyond the names of the attorneys (Mr. Biegler and Mr. Dancer; there is also a Mr. McCarthy who is mentioned) and the fact that the original judge on the case, a Judge Maitland, was taken ill, and the new judge was from Lower Michigan. There are references to this being a sensational trial. Here is an excerpt from my transcription:

> I come here on assignment from Lower Michigan to sit in place of your own Judge Maitland, who is presently recovering from illness. Now I have no desire to upset the folkways or traditions of this community during murder trials whatever they may be. . . . I had not realized there were so many among you who were such zealous students of homicide. In any case I must remind you that this is a court of law and not a football game or a prize fight.

Beyond this there are the judge's exhortations to the attorneys and the gallery to quiet down, to act more civilly, a couple of rulings on objections and witness testimony, and a congratulations to the prosecutor on a particularly spectacular prosecution: "This is the first time in my legal career that I have seen a dead man successfully prosecuted for rape." The actual prosecution, the actual witness testimony, the actual objections—in short, any voice aside from the judge's—are not in evidence. There are only short silences during the spaces where other people apparently responded, indicating that this is an edited version with the long silences and other voices removed. I didn't know what to make of it. It felt like there was a decent chance that this was a recording from the courtroom of the murder trial on which I based some of my first book. Strange. Maybe I'm reading too much into it, I thought, making everything about myself.

A damaged tape. An audio recording of a section of an Upper Michigan murder trial. The trial, the trail—they both appear to end here.

Then there is more: "I suggest that both of you gentlemen invoke a little silence and let the witness answer. In fact, I order you to."

"I'm going to take the answer."

"Take the answer."

"Gentlemen, gentlemen. There has been a question and an objection. And I must make a ruling, which I cannot do if you keep up this unholy wrangling. We are skating on thin ice, I realize. But in all conscience, I cannot rule if the question is objectionable. Counsel is not asking for the results of any polygraph test, but the opinion of the witness based upon certain knowledge possessed by him. Take the answer."

You want to give it a listen? The MP3 is on my website at otherelec tricities.com/vp/mix.html.

It's pretty freaky, actually, when you just listen to it, not knowing what it is. Turn the lights out. Look out the window at the canopy of whatever deciduous tree you see and the moon rising spookily through its bare wintry branches. Make sure no one is paying attention to you.

I listened to it over and over, filling the silent hisses with speculation.

I spent a couple of hours trying to look up information on the murder trial of the man who killed my high school acquaintance, just to see if this was it. I found very little.

As it took place before the explosion of the web, there's almost nothing online about it. I wonder whether the trial transcripts are public record, whether they're available for researchers. The court transcriptionist surely did her (I've never seen a male transcriptionist, but they must exist) job for a reason. These transcripts must be open to lawyers who might want to prepare an appeal, or something. I resolved to find out more about this, then promptly forgot.

The roots of the tree that should in nature grow the sweet oranges most of us enjoy eating or juicing are susceptible to a bark-destroying virus. The roots of the sour orange tree, however, resist the virus. So in Texas or Florida, for instance, growers graft sweet orange branches—scions—onto the trunks/roots—understock—of sour orange trees for protection. Farther north, orange scions are usually grafted onto rough lemon understock for a similar result. Oranges are now so hybridized that the seeds of an orange—if planted—will usually not produce the same kind of orange tree.

For those of us who fetishize the tree as the epitome of natural, understanding that the modern citrus is essentially a remix, a cut-and-paste job, comes as a bit of a surprise. There's not a whole lot natural about domesticated anything anymore, which is one reason why "natural" on food packaging doesn't usually connote very much. (Neither the USDA nor the FDA has rules for what "natural" may or may not refer to.) I don't spend much time close up with my food, and certainly not fruit trees, and haven't bothered to investigate the joints where the understock meets the scion.

It is not particularly difficult to make your own fruit salad tree if you're adept at grafting. It does take a lot of care and careful pruning, though, since fruits mature and fruit at different rates and times, and you risk having one fruit take over your tree or become too heavy, unbalancing your tree and bringing it down.

The term for grafting scions on the understock of a different tree is *topworking.*

«

Maybe six hours later, after feeling entirely engaged in the mystery, I figured out what might already be obvious to you, what would be obvious to denizens of Upper Michigan (or aficionados of film or murder mysteries) of a certain age, that the microcassette recording is in fact a greatly condensed and edited version of the audio from the 1959 film *Anatomy of a Murder.*

It took me a while to get there. My wife suggested that there's no way anyone was recording the trial from the inside. True, I thought. It's suspiciously articulate, and I didn't hear the accents and Canadianisms, the yas, the trills of ehs, and dropped prepositions that usually signify Upper Michiganders, or as we call ourselves, Yoopers. And the more I thought about some of the lines, the more they sounded like written dialogue. At that point I had not yet seen the film, though the book on which it is based is set in Upper Michigan and is probably the most famous rendering of my peninsula, if you don't count the crappy Ben Affleck heist movie *Reindeer Games.*

And with that revelation, the door slammed closed, one part of the mystery solved. But then: why only selections from the replacement judge character's comments?

And why unmarked? Why a microcassette? Why from Nebraska City, Nebraska?

And who sent it?

Where I am from there are a lot of unexplained things: that Paulding

Light, the Mining Hall Disaster, the strange phenomenon of paradoxical undressing, crimes unsolved, disappearing girls, unresolved deaths. In a relatively remote place like my part of Michigan you learn to live with the fact that not everything is understandable. That's part of the irreducible mystery of the state, itself obscured much of the year by weather of one sort or another.

Much is obscured by trees and snow on trees, falling to cover over our tracks as we set out for a winter ramble among the fallen trees, the rabbit tracks on snow, the marks that suggest the occasional wolf or moose had come through here just before or after us. Some of it is clouded by history or the passing of time; some is erased by willful obfuscation. The speculation we engage in to get at the roots of those stories and selves now lost to history is memory topworking.

«

My favorite mixtape, which I no longer own, sadly, because it was lost in a move, was created by a guy I don't know for a girl I don't know. It was staged as a radio show, with commercials and bits and jingles the guy improvised himself, using different voices, between the songs. It was an impressive gesture, clearly scripted and rehearsed, technically very sophisticated. Since I found it at the decrepit St. Vincent de Paul thrift store in Grand Rapids, Michigan, it must not have been sufficiently beloved by the recipient. Or possibly the recipient died, or was killed. Or maybe it was never sent—the gesture discarded in a moment of hesitation and second-guessing, a sweet, powerful regret most of us know all too well. Or perhaps it was well loved at the time and was only later discarded as she forgot about the he, or didn't care, or maybe got rid of her tape player and either committed it to digital format, or more likely didn't, that's the feeling I got, perhaps because the mixtape seemed a little excessive, by which I mean obsessive, which is the way all mixtapes are if you're serious about making them. As a social ritual it's still a lovely but strange one, and it's not always welcome, as you find out if you've made enough mixtapes, or if you've misread the social cues preceding the presentation of the mixtape, which you might have done because you were concentrating so hard on the mixtape you were making.

Though I use the terms *mixtape* and *mix CD* interchangeably, I probably shouldn't, since the technologies are so different. The track-by-track skippability the CD brought us, along with its futuristic laser shimmer and Sharpied CD title, differentiates it from the mixtape, which required much more work to produce: you had to do it manually, cuing and taping each song from the other source, being careful about song times, splicing here and there, adjusting intros and gaps, taping over things so that occasionally you got a little history of your magnetic tape poking through the hiss that signified silence.

Erasing an analog object like a mixtape is never a full erasure. With the CD an actual silence—a digital zero—can be achieved. We give up the two-sidedness of the mixtape; we give up the physical act of having to flip the tape and press play. We give up having to occasionally wind or rewind the tape manually when the tape got messed up. We forget these things in our desire for the convenient format of the CD, which is of course on the wane now in favor of the (frankly superior, let's be honest) format of the MP3, where the music has little to any physical presence at all. It's not a shock to see the CD discarded. I've thrown away so many burns I've made because they don't last, either, not more than a few years, often, even when they've not been scratched or used accidentally as coasters. Finding someone else's mix CD in the thrift store or on the street, or even receiving one, still gives me a thrill, but it's not quite the same as the weird analog and homemade intimacy of the mixtape with the handwritten tracklist.

Thus the mixtape is a particular devotion offered not just to the recipient of the mixtape but also to the technology itself, an offering from and to the double-tape deck itself, and to posterity. I often made copies of the mixtapes I made for friends because I liked them so much. They're abandoned now, rashly, probably, when I decided my CDs were the future, which have now been replaced by my return to vinyl and the MP3, though I'm smart or neurotic enough not to fully believe that anything is the future, not really, so I haven't thrown those CDs away. I think of those tapes sometimes, given to the trash for future dumpster divers or anthropologists to sort through. They've been donated, too, to Salvation Armies; Goodwills; Alabama Thrift Stores; St. Vincent de Pauls; the White Elephant in Green Valley, Arizona; Lutheran Thrift; Deseret Industries Thrift; Humane Society Thrift; 22nd Street Thrift Store; Casa de los Niños; Miracle Thrift; flea markets; and installed in various libraries around the country. Perhaps one ended up in the Nebraska City, Nebraska, Friends of Faith thrift store, on Central Avenue, just across the street from the Otoe County Courthouse, between L. Brown Custom Cabinets and an Allstate insurance office, where my tape might be speaking to someone else this very moment, perhaps even you, reader.

Making mix CDs is thus a kind of long play for the future, but also a convenient fudge, a topworking of one technology on top of the techniques implied in and learned by dabbling with the other.

《

One of the reasons I love shopping in thrift stores is the history, the happenstance of it. Many things at thrift stores are messages placed in bottles for whomever to find, whether or not the giver or recipient knows it. Maybe you can call it providence. There are plenty of ecological and economic reasons to shop secondhand, but I'm in it for the surprise.

What do we leave the world? What marks do we leave in snow among the trees? What magnetic trace do we erase or tape over? Which tapes are spared the magnet or the scissors or the heel of the boot? What books have we written? What websites have we created? Will anyone read the crappy poems we posted on rec.arts.poems in the early days of the internet, or will they persist as ghosts, the not-checked-out-for-decades copies of obsolete research on metallurgy I page through in the university engineering library before they're on their way to storage and probable discard or pulp? What music offerings have we left, hopefully, our faces lit with hope, with expectation, for potential lovers or friends, or in some cases perfect strangers? What have we grafted onto what rootstock; what have we planted for some future resident of this space to enjoy? What have we plastered up in the walls of our old houses that we remodeled? What scrawls in wet concrete sidewalks of our old neighborhood? What initials have we paired our own with cut in hearts on bark of the biggest trees out back of the school? Does our thinking of the future imply that we believe in a future after the world has heated, combusted, blown up, forced our civilization off it? Have we left answers, or will we leave questions?

《

Coda: Three years later I figure out the second big question—who you are, mixtape sender, mysterious stranger, crypto–Upper Peninsulan, old friend. Chatting, our housesitter mentions that she was at a writing residency last year in Nebraska City, Nebraska. A small door opens in my brain.

I inquire. It turns out there's an artist/writer residency there, the Kimmel Harding Nelson Residency. A residency? In Nebraska City, Nebraska, home of Arbor Day? Yes, a residency. They have a list online of their previous residents along with their dates of residency. I scan the names. It has to be someone there on a residency. That makes so much sense. You do strange things on residencies. Hide things in public spaces. Conduct interventionist art. Post random projects to friends anonymously. When you limit your inputs like you often do at a residency, you start to generate more unusual outputs. See also Oulipo. (See also the essay "Space" on my website otherelectricities.com under Vanishing Point.) You want to have a personal conversation with others who have shared the space, or who will occupy the space after you.

I know a lot of the names. I don't know what that says about me. But one in particular catches my eye, and the dates line up, and the last big question of the mystery is solved (a few of the smaller ones continue on, like a grace note ghost). Of course my friend from Alabama, A., is the culprit. Well played, A.

I'm in Tucson when I figure it out at last, contemplating the sound of wind through the windmill palms that tower with the ocotillo in my front yard. It's a lovely sound, one you just don't get in the North. I love the sound of wind through pines, too, or the rustling of the maples, oaks, and poplars in the fall as they go brilliant and lose their leaves, suggesting the approach of winter. But the palms have a peculiar beauty. They don't need much. You don't want to water your palm, since the roots will rot. They're designed to catch and hold their water in the crown of sharp leaves, where the heart of palm resides, rising with each year's new growth. Trying to transplant a small palm from my backyard to my plant-obsessed friend Jon's makeshift Japanese garden, we had to cut its root ball away from its wide network of roots. In this part of the Sonoran Desert, plants' roots spread wide, not deep, because of the caliche, a superhardened clay that's everywhere a foot or two beneath the surface.

Pulling it out we drew blood, too, since everything in the desert is sharp, thorned, serrated, spined, resistant to meddling. We left a little of our analog selves in the space left after we got it out. After a year the palm died in his yard. We're still not sure why. He will presumably pull it up and replace it with something native and gorgeous and complicated, since that's his wont. The memory of those new roots, those old roots, will be gradually erased.

It's bittersweet, I suppose, to close this open door of mystery, but more sweet than sour, as I am the agent of the solution, lucky in my stumble. The world offers so few of these rewards for our attention that we best

take them when they're offered, before they disappear back into the trash,
the sidewalks filled with other rotting oranges, the thrift store, the lumber
pile that might get pulped to paper in Wisconsin, on which we might write
or rewrite history, the whiteness of blizzard or memory. I'm going to take
the answer.

Facing the Monolith

It's submerged in nearly every sentence, diphthong without which it's hard to go for long (ask the Oulipo). It, a tic, a blip, a spear to pierce the Goodyear Blimp, an exclamation point without a dot: you can't avoid an I. Those Is, somehow American, manic, upright, gaze at the everything around us, always thinking, being, wanting to find their way to something biggie-sized and tasty, always gerund, processing, grinding up an us into component bits of light, but at the bottom of the can of us there is just us.

The world is filled with them, jutting, jousting, rutting, roasting them on television cooking and other shows. Sometimes it's easy to believe that without I there would be no world. Certainly there'd be no universe. The internet is not the universe, though some days it seems like it; it is another space in which we can separate Is from bodies, let them erect themselves, let them do their thing.

I receives enigmatic sexts from senior citizens concerned about our eroding communications standards, our sagging breasts, the proliferation of poetry, and the increasing use of the emoticon and the word *like*, which is unstoppable, but which I like. I may lament dropped apostrophes in emails, television ads, possessives repossessed by teens who think of everything as theirs, including memoir, including technology, the world's best worlds, including individual experiences that may seem idiosyncratic but are not.

«

What makes an I? What makes us display our Is? Why can we sometimes not believe our eyes? And what good are eyes, are Is, if we can't believe them? Is the self an atom, indivisible without catastrophe? Or a conglomeration of unlike parts, a rebuilt Hardy Boys jalopy? (The Hardy Boys novels were not written by an I—their "author," Franklin W. Dixon, like Carolyn Keene of the Nancy Drew series and plenty of other "writers," is a construct, a convenience, a conglomeration of nameless, ill-paid ghosts.) Is I a bunch of flowered turn-ons, measurements, and pet peeves? Is it a wiki? A palimpsest? A set of sexy Russian nesting dolls? Obviously we believe in I. We have to believe in I. We decide to believe in I in this culture. But I can't shake the feeling that I is only a shared and useful assumption.

And well, yes, part of my interest in memoirs, in YouTube, in personae, in the public display of I is because I envy them, unrepentant, unashamed displaying themselves—live! nude! girls! real! wild! hot! authentic! living! unexamined! life!—for you.

I can't imagine a life in which I was unself-conscious enough to try to tell my story unmediated. I've tried to be a good midwesterner raised sort of Protestant (which is to say, Protestant) and filled enough with shame (and therefore its opposite, pride and its accompanying exhibitionism, that sudden panty flash that taboo zest that rush of yes and more than yes) that I just cannot imagine myself into that kind of consciousness at all. Lacking self-consciousness is a big part of what separates the celebrity from the noncelebrity, studies show.

Like any other neurotic I become necrotic with time. The half-life of I is such that it decays into dandruff serif flakes, skin cells, yesterday's brains, who we used to think we'd be.

«

Talking about I is an undertaking, meaning talking about decay, the inevitable end of each I back to the flatness and underneath of the caverned earth. It is talking about shame. It is talking about voice. It is more than that, sure: it's also about eye and pathways of brain, and where the brain directs the eye to look, and then what the eye filters to the brain: the raw optical data of seeing becomes processed, constructed, becomes what is perceived, namely, a fiction. There are many minds devoted to this processing and perception. But for now, I must simplify: the expressed I is a simulation, a function of voice.

Isn't that what writers are instructed to be in search of? Isn't that what blurbs and reviews laud? A wholly original voice? Sui generis, godhead, in italics or roman like the type, the numeral, or the vomitorium?

Students in creative writing programs are toiling by the thousands trying to find their voices. Meaning, partly, trying to select their voices from the thousands of voices they encounter in books, in life, in workshops, at readings, in songs, at bars, chat rooms, online. What is the range from which they might choose? How new can you be and still be intelligible or interesting?

Then there are those self-styled writers who claim they don't read because they don't want their voices to be influenced or curbed. Indeed. Though when confronted with a strong enough voice, it does happen. I read DeLillo, I write a DeLillo-ish story. Same with DFW. Kincaid. Didion. Kelly Link. We become possessed, we no longer I but a kind of nested us. Isn't that what we're after, this doubling? If we want to learn how to possess, we must first be possessed.

«

Consider the case of musician Tom Waits, who often sounds possessed. His voice is a unique one, is it not? A signature style? He has developed it over years of songwriting and performance. Like Dylan's, Springsteen's, or Björk's, his voice is distinctive, unmistakable for any other.

(He might be faulted for the overmythologizing of his voice, but that's another argument.)

He refuses to allow his songs to be licensed for use in commercial advertisements.

Does he believe he does not want it diluted?

Does he not want it to endorse? To condone?

Waits has often been asked to license his songs for ads. Several times, after his refusal, ad agencies have used soundalike singing jingles sometimes very similar to his songs. Waits successfully sued Frito-Lay for this practice, after they used a Waitsish song for a Salsa Rio Doritos commercial. He successfully sued Levi's for using a Screamin' Jay Hawkins cover of one of his songs in an ad. He sued German car manufacturer Opel. He successfully sued German car manufacturer Audi. Also MP3.com and the company Third Story, whatever they do or make.

The theory behind his lawsuits is that an artist is entitled to the right of publicity, to not have her identity associated with a product as an endorsement without her approval. The Frito-Lay lawsuit was won on the basis of "voice misappropriation."

According to the judges' written opinion on the unsuccessful appeal of the Salsa Rio lawsuit, "The defendants argued at trial that although they had consciously copied Tom Waits' style in creating the Doritos commercial, they had not deliberately imitated his voice." In their minds, while Waits's actual voice was protected, his style was not. The judges didn't see the difference, however, affirming the legal protection of a voice (in California law anyhow), citing a previous judgment in a lawsuit by Bette Midler: "What is put forward as protectable here is more personal than any work of authorship. . . . A voice is as distinctive and personal as a face."

«

We are under no obligation to consider legal definitions of either style or voice when we're talking about a writerly I, but it's useful to think about them. The court deems voice to be unique to an individual, a function of the physical person, and it's therefore protected. In prose, though, we don't have the timbre produced by the tissues of the body, so when we say "voice" I think we mostly mean "style" as it shapes and is shaped by content—two strands of DNA, inseparably wound and reliably identifiable by careful readers and digital algorithms.

But if you add up enough elements of style or content, don't you end up with a voice? It's not as if Waits is the first singer to sound rough and worn (try listening to some blues), but part of what makes his rasp "distinctive" is how little it is like most popular musicians in the era of the pitch-correcting processor Auto-Tune and multitracked, overdubbed production.

One of the more entertaining facts of the Frito-Lay case is that the song they tried to license was "Step Right Up," a song Waits says is "an indictment of advertising." Of course advertising is excellent at divorcing surface from content: witness the country cover (note the change of style necessary to change the context of the song) of Morrissey's apocalyptic mope, "Every Day Is Like Sunday," which was used briefly to promote the NFL's *Sunday Night Football*. Or consider the common public misunderstanding and misuse of Springsteen's "Born in the U.S.A.," or the use of Iggy Pop's ode to heroin, "Lust for Life," in an ad for Carnival Cruise Lines, and I'm sure this list goes on and on, and this is all highly entertaining for those of us with a deep appreciation of irony, which is partly an understanding that voice is a doubled thing with an edge, not always directly aligned with lyrical content.

Currently content is protected by copyright, probably a little too rabidly for my taste.

And what does "original content" mean?

«

Is the I what's left when the rest of ourselves, all the edifices we build to protect our most vulnerable parts, washes away? Or is it the lowest part of our riverbed where the water collects when the rest of it is gone? I think of a friend who told me that only in the past few years has her life eased, in part because her libido has finally waned. It doesn't drive me like it used to, she says. I think but am not sure she is relieved. Or I think of another friend who's just gotten weirder as he's gotten older, as he's encircled himself out on the lake with all the things he wants and none of what he doesn't. I'm not sure if he's happy, exactly, but he's become the hermit that maybe he was always meant to be. Habits grow and become routine and begin to calcify. I'm sure they'd notice that about me, too, if they looked, and maybe they do and are just too polite to say it. You get comfortable among your particular mess and the less and less you deviate from it the happier you think you are. And maybe you are.

«

Evidential languages embed how things are known into the way they're told: when I say I know that the teddy bear cholla can put the hurt on you quite speedily, an evidential language would embed how I know it into how I say it. I know because I have stumbled or was thrown into a cholla (btw, that hurt, Dad! Enjoy the public spanking in the memoir). Or because I saw it happen to someone. Because I heard it happen to someone. Because I read it in an essay, and we now know reading is a kind of simulation. Because I ran a simulation. Because somebody tweeted it. Sent it through the filter of the telegraph or the telephone, which trims the extreme upper and lower frequencies from our voices before transmission, rendering them less identifiable, which might be why people often mistake me on the phone for a woman. In English we might say "I heard that x" or "It seems that x" or "I saw that x" or "I concluded that x," but it is not required, so mostly we don't if we can avoid it. We just say "x," and doubt and cry, accuse, investigate.

«

I, the ninth letter, missing, buried neck-deep in the strata: its stately Ionism, its appealing prick-like jutting. English is the only language I know of that renders I as a singular, monolithic letter, even if it is a diphthong in which, as the Spice Girls tell it, 2 become 1, or, as its etymology suggests, two thoggoes (voices/sounds) are fused. I as the nominative singular probably descended from the Old English *ic* when, around the fourteenth century, it lost its *k* sound into the *ch* sound, which then attenuated into nothing at all. So I went solo and picked up the diphthong around the time of the great vowel shift, about the time it was anointed with capitalization. Though some other languages capitalize the equivalent of both I and you, English is alone in capitalizing only I. Too, I can mean a number, i another. Imagine. Anything could be buried in its crypt. Memory, sure. Fantasy, sure. Maybe even fact. The stories we tell ourselves about our pasts, from which we construct self, and what we call the future. "We think of our future as anticipated memories," says behavioral economist Daniel Kahneman. Experience is not what we think it is. Or, it is, actually. How it's remembered matters to the brain more than how it was. This is why we're storytelling-special. We examine, reconstruct, pump it through the algorithm. We think: we make it so.

«

The more you press on it, think about I, about what we present as our individual pieces of I, the smaller it gets. You start shaving away elements of style, grammar, repeated content, genre, learning, shared linguistic tics. You shave away bits of "individual" experience that, it turns out, lots of people share—alienation! depression! desperation! repression! frustration! salvation! You peel away layer after layer of shared intellectual pretension.

Lots of us played Dungeons & Dragons. Lots of us played a chaotic good dwarf. Lots of us stuffed our faces with Salsa Rio Doritos, listened to Tom Waits, and wondered about the weirdness of the world. Lots of us had a childhood friend die. Fewer had a childhood friend murdered. Lots had a parent die when we were young. Fewer haven't been to a funeral since. Some of us like the band Low. Some of those who do also like the Sisters of Mercy. Far more like (or liked, at any rate) the Spice Girls, for different reasons.

Are we a confluence of events? Of likes? Of fanboy crushes? Are we defined by our dislikes? Our traumas? Our moral objections to sleeping with students? Our high horses? Our creepy lusts? Our desires to increase our busts? Our deep hurts? Our dirt? Our handfuls of untold secrets? Our aversions to memoir? Our obsessions with our mothers? With one another? With fucking? With the glorious mishmash of the word *motherfucker*? Are we the production of our bodies? The libraries of books read, video games played, songs listened to, drunken conversations had? Our constellations of pornography or recurring fantasy? Our friends on Facebook? Our Netflix queues? Our scattered cell phone conversations? Our vocal tics? The people we always dreamed of sleeping

with? The people we slept with? The people we sleep with every night in
body? In dreams? (And is that sleeping with if it's not a real other I?) The
people we regret we slept with and won't admit to if pressed?

«

This last week I have been in residency at the Atlantic Center for the
Arts, in New Smyrna Beach, Florida, teaching nonfiction to teens. The
complex is cut out of prehistoric woods: three master artist cabins, a gallery, several art studios, and assorted other buildings, all connected by
boardwalks, like a spiderweb or a brainstorming idea map, like the kind
we were told to make in school to explore and connect our ideas, as if
seen from above. The buildings are mostly locked. There are two kinds
of locks on the buildings: the keylock and the keypad lock. Everyone
here knows the keypad code, so all involved—master artists, students,
staff—can open the buildings that are not keylocked.

A few buildings, though, are keylocked: the black box theater, the
sculpture studio. There's no reason we should be in these buildings,
we're told, but if we need to, they'll unkeylock it for us if we ask. Half
the time I spend here I am wandering around, checking buildings to see
which ones I can get inside. It's as if I were in high school again, stealing
master keys, trying to access any kind of space that I see is beyond my
current level of authority (the same authority that gives the author her
voice and thus her power). Same with my behavior in video games. I (by
which I mean you too) get acclimated to checking every door, talking
to every non-player character (NPC), trying to pick up every object, test
each fork of the skill tree, the conversation tree. This is how you find
new things in games, how you learn what is allowed and what is not,
which is what we all want to know about the world. Every step here I am
in a game, I am that game I, isometric, slightly behind the avatar that
I quickly learn to conflate with self (hangdog, I tell my wife, "I just got
fragged"), wandering, accumulating.

«

It doesn't take long before we find our selves between them, these Is, the
ones on screens: laptop, desktop, smartphone, Xbox. Like pillars or pro-
tagonists in stories, they rise on either side of us, taller every moment.
We are diminished. We creep as if spies among the spires. Isn't that the
effect we were seeking, to triangulate our selves in the trough between
the two of them, this book, that one, this brain, that one, this fool, that

dumb-ass one, yesterday, tomorrow, and by looking up and seeing something recognizable and recognizably outside us, we are reassured?

«

I'm serious. This is serious stuff.

Pressing on I—interrogating it—is a valuable task. So we should laud our memoirists, our personal essayists, our vulnerability artists, makers of our labyrinths, the kids in their bedrooms filming themselves for webcams or YouTube, for their attempts to get at what I is or can be or might be, what it might look like anyhow, or what they want it to be at the least, even if by omission, by incorrect assumption, by unsupervised play.

I as playpen.

I as boundary.

I as foundry.

«

When I is the size of a colossus and a long way off as it is when we are teens trying out selves, then placing them back on the shelves, it's smooth and huge. Get closer and we can see the cracks in its base, its many pockmarks, the scars from zits or asteroid hits visible in the high-def. This I's used, we know. Others have been here before. They have been hurt in this space before, in the same way before. They have spray-painted their names on the column. They have nicked off chips to take home, to remember. A souvenir, they think. Like the tourists who cut off a piece of the Humongous Fungus, the world's largest contiguous living organism, in Michigan's Upper Peninsula, and, by so doing, reduce its size a little bit. The more tourists come, the smaller it gets, until it will become too small and lose its notability, and tourism will then slow, and then it will grow again. There is an equilibrium point between shrinking and growing, thinking and showing, between being remembered and forgotten, that defines its constant size.

So you look up at it. It's natural. We're in equilibrium. You should take a chip home, have a story to remember this. Perhaps if you plug your story into the world it will grow into a monster if you give it long enough and feed it well enough.

«

Secretly what I fear, and maybe what we all fear, about pressing on I is that if we push it too hard it might disintegrate. If these Is turn out to be fiction (entirely possible) then what is to say we have an I at all?

And where does that leave us? Not anyplace good.

If we can't conjure an individual brain, individual experience, individual voice with language, what good are all these lines?

What if I turns out to be not a self but Auto-Tune, all influence or house-style guide, like "author" Franklin W. Dixon, a ghost collection, a grab bag of tics and tricks. So much for originality. So much for the idea of the author. So much for genius, sui generis.

It's instinctual, I guess, that we're made to recognize ourselves in the mirror. Looking good, I think: slimmer, fitter, a little balding, maybe, but also maybe more memorable, bigger, puffy like a thrush or heffalump. In that moment we are aware of I but also of background, context. World and I, we think, and that implies a self, a mechanism for seeing and being able to recognize both World and I. Here's what I believe: the way to talk about I is to talk about world, not (just) to talk about I. I sees world through eye. And what we see and say about the world says a whole lot about ourselves.

I think it says enough.

World includes I, after all.

«

The Humongous Fungus is believed to be the biggest individual organism in the world. It is fifteen hundred to ten thousand years old. It covers ninety-one acres, mostly underground. It weighs at least a hundred tons. Going to see it is tricky, since the vast majority of it (like many plants and fungi) is underground. You can see only "tiny offshoots that poke through the surface in the fall, edibles commonly known as button or honey mushrooms" (according to the website for the Humongous Fungus Fest, in Crystal Falls, Michigan, a city named for clarity).

I've actually never seen the fungus though it's not far from my hometown. I spent a week one summer working at a Bible camp just outside Crystal Falls, where I pretended to be the brother of a woman I might or might not, in retrospect, have been lusting for (so I could show up at the camp and get some work, which consisted mainly of maintenance, torching hornets' nests, and, for some reason lost to me now, shellacking a dead squirrel we found on the side of the road and mounting it on the hood of the camp truck). Oh I, you ass, your wacky stories, your delinquency, always trying to stand out. We all did that. Didn't we?

«

Well, the Humongous Fungus *was* believed to be the world's largest (and oldest) living organism as of 1992. About eight years later another claim was made in Washington. And two years after that, another, larger one was discovered in Oregon's Blue Mountains. The science behind determining what constitutes an individual organism is probably not worth going into:* suffice it to say that this is one massive thing, and suffice it to say that what was once a true statement ("fungus believed to be the biggest organism") is no longer a true statement, so its truth-value is partly temporal, contextual.

The world changes around you quickly, even if you don't notice.

«

Well, that didn't take long to get to the asterisk, did it?

* "All the vegetative isolates had the same mating type, the same mDNA restriction pattern, and had the same eleven RAPD products and five RFLP-based markers, each marking a heterozygous locus" (Tom Volk, glossing the paper by Myron Smith, Johann Bruhn, and Jim Anderson published in the journal *Nature* announcing the find). If you are down with this, you're a smarter woman than I.**

** "I could never be your woman" ("Your Woman," by White Town, good song).

«

"You've changed" is what my friends say when they see me, my new configuration of facial hair, my new and fatter ass! my new dentistry (no longer do my front teeth define me in their flaws, I think, though I don't know whether anyone else ever cared, and my self-consciousness about it always pushed me to look at the teeth of others when I talked with them, and I bet it made them self-conscious too: Is there something in my teeth? Are my teeth fucked up? Who is this fuckup who's looking at my teeth? Or maybe he's thinking about my mouth in a more sinister way, or doesn't want to look me in the eye, and what is wrong with me so that he won't look me in the eye or think about my mouth in another context?). My thinning hairline, my proportionally complex mustache, as if to make a claim on identity, memorability, my settling into the outlines of my own body. But, wait, what changed? Am I not the same? Am I still who I was? Or do I contain that old layer after layer, like wallpaper? Perhaps we should go to the yearbook? Or perhaps we won't. (What's a yearbook, Dad?)

«

Even the palms in my front yard, beautiful and majestic, have been shaved, like a long-furred cat for summer heat. They look like Is, these palms that sound like the sea when they sigh in the wind. These palms that rise from the ground and serif out into the Arizona sky, deckling its edges. A guy came to the door today and offered to shave them for twenty-four dollars each. In truth, they have needed shaving for a long time. Their fronds spill onto the yard when the wind shakes them down, and I have to pick them up. They lose and lose, and yet still seem to grow.

Now, I know that palms, though beautiful, are barbed (try transplanting one, like my friend Jon and I did: enjoy your injuries). Everything in the desert is dangerous. The tiny fronds are spined to keep animals from eating them. They drew my blood, Jon's blood, and who knows, we might be accidental blood brothers now, part of each other now, halfway to a story now, trapped in a cave, about to solve the mystery of the Hardy Boys and the Nameless Scribes Who Constitute the Fiction of One Franklin W. Dixon as we carry the plant and its root ball to my truck.

The sun and wind here will grind nearly anything down to nothingness in time.

Every plant in my yard draws blood, as if to say, "Who is landscaping whom?"

«

I understand the term is *manscaping*. I had been watering the palms. I'm trying to be a better citizen, responsible by unwritten social contract for yard work, hair, and trash removal. Even though here we have no lawns, still when we get water, the plants grow. I cut or burn them back; else we won't have a yard but a wild. All world, no us. We need some semblance of control. We need another hero. The electric hedge trimmer fills me with the sound and authority of the chain saw, the authority of the image of the Big Daddy, shirtless and glistening, tending to his yard, authoring a novella in Norwegian about hunting elk with forks, and in this way we all want to become our fathers, even if we lost them, forgot them, or had them killed. Even with the trimmer, the project, like most involving self-discovery, is painful. It's loud, trimming the bougainvillea in the side yard, and thorns fly everywhere. A face mask is required. Goggles. Heavy shoes.

«

Eventually we'll have the palms not only shaved but skinned (in the context of palms, *shaving* means cutting off the big fronds but leaving rough stubs behind; *skinned* means trimming them all the way down to the smooth-looking bark). They, too, will be manscaped, Old Spiced, golf-clapped, shaved, fresh-smelling, and ready for their dates.

(These are not date palms, however.)

(The transplanted palm died a year later, even under Jon's expert horticultural care, as if to say, Well, I was something, something special, then you dug me up, and I am no more.)

«

After a year of trimming, I decided to just raze the bougainvillea, dig its roots out, and start over. I trimmed it, and then I started cutting chunks out of it, accumulating many tears and welts and lo, I did shout as I was cut and as I cut. It was once beautiful, the bougainvillea—or really it was two bougainvilleas, though I believe after long cohabitation they had merged: And did they notice their entanglement and believe themselves still disparate but less so every day? At what point did they give in to this inevitability? But they had been neglected for decades and had become encrusted and gnarled and thorned. Each was now the size of a small car, the kind that's not fun to drive and has an iffy safety record. They were huge and wild and showed no evidence of care or a human hand.

It took me a week to cut them down to their trunks. I did not sleep. I could not sleep with them outside my window, resisting me. I knew this had gone way past the point where I could turn back or explain how I felt and what I was trying to do to anyone else, not least my wife, who wondered, I am sure, what had become of her mild-mannered husband and what maddened plant-hacking despot had taken his place. The plants were signifying something I couldn't articulate, and they had to go. Eventually I chopped them back with an ax all the way to the ground, and it took me days but I dug up their interconnected root balls, and I raised them to the sky and heaved them over the side of the backyard wall triumphantly and god damn if I didn't feel like a protagonist right then. I sat for a good long while looking at the hole.

Then I filled in the hole.

For the next several weeks thorns expelled themselves from my body bursting occasionally through my outer layer, but I'm convinced some of the plant remains inside me no matter how hard I try to dig it out. I scarred myself twice before I gave up this self-digging practice. The internet tells me they'll come out eventually—it's just a matter of time—but

I am not convinced. I believe in some small way we too have merged and I have become embiggened against my will. I am learning to live the plural life.

«

You should not skin a palm all the way up to its blossoming top. You need to leave a foot or so of outgrowth to catch water and channel it down into the trunk, so it can do its desert-survival thing, so it can grow. Don't water palms, either, or their bases will rot, and they will soon be pulled down and become horizontal, fallen like a body or like the sky. Palms store their own water. They are well-adapted plants. They are rooted against wind or monsoon storm.

«

Whatever you want to say about the self, it is persistent. It will do nearly anything, anyone, anytime to survive. Our Is are built, or grown, or designed, or evolved, whichever you prefer, to withstand storm, to withstand a storm of attention and excavation, erosion. These caves go on forever, or close enough to forever that it might as well be forever, since we are not big-brained enough to comprehend it all. This must mean that either (1) there is something essential there, or (2) there is nothing essential there at all, but the complexity of the network is such that it is permanently (we can only hope) beyond our ability to unravel.

«

Or perhaps what we learn from the palm is that, like the bougainvillea or like the self or like the voice, it's not so easily quantifiable; it's difficult to transplant, to cut off, to isolate completely, to circumnavigate. Its roots are almost unimaginably vast, and its sharpnesses will penetrate and become part of whatever tries to pull its root ball out. Removed from our worlds, our histories of self, the things and songs we love, our spectacles or the spectacles we have become, the outlines of our lives— that constant backward looking, searching for what we might contain, or in what we are contained—we might well disappear.

Little Angles

My daughter skips the opportunity to go to the All Souls Procession to walk and mourn her favorite cat, Napoleon, because she is unwilling to burn his picture. I explained you only put in the urn what you want to put in the urn, something to burn, that you can keep or part with whatever you want. They'll burn it all when we reach the end of the procession, and that will be the end of it, the burning: some transmutation happens or maybe some transmission when the words we put there on the paper burn.

It's just a copy, I said.

I don't care, she said.

So instead we went up the mountain with all the darkness underneath the trees and collected leaves and a short stick and a big chunk of pine tree bark and brought them back to the valley where we live.

We have few deciduous trees in the valley, so to get this kind of darkness you have to get above the saguaro line and up a couple of thousand more feet where the pines begin to grow. There we discussed the difference between the aspens that lose their leaves each fall and a white pine we saw that had gone entirely brown. *That* wasn't coming back I said, the pine. When an evergreen goes all brown, it's dead, I bet. A little brown is fine. All brown is not. That's why they call them evergreens.

Then I missed my Michigan some.

Then any bit of brown tree she saw began to thrill her: I saw another dead one!, she yelled from the backseat.

It was like we had driven into the land of the dead.

Seeing dead pine among the green *is* surprising: because they don't deleaf in fall (or, well, they don't leaf at all, not having leaves, but they do drop some needles), I'd sort of assumed they never died, which didn't make much sense, did it? After all, I'd thrown what felt like thousands of fir branches on campfires to watch them crackle, a little fireworks of the heart and of the Michigan night.

So we walked among the woods and gathered leaves instead. They were brown and red and yellow. I think we missed the real burst of fall colors but didn't tell her so. There was still plenty of evidence to be found, and besides, she wouldn't know.

I wondered, too, on the way back down as we lost six thousand feet of elevation and our ears popped and popped (or mine did: I've never asked her if she, too, shares this discomfort slash miracle) why exactly the GPS represented everything to the right of the road as gray, and everything on the left as green. The green meant national forest, so the gray must mean something else, and it was the edge of the mountain it was tracking, but still below that there was more road and more national forest, and in this case the forest was a delineation of a protected space and not a statement made about the presence of pines or not. My best guess was that it was trying to tell something to me about the contour of the mountain we were driving on. I love the GPS because in the age of smartphones and their powerful navigation it's easy to remember that they only work where there's signal, which isn't everywhere, and besides I like what it has to tell me about where I'm at, even if it's just tracking the edge of our safety, snaking down this road.

I felt a little ashamed trying to pressure my daughter to go to the All Souls Procession. For starters, trying to pressure her to do anything is usually counterproductive, and besides I realized that she doesn't seem to need to sort out all that much about the death of Napoleon or death in general. She seems to get it mostly. I did the math: I was only two years older than she when my mother died, and I didn't have it figured out at all. Still don't in fact, which may have been why I conflated my impression of my daughter's need to attend an event like this and figure out something about the way some people mourn with my own, and why these public celebrations of the dead fascinate me the way they do. While my interest masquerades as essayistic at times, what I really want is personal: to understand how to get it to pass: that mourning feeling, if not the memory itself or the fact of loss and the frustration at my inability to get it—or anything—to stop.

What my daughter wants is to keep it where it is, collocated with her stack of pictures of the cat and the wall she writes on in the backyard right above where we buried him. And she knows how to do it, even if

I don't. If she keeps the picture, then she'll have the picture. But if you burn a copy, I tell her, it's just a copy. You'll still have some.

She asked me on a run the other day what I remembered, and I had no idea how to answer that. I remember a lot, I said, too much to tell. She said she would always remember Nino, as she called Napoleon. I would, too, I said. He was beloved. But not all things that were beloved are memorized the way she wants to memorize him. If you look so long at these pictures of him, you can almost believe that they're real.

We brought a bunch of fallen leaves we found on the ground under the trees up the mountain to our sunny valley as a reminder of seasons, which is to say, I suppose, of time passing. I have a hazy memory as a kid of picking flowers with my mother in Michigan and pressing them in books and later encasing them in contact paper to preserve them. I don't know how long they lasted that way, or what happened to them after that. My daughter and I haven't yet done anything with the leaves we gathered: it was more about the act of gathering them than planning for any particular outcome, though I wonder if I was subconsciously echoing and trying to re-create that memory. Re-creation is a kind of preservation. (It's also a kind of destruction in that it layers one memory atop another.) I scanned them later because sometimes when I don't know what to do with something I scan it; that way I'll have it in as high fidelity as I can for later use, even if the thing itself continues to decay. They crumbled a bit as I pressed them flat on the scanner, and I didn't want to try to unfurl the lower left corner of the maple leaf (you'll probably be able to see that fold at the beginning of this essay) for fear of breaking it. I look at these leaves now on my screen. I mean, I look at the pictures of the leaves on my screen. I know a scanned image of leaves is not the leaves themselves, but it will also remain preserved for as long as I am careful with the data. If I stare so long at these pictures of leaves, I can almost believe that the data is all I can feel.

I just listened to a story on a podcast I like a lot in which a woman talked about creating, as a teenager, a digital replica of her grandmother, the most important person in her life, who had just died. She'd spent hours in the computer game *The Sims* (in which you create characters and put them in domestic situations) customizing a character she'd made to resemble her grandmother as closely as possible. It took her a year, downloading all these mods in order to make her house exactly like her memories of her grandma's house, and her grandma in the game a more perfect analog for the grandma she remembered. She used a stop-time feature in the game to stop her and all the other simulacra in her family she'd created from aging. She liked it that way for a while—a couple of years is what I remember—but eventually she understood that she'd have to turn time on again in order to grieve, and so her digital grandmother died, and so the woman grieved, and it was hard.

It's an intensely emotional listen: you can hear the woman's voice breaking throughout among her sniffling and crying. It was hard for me to listen to, in part because I kept wanting to comfort her and kept being unable to; I wondered why this messy take was the audio they used in the story.

You should give it a listen. It's episode 129, "Autumn," of the podcast *Reply All.* Instead of listening, though, if you were to download and read a transcription of that episode, you'd strip all the emotion and all your discomfort away. I'm reminded of just how intimate audio is, particularly when you're listening to it as part of a podcast, which is more often than not right in your earbuds, unmediated even by the bit of air between the speakers in the car and and the ears that are listening.

And yet in spite of all that extra rich data that analog delivers, the detail I'm left with was that the *real* memorial to her grandmother exists only in the game, a grove of digital trees planted in her memory in the backyard of her digital house, and how the light looked coming through it.

My Monument

Seepage

Even in the most interior room of the house I can't avoid the warbling Christmas music coming through the walls, the windows, and the skylight. It tinkles jauntily from the speakers in the neighbor's yard. It's so constant that even when I can't exactly hear it—after eleven at night, or from the New Year to Thanksgiving—I can't be fully sure it's gone. By repetition, these unfaithful versions, played too quickly and without human voice, become the norm for me, just a given, always present, a dubious gift that's always there until the season has gone and folded itself up again.

Scope

My Rudolph is by far the largest Christmas decoration on my block. Also: in my neighborhood. Also, quite possibly: in Tucson, Arizona. I have never seen a larger Rudolph in person in my life, though I am sure some exist in the parades my grandmother used to watch on the black-and-white television on holiday mornings.

Fifteen feet tall and motor powered, erect, huge, a monument to or against something, above the roofline of the midcentury ranch house in the front yard, between the rosemary and the ocotillo, the palms and the agave, he stands as long as I will have him, usually the day after Thanksgiving until the holidays have finished.

His body, tethered by eight cables dug into the ground so as to resist the wind, supports an oversized, rotating head that overlooks my two neighbors' houses, which between them display 104 inflatable Christmas decorations with not one duplicate. Their cheer is maximal.

Seen from their perspective, my Rudolph might be perceived to be shaking his head slowly in disapproval at their displays. Or perhaps everywhere they see approval: the confused coyote fencing with the inflatable gift-bedecked penguin in the wind, the shrieks of unidentified children from a street over, even the way their tea leaves dry in their cups—yeses are all around us all the time.

Time

Here in the snowless world, to decorate for Christmas is to make a statement about anachronism. Because so many of us are transplants from our colder elsewheres, by erecting our decorations we are also making our little shrines to home. In this city it's easy to forget what time it is, what day it is. A month might go by without sighting a cloud.

Vowels

To be clear, the neighbors' two yards together, with every square foot stuffed full of Christmas, constitute a startling display. On December evenings I watch cars drive by our little cul-de-sac and slow then brake, then stop, then back up. I watch the faces of the drivers fill with surprise, amusement, and even a little bit of awe. I watch them illuminated by, say, the giant inflatable dachshund wrapped in a bow and dotted with presents, delivered, evidently, by several smaller dachshunds. I watch the kids' mouths in the back seat go o o o o o.

I've spent some time out front of their houses going o o o myself. When I do so I can often see the neighbors, inside with their blinds open and the lights barely on, watching me watch the show go on.

Moral Relativism

My Rudolph, my menagerie of one, was purchased from the ridiculous Hammacher Schlemmer catalog for $399 plus tax and shipping: an improbable and indefensible amount to spend on an ornament. Is the nervousness I feel admitting to this number shame or pride, or some mixture of the two? I don't know exactly how much it costs to run, to keep it lit, to hold its sentry post until I shut it off and it pitches forward and deflates into the cactus as if it's run aground and been abandoned. To estimate, my electric bills since purchasing my Rudolph have so far run about thirty dollars more per month. Powering him costs less than a dollar a day. For a dollar a day I know I could be feeding starving children, too, as the mailings I get remind me. The juxtaposition does not ride comfortably.

I do not mean zoo. A menagerie is kept by an aristocratic family for the display of wealth. A zoo is theoretically historical or scientific, displayed for the education of the public. Louis XIV constructed two menageries: one at Vincennes and one at Versailles, in which lions and bears and bulls were brought out to fight for the royals' pleasure. I am not aristocratic, and what little wealth I have I try to wear lightly if at all. Having said that, my display displays something, I am sure: my relative privilege, my generosity, my pleasure at making the big gesture, my settling into my role as neighborhood foil, my lifelong pleasure at pageantry, my civic participation, my folly.

Considering the Spectacular

My two neighbors are both of grandparent age, and it's hard not to read a little desperation in their displays, as if by overstuffing their yards with festivity their houses might become homes to Christmas itself, and their grandchildren would come to them and stay as long as they might like, being offered sweets on plates and filled with love until they burst into the air like released balloons.

Watching the neighbors' installation is a pleasure I cannot recommend to you enough. To their credit, these neighbors are timely in erecting their shared spectacular. Every year, the day after Thanksgiving they put up their comprehensive kits. If he has the day off, Mike, another neighbor across the street who once tried to sell me a sword, blasts seventies AM gold with the doors open and drinks can after can of beer and peers at the whole production darkly from inside his house. It is important that someone keeps an eye on the spectacle as they arrange and stake inflatables and wire everything together into the dedicated outlets.

Their industriousness would make the squirrels we generally don't have down here proud if they existed.

Considering Perversity

Really, though, I read the neighbors' warring displays as being about not being humbled by time. There is a perverse and stubborn quality to them: once you've had them up one year you feel the need to continue erecting them against the world. It's a refusal of circumstance too.

Through our displays we are saying no to taste, and to restraint, and yes to erections. We are saying no to self-control, and to decorum, and yes to demonstration. These are the ways in which, we say, we are not bound. The longer I live in this neighborhood, the more I'm starting to get it.

Considering Desperation

It is also hard not to read *my* display as a little desperate. What is it a monument *for* or *to*? Or must a monument be always in some way dedicated to oneself? It is true that I purchased the thing after the birth of my daughter, so on some level it's a parenting kind of proving something that I'm doing. But I believe I'd been committed to this idea long before; I'd begun my travel down the path. I've always loved the big and foolish and public. I admit I purchased it partly with irony and partly with money, but I've long since left that. Becoming a parent perhaps allowed me to justify some of the impulses latent in me for some time.

At This Time of Year

Spare a thought for the other reindeer, those we mention in passing, as background for our hero. The whole set—Dasher, Dancer, Prancer, Vixen, Comet, Cupid, Donner, and Blitzen (to use the most popular present spellings)—have been with us since 1823 thanks to Clement C. Moore's "A Visit from St. Nicholas," better known to most of us as "'Twas the Night Before Christmas." They have served the season and the story well for a very long time. Rudolph himself debuted in 1939 in Robert L. May's children's book for Montgomery Ward and has taken pride of place in song and story and stop-motion animated cartoon thereafter.

Probably, if you're like me, you sort of know the others' names, but only because they bullied Rudolph and got the ass end of his comeuppance.

We will all eventually be washed away and rendered obsolete, background for someone else's heroism. As such they, not Rudolph, may be our better analogues.

Parenting

And spare a thought for Rudolph's parents, who were horrified by their son's mutation in the stop-motion Christmas special: that nose, so wild and red and lit. What would become of such a creature? To stand out is to be strange and be estranged. Should we forgive them for wanting their kid to have a normal life? And what is a normal life exactly?

Considering the Restoration Spectacular

One of the most memorable features of English Restoration theater was the Restoration spectacular, or machine play, in which the focus was on special effects and visual impact, not individual performances. These plays featured mechanically moving waves, flying actors rigged by wire, movable and quickly changeable scenery, elaborate stage costumes, simulated fire, simulated thunder, roiling seas, and elevators, just to name a few. Movement was the feature. The productions would often be incredibly expensive, that fact itself a draw to theatergoers looking for something beyond the everyday.

If this is reminiscent of the past few decades of popular film, with its increased reliance on computer-generated imagery and special effects and epic sweep, it's no surprise: we still desire something beyond the everyday; we're still hungry for spectacle, the sort we would rarely encounter otherwise in their lives (or in our case on our relatively small rectangles of screen).

Opacity

It's hard for me not to love a machine. What's not to love about a thing you can take apart and figure out? Well, that's theoretical. The machines we're most impressed by now are increasingly digital (computers, cars, computer-controlled cars), and their complexity resists all but the most tenacious tinkerer's desire for knowledge. It's sad to know that we are in an age of opacity. Yet we can still know, if we're willing to take apart assembly code and if we can read machine language, if we have the proper diagnostic tools.

We live in an age of engineering wonders. (Perhaps we have always lived in an age of engineering wonders.)

As in our excitement for the Restoration spectacular, we still thrill at technology's ability to simulate. For instance, every Christmas, La Encantada, the fancy open-air mall in the Tucson foothills, generates artificial snow. Since we get only a dusting of actual snow in the valley about once every four years, it is quite a draw.

Those who go to see the spectacle are advised not to let the artificial snow settle on their tongues, since the flakes are in fact soap.

Irish Spring

I am reminded here of the sensation—taste, but not just taste, also the feeling of its fullness and the aroma and fatty presence of the bar—of soap in my mouth. As a child of course I loved to swear. It was wonderful to see the power a word could hold, how I held it in my mouth and then released it out into the world. Even then I thought soap in the mouth was an unusually metaphorical punishment. I most vividly remember Irish Spring. It did not—and could not, obviously—wash away a word.

Irish Spring

Originally introduced in Germany in 1970, Irish Spring currently has nine variants: Original, Deep Action Scrub, Clear & Fresh Skin, Moisture Blast, Hair & Body, Aloe, Icy Blast, Clean Scrub, Intensify, and Signature for Men. Seven (Reviving Mint, Mountain Spring, Waterfall Clean, Fresh, Vitamin, Sport, and Irish Spring Deodorant Soap Microclean® with Microbeads) have been discontinued. That list walks you through a little subhallway in the museum of American culture and its yen for variation and recombination.

Opacity

You can imagine, then, if you love machines, how you might love a giant inflatable Rudolph. From the exterior it looks solid, but inside it is nothing but forced air. It turns its head, but when the wind catches it, it appears to bob up and down in excitement or approval. It folds down into a backpack-sized box. My daughter hugs it with all her might and makes no dent. It is easy to displace your affections for a machine when you are a parent. This explains in part how one of the ways my father demonstrated love was to get the oil changed in our cars, to check the belts and brakes. That practice also conveyed a subtle assessment of my brother's and my half-assedness when it came to maintenance: if we had kept it up, there would have been no need for him to perform his love this way.

For sure it is part love I am developing for my Rudolph, and it's made more rational now that my daughter loves it too.

I have the ambition of being completely inside the thing one day and letting its glorious rushing, like Calgon or a Klingon, carry me away.

On Figures of Speech

It's marvelous! we say. It's spectacular! we say. It's awesome! we say. Yet we are not ground to silence by our awe. We do not mean we marvel at the marvelous. Nor do we mean it is a marvel. I am not sure marveling is in our emotional repertoire any longer, but I wish it was. If we marveled more, it would mean being humble in the face of the unknowable or vast.

What is the bandwidth of our awe? Has it increased or diminished as we've aged, as our age has swallowed every marvel available to it?

I think here of cyberpunk literature like, most famously, William Gibson's *Neuromancer*. Countercultural at the time, now most of its founding principles (the experience of being nearly always online, ubiquitous and embedded technology, information as currency, the rise of multinational corporations, and other seemingly dystopian predictions) are familiar enough in America so as to be uncontroversial. I wave my smartphone at McDonald's to make a payment and the interaction just slips by.

Plus, thanks to the 1980s mainstreaming of *awesome*, the word shook off its connection to awe sometime ago. Are we so inundated by spectacle that we have forgotten how to let one overtake us?

Perhaps my neighbors, in their quest for excess, mean in part to remind us of these capacities.

The Pleasures of Home Ownership

To own a house is to understand your capacity to mock a neighbor.

Three years ago, I had mocked these Christmas neighbors publicly by wrapping the four female mannequin bottoms that usually sit out by the pool with pink lights and stationing them in the front yard, abutting the curb. Sadly, my display's effect was lost in the dark: you couldn't tell what the lights were wrapped around: they were just a clump of crotches illuminated by pink lights, a vaguely Christmassy amoeba floating off the ground. My gesture was both too arch and too indistinct. Plus I like my mannequins and feared they might be stolen by sexed-up youths. I took them down after a couple of nervous nights.

Also, mockery is easy. I understood it all too well when I was deep inside it.

I tried again the next year. I found a broken, white-lighted, three-legged reindeer at Goodwill and put it in the yard, staking it so it would stay upright. I had the thought to assemble a flock of other broken Christmas animals that could gather on their sides, blinking and clicking and trying to rear and sadly make gestures at flight in response to the tour de force next door. My wife was not in favor of this idea. She called it cynical. But one on its own is fine, she said, cheerfully. In the dark you can't tell it's broken.

This is one of the problems with the dark.

My Fear, in Part

If I were to give in fully to my neighbors' urging, there would be no end to it. In the country of muchness it is good to know your limits. One neighbor, on seeing that we didn't decorate for Christmas, offered to colonize the front yard with his decorations: he said he had too many for his space and he would be happy to share with us. This was surely true, but immediately I could see the creep that might take place: every corner of my yard lit up and moving. He offered to make use of the excess space on our roof, on which he could land his huge Santa balloon and his Frosty helicopter. But then, I thought, I would not be able to see the entire scene without leaving the safety of the house.

Then I wondered: Who was this display *for* anyway?

The Pleasures of Home Ownership

It's hard not to watch the neighbors from inside the house. Surreptitious spying is what having a house is for. Apartment buildings in a denser city offer better voyeurism and less privacy, but to own a house is to worry ceaselessly about its value as it's buffered in the financial winds. To own a house is to set an alert on Zillow and to track the other listings in the neighborhood, to map the foreclosure signs and to grind your teeth with each dip. When values rise we feel somehow responsible, as if that gutter cleaning we did two years ago or the repainted back fence ended our suburban blight. To own a house is to start to pay attention to things you thought forever beyond your care: escrow, drainage fields, the woes of subdivisions, the shitting of crows on deck chairs as they line-roost

above the patio, the patio itself, the o sounds you make without thinking
while watching a tanned, lithe body floating in the next-door pool.

Front Porch

Tucson is not a front-porch city. No one slumps on stoops and remarks
on the patterns of the neighborhood. Instead, the backyard is our glory,
often not obvious from the street. That's where the pool and grill and wall
and all the livable outdoor space and shade are, and that's where we sit
behind our walls so as not to be seen with our tops off or doing whatever
else we do in private. That's what makes the Christmas display so shock-
ing: here, we think, is a public show made for all of us.

Boredom

In my in-laws' neighborhood in Minnesota no one has a pool, and in
the winter no one is outside, except to move snow from the road to the
yard or the yard to the road, and inside it is somewhat warm and dull,
and in this embrace of dullness the Hammacher Schlemmer catalog
occupies a prominent place. Like my own parents, my wife's folks line
their home with catalogs for the winter: dispatches from Lands' End
overflow baskets in the living room; L.L.Beans cover the distressed
coffee table. Everywhere there are old copies of *Consumer Reports*
that assess products' fitness and reliability. Perhaps it is a practical
choice: if their furnace were to quit, as it did a couple of years ago in
the middle of the winter, they could stay warm by burning catalogs for
weeks until help arrived. That is, if they could bear to part with such
abundance.

The Migration of an Apostrophe

Lands' End: what a name! the end of lands! what might be delivered to
us by UPS or USPS from these frontiers! Can you guess it might come
in monogrammed flannel? How many of us can even imagine the end
of lands, the edge of the known world, where we might encounter dark
spaces on the map?

    As it turns out, Lands' End evolved from a sailboat equipment com-
pany, and was named after Land's End, an English landmark, as far west
as you could go in Cornwall, a geographic spectacle. The movement

of the apostrophe was a typographical error in their early promotional material that got stuck and never moved again.

Lands' End was bought in 2002 by Sears.

As I click through citation-links to read the business news reporting the purchasing and later (2014) spinning off of Lands' End by Sears, I realize the URLs have changed and where there once was land is now just emptiness and water.

Luck

I'd like to clarify, because it's important: I *happened* on this catalog. It did not come addressed to me. To have received a Hammacher Schlemmer in the mail means you've lost your way, that the countercultural tendencies you once prized are no more, or are at the least very badly attenuated. But to stumble on a copy on your in-laws' coffee table as you vainly search for a whiff of the neighbors' unsecured Wi-Fi to check your email while drinking is perfectly acceptable and speaks nothing of your slippage. So, bored and more than a little cold, I leafed through it. This was a year ago.

It claims it is "America's Longest Running Catalog . . . Offering the Best, the Only, and the Unexpected since 1848." I don't know what else would supersede its claim to longevity. Wuss-ass Sears has only done its thing since 1888. How long have you or your family done anything? When I first saw the claim I misunderstood: I thought it was a catalog serving marathoners.

Order

I've always believed myself to be an agent of chaos more often than an agent of order. I think this comes from spending too much time with Robert Anton Wilson's *Illuminatus!* trilogy when I was a teenager and listening to weirdo British dance artists/anarchists the KLF. I know this assessment, like the feeling a giant Rudolph might theoretically give you, is overinflated and probably waning. It's for sure an easier self-assessment to have before you become a parent, at which point you become by default an agent of order, because you now have under your protection an undeniable agent of chaos and something of a spectacle, as I am reminded as my daughter shrieks at top volume and assesses the crowd's response.

I now understand it takes a lot more effort to build a thing than to tear it down. But still I admire the force of the impertinent. The difference is that I want to move past it—make my dickish mark—and build it into something for the neighbors.

Muchness

The Hammacher Schlemmer catalog is a monument in itself and to itself, a monument to monuments. The contents are spectacle enough for most of us: the Drifting Adult Trike, the Hands Free Hair Rejuvenator, the 1959 Corvette Billiards Table, the Authentic Baseball Glove Leather Chair, the Human Bowling Ball, the Gotham Golfcart, the Bike Snowboard, and so forth. You may buy a theremin made by Moog, a belt buckle made from a nine iron, or a Live Video Feed Surveillance Clock, so as to keep tabs on your thieving relations when they visit for the holidays. Otherwise your catalogs will just keep disappearing and where will you be when the cold comes?

I see your eyes widening, your heart quickening, as if you've just been caffeinated. I feel that way too.

Aside from excess, the catalog's central theme is products identified as being the world's largest (Puzzle, Scrabble Game, Write On Map Mural, Toe Tap Piano); world's brightest (Watch, Flashlight, Vanity Mirror); world's lightest (Carry On, Luggage, Purple Carry On, 1,875-Watt Hair Dryer, Impervious Luggage); world's thinnest (Calendar Watch); world's smallest (Automatic Umbrella); world's longest (Zoom Binoculars); world's most detailed (Globe); world's fastest (Amphibious Car); world's only (Counterbalanced Turntable); world's most secret (Locations); world's first (3D Printing Pen, 3D Printing Pen Stand, Flying Bicycle); world's softest (Flannel Sheet Set); world's best tabletop Christmas tree (Prelit Fraser Fir, Prelit Noble Fir, Douglas Fir, Concolor Fir). This is not even to get into the things not labeled World's Best but simply Best (Bug Vacuum, Talking Scale, Interdental Cleaner, Gel Infused Cooling Radio, Freestanding Heated Towel Rack, Double Belgian Waffle Maker): monument after monument.

I ask a Hammacher Schlemmer representative what percentage of catalog subscribers end up ordering an item. They won't release that information "because we are a private company," they tell me. Well, how many subscribers do you have? Same answer. I find this opacity both strange and compelling. It's like touching a monument's slick, black wall and trying to see through it but only seeing my own searching expression.

Ryan Bradley writes in the *Los Angeles Times* about his fascination with the catalog, "The first issue arrives in late October. I read it cover to cover. I do not buy anything from it." For most of us, one imagines, this is true. Sometimes it is enough to marvel at the marvels. That is what they are for, after all. The catalog itself *is* the publication. It's an exhibition: you're here to *see* and to *imagine*, not necessarily to buy. The catalog *is* the spectacular. Reading it you begin to feel that by browsing or owning a copy of the catalog itself you demonstrate your discerning taste: you yourself are special, the world's only, the world's best.

Plus, I think you must be in on the joke. Bradley asked the CEO of Hammacher Schlemmer how many people had ever purchased the $30,000 hammock. The answer was, quite obviously, none.

One wonders, then, if their more outlandish items even *exist.*

If you are on the mailing list, you receive news of the world and of its many marvels quarterly.

Idiocy

I don't need to tell you how our culture prizes size, speed, confidence, and incomparability. The catalog is a labyrinth of them. The superlatives make it difficult to read straight through. I had to stop to catch my breath before returning.

Among the many glories in the catalog, I spied a huge Rudolph. It did not claim to be the World's Biggest; it was simply "nearly two stories tall." In the photograph children cavort below it. That's a big Rudolph, I said to myself. What kind of idiot would buy something like that?

Just Desserts

I thought about it for a year, and when my neighbors started erecting their spectaculars I found myself still thinking about big reindeer.

So I looked online for options, as you do. In my search, I found other large inflatable Christmas decorations (I googled "huge Rudolph," "large Rudolph," "really big inflatable Rudolph," "yard irritation," and "Christmas lawn colossus"), but everything I found was terrible, like the "giant inflatable color changing Christmas tree" which looked like over-sized alien genitalia. In my browse I also found: a crappy fourteen-foot Santa train; a crappy Santa's reindeer stable; a half-assed (not literally) nine-foot Santa dog; a terrifying psychedelic snowman head; a ten-foot animated moose (what the moose has to do with the Christmas iconography I do not know, perhaps a vague sense of northernness, an orientation toward Ultima Thule?) with an ugly plastic sweater that did not cover its prominent ass or stupid eyes; a vaguely satanic eleven-foot inflatable non-Rudolph reindeer; a giant Christmas bear with an insipid face; and a whole lot of stoned, pathetic inflatable elves that I could imagine staring listlessly into their virtual neighbors' yard in hopes of being fed inflatable Doritos.

While I would purchase and attempt to eat inflatable Doritos or an inflatable dessert, I wanted none of these impostors. What I wanted was what had buried itself in my memory from that catalog a year ago. That is how consumer culture works, I know. It takes a year to register the punch.

So I traipsed to the website, where I was immediately distracted by the Only Outdoor Heated Cat Shelter, adorned with a negative review noting that "the hindquarters of our cat did not fit in." Another was titled "Still Waiting for Cat to Enter." Another (there are, in fairness, only a few negative reviews; the positive ones are not nearly as fun) explains: "My cat will not go near this house. If you are having a hard time finding a Cat House it might be because Cat's [sic] do not like a house."

I would like you to know that I did not order this item, in part on account of my cats' irritability and their oversized hindquarters.

What I did order was my Rudolph. Then I kept browsing, transfixed by this American netherworld.

By the time I got to the last couple of reviews of the Cat Shelter, I was drinking port by the Christmas tree. It was ten o'clock. My family had all been in bed for two hours. I found the white lights of the tree soothing, gauzy, suffusing me with our shared light, or perhaps it was the port or the view I imagined I would soon have of my Rudolph out the window that affected me this way. The tinkling of "Good King Wenceslas" from the neighbors' house was lovely and only a little demonic.

Historically

Of the Colossus of Rhodes, one of the seven wonders of the ancient world, Pliny the Elder writes:

> But that which is by far the most worthy of our admiration, is the colossal statue of the Sun, which stood formerly at Rhodes, and

was the work of Chares the Lindian, a pupil of the above-named Lysippus; no less than seventy cubits in height. This statue fifty-six years after it was erected, was thrown down by an earthquake.

Well, when one looks for errors in antiquity, Pliny is a great place to start. Like my brother, he has an opinion on everything, has heard about whatever you're looking for, and presents it as fact, carved in rock and unassailable. His fabulist descriptions have persisted for two thousand years: unlike my brother's, Pliny's mansplaining is historical. I suppose I can't predict how useful my brother may be to the future's desire for knowledge, so I should not yet count his contributions out.

Just Deserts

We live in a desert. On each side of the city is a mountain range. Where there was once water running year-round through the river now it is dry except when it rains or there's snowmelt in the mountains, and during the monsoon. Without the winter weather we have to make our own signifiers of the season.

A restaurant exists in Tucson called Just Desserts that only sells dessert. It caters to teenagers and college kids who want to get together to for role-playing games or complicated European board games that take an hour or more to set up.

Also I believe in time thanks to climate change fueled in no small part by all our internet ordering and our shipping and our global supply chains we will all get the desert we deserve. We'll have to learn to survive in it.

When It Arrived

I was doubtful my colossus would be big as I imagined. It showed up flattened in a box the size of a diaper megapack from Target. No way could that hold my promised monument. Surely I had proved myself a fool. Still, my wife could hear my glee-squeals from the front yard as I released it from confinement and its scope became apparent. Yes, this was the thing at last. I plugged it in and watched it rise and lo! it rose, and lo! it was humming and shining and it was every bit as large as I had imagined it; this is to say that it was good and the world felt to me very slightly improved.

Get close enough to a thing and it becomes impossible to keep the whole in sight, to retain whatever belief you had before about perspective. It's magic that stays magic.

Desire

I should love to assemble a monument to error. A catalog of swerves. A library of mistakes. Here's what we thought that we think no longer. Here's how and when and why we were wrong. We usually chuck the wrong bits of knowledge and retain and teach the rest, but what if we kept all that was false that we believed? Instead of studying the truth we could study the ways we erroneously believed.

Would we be humbler about our assertions then?

What might this kind of monument look like? A tall thing on its side, broken at the stem?

Our Cheer

Of course the neighbors were duly entertained when it went up, slowly erecting itself in the Tucson night, joining their displays. The neighbor's wife and the grandchildren could not stop laughing when they saw my Rudolph towering among the palms. The kids took selfies under his moving head. They staked out the yard to wait for the patriarch's return. When he exited his huge truck I could hear the laughter all the way in the back of the house.

They're Our Cathedrals

I do love a monument, a colossus, an edifice: the Pictured Rocks, the Humongous Fungus, the Mystery Spot, the last Big Boy before the Mackinac Bridge, the competing Biggest Balls of Twine, the Biggest Crucifix, the Biggest Pecan, the Biggest Ketchup, the World's Biggest Ball of Paint in Alexandria, Indiana, Sea Shell City Michigan's Man-Killing Giant Clam. I am drawn to them, to the way they loom, the obsessions they feed. I could navigate this country by their light.

Compare to the ubiquitous and spectacular cathedrals throughout Europe: also popular and well lit. They, too, mean to inspire our awe. In

America, even if we know that what we most admire will not be particularly old, it can be wild and odd and large, its very existence a question we mean to answer by stopping and tweeting WTF The Thing? Or, Big Ass Navel Orange: WTF. If we cannot have our unicursal labyrinth at Chartres, we can have a lower-back tattoo of it for others to contemplate as our shirt rides up.

Like any monument, this is not just a metaphor but a fact. As I sit in Starbucks number 19,981 (the number itself an edifice), I see a woman with that labyrinth tattooed across her lower back, her shirt having in fact ridden up. I'm gaping surreptitiously and hopefully not too obviously (while it is possible I am a creep [I admit I am creeping here a bit, even if in service of my art] I would prefer not to be labeled one). I wonder at her choice. Does she know the origins of this glyph, the labyrinth itself is in the systems of the body: circulatory, digestive, reproductive? To have it tattooed right on her body—and on the lower back, with its flirt/reveal— must be either ignorance or blissful knowingness, either way: American.

Chain Reaction

Tonight, while rereading Pliny's account of the Colossus, I realize my Rudolph has broken free from his moorings and is listing strongly to starboard. Is it odd to call him *he*, sexless and buoyant and empty as he is? Still, he is definitely meant to represent a he, the he from the story-song, even without the component parts of sex reminding us of his animal nature. Perhaps it is more untoward to call him *my* than to call him *him*. He is mine only by trick of fate or circumstance, my having seen him in the catalog and having made the commitment to order him to my door.

Now I see my Rudolph is on his side and nosing into the cactus, vainly attempting to turn his head, which operates through some kind of mechanism I have not yet sussed out. I could cut him open in order to understand it better, but in this case the knowledge gained does not to me seem commensurate with the destruction of the creature. When I go outside to right him, I see a stake has broken. In trying to restake him I break another.

The stakes with which he's moored are inferior, I complain on the Hammacher Schlemmer feedback form, hoping they will send replacements, hoping they will relay this information to the manufacturer. That is: these are not the world's best stakes. They break when struck. They

should be made of metal or a stronger resin. An email comes the next
week with an apology, but notes that the item is now out of stock.

Perhaps my Rudolph is the last one made. Perhaps my Rudolph was the last one born. Perhaps my Rudolph will be the only Rudolph of his size and quality, the only one to rule our shared Arizona night.

Customer Service

As much as I'd like to think it, my Rudolph is not the only one. The following November I get an email telling me they are back in stock. I call and ask for a replacement patch for the tear that's opened up on his flank.

I expected some resistance.

Hammacher Schlemmer prides itself on its unconditional lifetime guarantees, the sorts of things that would impress a dad, my dad, for instance, or yours, and it impressed me even as I wondered about the costs of the policy. Sure, they said, it'd be easier to just send it back: we'll replace the whole thing.

This is rare in a culture of speed and disposability. I remember how amazed I was when I bought an expensive suitcase that the company happily repaired multiple times: this didn't feel very American, I thought. Or how you can take a J. Crew or Banana Republic jacket back to the store to get it mended or replaced if it ever tears or stains—even if you didn't buy it from them new.

You may sense a little aspirational class privilege in these opportunities. None of these stores are really all that exclusive or expensive, but they're a cut above Walmart. Each feels more than a little colonial. Their items aren't made in banana republics, but they sure aren't made here these days.

In my search for Rudolphs I found he was, unsurprisingly, made in China. You can order him by the hundred or the thousand.

For a moment I consider cashing out my 401(k) to raise an army.

My new Rudolph arrived and was unboxed and grew and again was big and bad and glorious.

Size Matters Again

Tucson doesn't stake many World's Largest claims. We have the world's largest treasure hunt every spring at the Tucson Gem and Mineral Show.

There's the world's largest privately funded nongovernmental aerospace museum (a claim requiring quite a lot of modifiers). Improbably, we had the World's Largest Matzo Ball (488 pounds, in 2010), a record that may or may not still be ours. The World's Largest Airplane Graveyard is here. And perhaps most spectacularly (since randomly), until last year, when he died, Giant George, a Great Dane, was the World's Tallest Dog, according to the *Guinness World Records 2010*. He had held the record secretly for a week before it was announced publicly on *The Oprah Winfrey Show*.

One might wonder: What's the point in achieving or bragging about our size, if another contender will just keep building or breeding something bigger?

In This Way We Are Enlarged and Possibly Engorged

Edifices: they light our way. They rise high. They stand in for I or sometimes we. Usually the I rises above the we, but in the end the we—those who can stand under the shadow of the Colossus and feel themselves embiggened, made more than they are—matters more.

Historically

Pliny again, on the Colossus:

> Even as it lies, it excites our wonder and admiration. Few men can clasp the thumb in their arms, and its fingers are larger than most statues. Where the limbs are broken asunder, vast caverns are seen yawning in the interior.

Part of what we admire is its inscrutability, its brokenness, the space inside the fragment and what we might imagine in it, the space between the world it was erected in and our world today, our inability to know it fully. We marvel and we are filled with awe. We're stilled with awe, we and our awe in a bright white room, quiet, imagining it. So we are silent and look inside. What have we seen that is too large or beautiful or broken to imagine? The undersides of complicated interstate cloverleafs in cities from below, weaving, curling streams of cars onto other thoroughfares: even though they are concrete, I find them beautiful when on foot or passing underneath. Impossibly complex tangles of circuitry inside our machines when seen under the microscope (and so made large enough for us for awe), our cells' interiors, the impossible distances between stars in space. The man-made monolith means more, though: it speaks of the individual, her love for the large, for building something so big the world would wonder at its size. The Valley of the Moon, twelve miles away, weird and run-down Tucson theme park of the fantastic: the obsession of a lifetime for George Phar Legler, a spiritualist who believed the spirit world was just beyond the one we perceived and who devoted his life to building a place for children and adults to look into it and experience the sublime. Arcosanti, a futurist community north of Phoenix, designed and built in the philosophy of arcology, an architectural model fusing architecture and ecology, built by the recently deceased Paolo Soleri (who also drew sketches of nude models: "attractive ladies under 30" were invited to pose for him and would receive a copy of the finished sketch as well as, surely, a generous invitation to sex). When we apprehend the vision and the constructed thing we marvel at its reach—and foolishness. In this are we diminished? Would we prefer to drag the maker down to our level? Instead maybe we should aspire to such a spire and make room in our silence for astonishment and belief.

Now and Then

"Now and then out here a thing got so gigantic it grew unearthly."—Paul Monette, *Predator*

Pleasure in Outlasting

Tonight my Rudolph stayed erect and lit longer than my neighbors' blow-up golems and when I ventured outside into the somewhat cold I was not bombarded by their lights but only by my own and I felt a sense of pride (and then I felt a sense of pride at my sense of pride: Who knew I could feel pride like this? Who knew it could be so easy to feel myself so full?). My Rudolph continued to light the night after their displays had faded. Because my Rudolph is the only decoration and because it does not need to lead with its ostentatious brightness, when it is running next to my neighbors' zoo it does not seem bright at all. It does seem big. Its name might be Olaf in another life, but in this life it is identifiably Rudolph and all who see it are made glad. Children especially shriek at the sight of it.

I pull its plug and it pitches forward, almost as if it bows before me. Then it lists to the left and I need to hold it while it deflates so it does not fall into the agave plant. If it did it might be pierced and slowly open itself up in ways that would lead to its destruction, and I might have to invoke the lifetime warranty with guilt, knowing that in a way it was my fault. Instead, I hold it as the life rushes out of it. It's hard not to think of what it would be like to have a pet like this, a massive pet like this.

I give my oldest cat a pet because I cannot yet come to terms with what it would be like to have to make that journey with her.

The Speed of Shame

To leave my Rudolph lit after the neighbors have closed up their shop for the night: Is it rude? I wonder. It would be rude of the neighbor whose machine churns out the songs filling the cul-de-sac if its weird tinkling ran throughout the night, which occasionally it does. That it typically does not is a credit to his restraint, something his display otherwise does not suggest. Perhaps my Rudolph speaks as much of me, in the way of a flashy wife or midlife crisis car. Instead, I keep it lit in the spirit of the lighthouse keeper, in hopes that it might guide drunken drivers or *Edmund Fitzgeralds* home. As it goes with culs-de-sac, the cul-de-sac is hard to tell from the other cul-de-sac, especially in the dark, and though we know we should not drive home drunk, some of us do, I'm sure, there being few satisfactory options, and some of us are in need of drink.

I admit I do not fully understand the ways of neighborliness. I don't always pay attention to what's expected of me socially and am surprised to learn, say, that as the best man I was supposed to prepare a speech. I fumble through an ad hoc one. It will take years to register the shame, but I do so here.

Black Diamond

Just because a thing is big does not mean it is invulnerable. Consider the Death Star, the *Hindenburg*, the *Titanic*. In fact, the greater the size, the greater the desire to see the thing taken down. Thus in part the sad history of elephants in confinement and in the wild. They have been hunted and imprisoned and executed because of size. Take, for instance, Black Diamond, an elephant who injured his trainer and killed his employer in Corsicana, Texas, 1929. He was sentenced to death and shot fifty times before he went down on his knees. This is not an isolated story. There is the other famous one, Edison's electrocution of an elephant, essentially for being unruly, but mostly to win a consumer war and spectacularly illustrate the destructive power of a rival electric technology: alternating current, went the story, kills! Elephants in captivity were routinely abused for years in ways too horrible to enumerate in this space. Edison also electrocuted a series of other animals, mostly domestic dogs.

On Dogs

When my neighbors are gone for a night or a few, typically driving their RV into Mexico or to California, their dog, Honey, barks all night without cease. I can hear her through the skylight as I ponder my footsteps through my home in the somewhat-dark as the thirty-nine LED lights on household devices flicker like devotional candles. She's fed and watered, I'm sure, but sure sounds lonely. It must be tiring, with no one to register her complaints. I've tried going out to reassure her that she's heard, but she takes my presence as an offense and freaks out further. I wonder whether to tell the neighbors about the contours of her experience as I understand it.

Customer Service

In consecutive seasons, a light fails in my Rudolph's nose and keeps failing even after I replace it. Some engineering marvel! (They should consider LEDs.) I am willing to perform surgery to aid my animal, but there must be a short somewhere. One year they say, sure, we'll send another. The next year I call back with the same complaint, and they say, sure, they'll send yet another, tell me to send this one back, too, just stuff it back in the box. A year goes by. Repeat. I wondered: How long could this go on? What kind of business model *was* this anyway?

The reviews online suggest that you can keep doing this as long as you need. One purchaser is on his (or her, I suppose) seventh Rudolph.

However, as I found out the following spring when I called after the holiday to complain, Hammacher Schlemmer said they were out of Rudolphs until November. You can either tough it out with the tears and the busted light, they said, or you can wait until the season begins again and call us back and we'll replace your Rudolph then, no problemo. Or you could send it back and we could refund it now, they said, pointlessly, because of course I had realized I didn't *want* a refund—I wanted my Rudolph. How many of us are willing to send the thing back and give up the performance entirely?

At this point I knew I had a problem. I had developed feelings for the thing. And I'd developed a commitment to the performance. I found that I was becoming someone else, someone a little more civic-minded, someone paying more attention to my neighbors and their treasures— and my own.

Persistence

They are not forever, even if Hammacher Schlemmer guarantees them. What stays that long? Even Hammacher Schlemmer has only occupied this space for 165 years. Even the Colossus at Rhodes was in ruins by the time Pliny witnessed it.

Plastics will last in ways we have not really accounted for in our reliance on their disposability. Much of the rest of our accumulated human meaning won't, however. Our books will be pulped, our hard drives erased, the trees in whose trunks we carved our names felled in windstorms, all our collected downloaded music gone when our sub-scriptions elapse, all the muchness that spreads out before us slowly vanishing. Maybe what will persist will be our songs, as performed on a little box in someone's yard somewhere from Thanksgiving to Christmas each year. Maybe it will be a recording of the lonely barking of the neigh-bor's dog. Maybe it will be the aggregate electronic hum of our collective electromagnetic fields.

As I try to reerect my Rudolph after his most recent mishap, my neighbor Robbee comes to lend a hand. (You might be surprised how unwieldy my Rudolph can be even though it weighs little.) As I complain about the cheapness of the plastic anchors, my Rudolph tries again to rise. I am ordering a more hard-core set of stakes for him, I say; I'm done with these. Robbee tells me with a note of approval that, yes, we each must maintain our units.

Perspective

From my vantage point in the living room I see the lights on in a few neighbors' houses. Tucson is a dark city, which means there are fewer surface-level lights in order to accommodate the needs of the astrono-mers at their observatories charting light from stars. My Rudolph does not yet threaten the astronomers, but if I were to increase it tenfold, or a billionfold, it might cast some small glow onto a star eventually.

I consider, as if floating above some other northern city, the sprawl-
ing of the lit-up interstates as fathers drive their children home through
snow on winter nights, thinking themselves safe. What is safety, I wonder, when at any moment our life could be torn apart?

I wonder if in the future the sheer sprawl of everything might not be
the feature we expected it to be before. Perhaps in the era of our own
surveillance we might learn to value subtlety, secrecy. It does seem un-
American as I write this sentence, unfortunately. Even as I write it I feel
like I am being logged, if not blogged.

Citizenship

With the installation of my Rudolph my neighbors have become notice-
ably warmer to me. Perhaps it is also the recent birth of my child that
signifies my commitment to what weak bonds we offer in neighborhoods
in Arizona, state made of walled backyards and thorned flora, concealed
handguns and sprawl. I didn't think I'd miss the way the Midwest teaches
you to interact with others, what with our porches and our occasionally
bearable weather. Perhaps this is why I have installed my Rudolph: not
simply for my own pleasure but to signify that I am here, my neighbors,
my fellow citizens. I choose to participate. I want to know your names.

The Nemesis

Christmas is a nemesis for those of us who depend on our families for
emotional reassurance during the season and do not receive it. It is an
annual opportunity for each of them to fail us in their way. It would
be healthier and in general better not to rely on them, we're aware, to act
for a month like we are psychologically robust and do not count and
recount every slight, but by now we know action trails intention. To my
brother (who dearly cares about such things) I believe each holiday season is a reminder of our insufficiency as a family, our straying from his
increasingly specific expectations.

I can predict my Rudolph's failures even if I cannot predict my own.

Citizenship

And what of the other reindeer? We know their names only for their
cruelty and slights, their insufficiency, their collective inability to figure

out a way to lead the sleigh through fog. What if they had good reasons not to let poor Rudolph join in any reindeer games? Perhaps they feared his best-known feature and wondered what kind of creature's nose lit up from within? Was he irradiated? Contagious? Haunted? What if as a beacon he drew other reindeer to him and caused pileups?

There might have been no way to know.

Utility

Does my Rudolph guard the house? Does it keep my family safe? Would you be more or less likely, as a burglar, to break into a house with a fifteen-foot Rudolph lit and glowing out front? Less likely, I believe, just by virtue of wondering what sort of person would buy and proudly display such a huge ornament. It stakes a claim on presence in a neighborhood that I—if I were a burglar, and lo, I have indeed burgled, so I know a little something of what I speak—would steer clear of. A few weeks ago I was walking a street away and was accosted by a neighbor who asked me if I had heard of the recent rash of burglaries. I had not, and so she told me some stories. Two houses on that block had been broken into in the last two weeks. No one had yet caught the perpetrators. All they had stolen were guns and cash.

I admit this took me a bit aback. I did not buy my Rudolph as a theft deterrent, but I believe he could act as such. If I were casing the street I would steer clear of any house exhibiting a spectacular. And besides, from behind my Rudolph looks more like a giant dog. When the neighbors have extinguished their displays, its significance is obvious. Like Cerberus, it means to say I guard this street and your ass shall not pass. I hold your lives in hand. I will keep you safe. In this land of guns safety is no small concern. After my congresswoman was shot in the head at point-blank range, I thought about the safety of myself and those I love. When I heard the break-in stories I thought more about safety. When my car was broken into—twice—within a couple of weeks I thought hard about our safety. But safety is not the only consideration. Sure, I could barricade myself inside my house and stockpile guns and cash and grumble on the internet. What a way to live that would be. I guess I choose to face out into the street instead. I choose to display a smile, even if it's a weird one.

In a world where there are few checks on the insane or unbalanced—in a place without the social safety nets you might find in the cities on

the coasts—in a disconnected place, a place built on disconnection—
perhaps this yard art gesture is enough to say to my neighbors that I
care for you. I am part of you. I am participating. I am watching and
I am listening.

The Pleasures of Home Ownership

To own a house is to fear the breaching of its walls. To be responsible
for a colossus is to fear invasion, to fear its toppling, to fear its becoming
ruin. Of course all of this eventually becomes ruin, but our most important job as humans is perhaps to resist ruin.

Being and Nothingness

Some nights I think about inhabiting my Rudolph, wearing him as if he
were a huge suit, like the inflatable sumo suits you can rent for parties
and use to try to body-slam your friends. What is the difference between
displaying him outside the house and wearing him? I wonder. If I could
stride down the street in him I could be happy then. But that's not possible, of course.

What is possible is that I could actually step into my Rudolph if I
so chose. He has two zippable access points: one in the belly and one
in the neck, just where you might begin your evisceration of an actual
reindeer. These zips are not large and I am not small, but still I am
confident I could push myself inside him if I needed to, a sort of reverse
birthing. I think about possession, what it might be like to take hold of
another body, to wear another's skin, to feel like I fit in. I don't think it
would physically harm me to try to get inside my Rudolph, though the
force and sound of all that air in the interior would not be appealing.

Maybe I am inside him already. Maybe in wrapping myself in thinking about him I wear him like a spirit suit.

What might it be to be so vacant and so large, so tethered and so
buoyant?

I would be hobbled, I am sure, inside the suit. It is made to be ser-
viceable by a human, in the case of a bulb going out in the nose, for
instance, or in the case of significant tearing. I could almost fit myself
in one of his colossal legs and peek out. But who would let me out if
I got myself trapped inside? I could call my neighbors' names, the ones I
know, but there is the Christmas music to contend with and the sound

of air, and besides it can get somewhat cold down here, so I couldn't be assured of my rescue.

Thinking about Rescue

A fire truck comes through the intersection at the Starbucks with its siren and its lights. We all know what it means. Someone has collapsed. Someone has been hit. Someone is in grave danger. Someone has speciously dialed 911. One can't be sure, but it's hard not to take a moment and cross yourself, knock on wood, whatever you do to congratulate yourself that you're alive for now, that your marks in sand have not yet been erased, that you're not yet forgotten.

On Memory

And what am I to do with my Rudolph when the holiday is passed and he is no longer current for another eleven months? I must pack him away, I know, but to do so is a little loneliness, to be so enclosed, boxed in a plastic container for the longer part of the year only to be released again when the earth has moved around the sun again. I know my Rudolph will have no memory of this, the time between when he mattered and when he will again, but still I mourn a little. What do my neighbors feel when they pack away their displays for the year but a rolling up of what they hold inside? To know that their relevance is gone for another year, that it has lapsed, is no small thing. My relevance will lapse, too, and click into the emptiness of deletion or destruction or even the white noise and nothing of what we imagine death to be, so to venerate my Rudolph is to participate in the air around the cul-de-sac, to feel alive.

If the cul-de-sac is a little universe, I am not so ridiculous as to think my Rudolph is the sun, but it is true that if you were to drive west on Seventh street you would plow directly into it if like a fool or one transfixed you did not swerve or stop. So in that my Rudolph is the promontory around which the cul-de-sac is defined.

Well, this street is not properly a cul-de-sac, since it only seems to curlicue; in fact, after the turn it does go through, in a little loop, but that is only obvious to those who turn the corner away from my Rudolph and disappear. *Cul-de-sac* means "back of the bag" in French. In America it is what "court" denotes. Vanishing down a little research hole I find that Tucson is the exclusive domain of the "stravenue," a ridiculous portmanteau indicating roads that run "diagonally between and intersect a Street and an Avenue." This is a dubious victory for my Arizona home. I propose a term: the faux-de-sac.

On Closure

It takes a little effort to pack Rudolph away for the season. In the matter of a few minutes, as he lolls and sags, and I hold and guide him—like a lover, I think to myself, this gentle quality of touching even though there is nothing underneath his skin, no nerves, no electricity to register the pressure of my hand—away from the cactus to the ground. As he lies there slowly expiring, air rushing out in part through the slightly porous canvas of his skin, such as it is, I think how odd that such a large creature can be condensed into a box and packed away. This year my neighbors struck their show promptly, overpromptly even, on the day after Christmas. To my mind you have until the weekend after the year turns over to accomplish this, but no, no dawdling for them. I wonder why but do not learn the answer.

Ennobling the Place

Let's turn one more time to Pliny:

> Within it, too, are to be seen large masses of rock, by the weight of which the artist steadied it while erecting it. It is said that it was twelve years before this statue was completed, and that three hundred talents were expended upon it; a sum raised from the engines of warfare which had been abandoned by King Demetrius, when tired of the long-protracted siege of Rhodes. In the same city there are other colossal statues, one hundred in number; but though smaller than the one already mentioned, wherever erected, they would, any one of them, have ennobled the place.

On Closure, One More Time with Feeling

Another year has passed and I'm already anticipating Christmas. It is August and we are on the verge of buying a new house, this one in the foothills of the Santa Catalina Mountains. The foothills have the schools and the silence and the views we want, and they're not the city.

I find myself more torn than I expected at the thought of leaving this neighborhood that I didn't really know I lived in until recently—this moment in this essay, maybe. Is that what my monument means to me?

One thing I've come to understand about myself as a result of becoming a parent is that I am far more sentimental than I had previously believed. Probably all my friends and family knew this about me and were simply too kind to tell me, or assumed I knew. You too. So thanks for that small decorum. I will sob when the penguin dies on the television show. Five minutes into the exposition for the superhero movie, when the protagonist's mother dies in his childhood I am a mess.

One thing I will miss is my neighbors' insane expenditure of Christmas energy, and the glee and irony it seems to inspire not just in my family but in everyone it touches, and that number is far greater than I would have guessed. Since we Tucsonans are a private bunch, we have to find our moments of community. This makes the rare moments where we all feel connected—as if we know each other and understand some aspect of each other's lives, and so we hold each other, whether in grief or fear or mourning—feel crucially alive. January 8, 2011, was one such moment.

Tragedy will do that, as you understand: it illuminates our likenesses and minimizes the rest.

From the new house, if we trimmed the gnarly mesquite, we would be able to see the old one in the valley below. Most of the year I believe there would not be so much to see, but from Thanksgiving through Christmas I'll think differently.

The foothills being a fancy place, a place of decorum and a dearth of yard ornaments, I wonder what they will think of my monument, because come Christmastime it will sure as hell be going up.

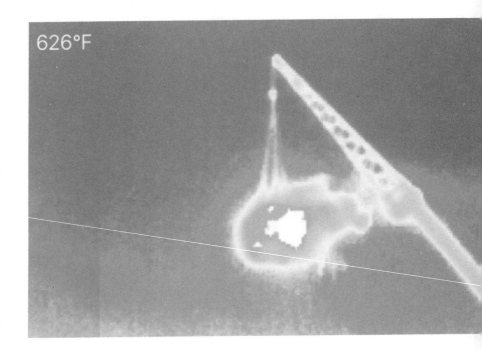

The Crane,
the Urn

And here I am after all on my own watching thousands of people dressed up like the dead walk to discharge their memories. As they exit the stage, their part in the procession done, I film them with my infrared camera. The makeup on their faces is skeletal and looks skeletal in infrared too. Some tote shadowboxes of photographs of their loved ones gone. Others push or pull wagons holding homemade altars. It is not silent, but almost no one talks. It is beautiful, I want to tell you, so I do.

About fifty feet in front of me I see the urn, now just a receptacle but soon to be a star, lit from within (an LED? I wonder), and guarded by a guy with a wizardy look, though I'm sure he's not supposed to be a wizard, just right of the stage. Women in fucked-up bridal gowns and haloed in lights wait backstage and talk to one another. A crane towers over everything. I see a loop of photos of the dead projected on the side of a building across a parking lot. If it's spectacle I wanted, it's spectacle I got. Or will get soon, I'm pretty sure. We are waiting now.

Through the infrared we are all traces of heat. I love its flattening effect, how easily we become data. Here we see the heat of exposed, unmasked skin. Everything else is not. My camera makes a familiar mandibular clicking sound.

The walkers have all finished their procession now.

Two figures begin to slowly ascend the scaffolding, one on each side of the stage. They settle on either side of the frame maybe fifty feet in the air. A group of dancers in some of tribal-looking gear takes the stage as a drum loop pounds.

I keep expecting something to start but it's all just buildup still. I go to grab a beer in an adjacent structure. I give some money to a woman on a huge tricycle and some skeletons on stilts: the procession's official (ha ha) ghost buskers. I gape a little. The stilts freak me out, which is, of course, the point. Here we are to be unfamiliar things, not to look hot or pick each other up or to reassure ourselves about our youth. If we're showing off I don't think we're showing off for those who have eyes to see. We're looking at each other but what we're seeing is something else.

Even the city no longer feels like itself to me, or maybe it's most itself. I'm reminded for a moment of my favorite Guy Maddin film, *My Winnipeg*, a kind-of documentary about his hometown and his family, both of which he mythologizes over and over to the point where you're really not sure what you should believe about Winnipeg anymore. Dozens of horses get frozen in lakes: it's historical or maybe it's not. The film proposes that the city harbors secret roads and alleyways, known only to locals, where they can go and traverse the streets without being seen by visitors. Probably this is a fiction, but it's a powerful one. I choose to believe that a chance remains it's a truth only locals know.

And here we are, we locals, we painted, grieving, fucked-up bunch of weirdos. And here we are, citizens, some of us who only came to party or watch something burn, and some of us to walk and set some part of ourselves free.

Maybe that's making too much of it, I think, but then I turn to see two giant jets of flame shoot up into the air and that thought gets cut off. I finish my beer and return to my post just off the stage.

A southern Arizona band I later learn is called XIXA takes the stage to flame and cheers. They're playing something hypnotic and southwestern that I can't identify and isn't on any of their albums (I'll buy them all in the week after to see). I stare there at the urn as the band plays on.

On either side of the stage, a metal tower holds a cradle. Each cradle cups a flame that shoots jets of fire.

The urn-guarding wizard escorts it to the hoisting point, and the crane picks up the urn to cheers. It slowly hauls the urn a hundred feet into the air. From here through the infrared the urn looks like nothing so much as an eight-foot-diameter twenty-sided die spinning slowly in the sky. It is like a moon. It takes whatever we put into it and shines it all back.

First the crane dangles the urn and then almost settles it into the cradle closest to me, asking for the flame. Of course it was a tease, I think, as it spins away and across the stage, moving toward the other side. My cradle flares and spits a fire jet into the night, as if in jealousy. XIXA plays. A sea of faces stares up at it. I stare at it too. Lowering, it teases the other cradle before it pulls out and hangs suspended above the center of the stage, where it sways slowly down.

It takes a solid minute for it to come close enough to touch or be touched again. I realize I'm holding my breath as it comes down.

A man is there with a flare held out to start the fire, and he waves it back and forth underneath. It lights.

A cheer goes up as it begins its ascent. The heat sensor on the camera suddenly spikes to 400 degrees. I had no idea it even went that high. Then it climbs higher. It takes longer than you'd think for the urn to fully catch flame, and then it's raised back up into the sky above all of us and there it burns, burns, burns, burns, burns.

It's sure something to watch. The video I'm taking now might convey an impression, but for me it's a diminished thing and is only good to cue the feeling in me later; it doesn't come close to capturing what it is like to be there in the crowd watching our stories burn.

The camera reads 626 degrees Fahrenheit, which is, I suspect, as hot a reading as it will ever give. I have a memory of pulling my portable GPS out on a cross-country flight and, opening it up, wondering a bit if I was somehow interfering with the plane's avionics, in order to gleefully register our velocity at over four hundred miles an hour, not that you'd ever feel like that from inside the plane. It's as if I wanted independent proof. I know that when the pilot tells me our velocity I do believe it, but I never quite feel it the way I expect to. I've always been this way: I learn only by doing, or by fucking up. Only once I measure it or am burned does it become real.

The song keeps rising for another seven minutes as we watch the burning urn. The acrobats are turning in the air on their drapes. I watch the temperature flicker between 588 and 626 again.

And then suddenly the progression shifts, and turns. In another minute the song ends. Something has passed, though I couldn't tell you what it is.

A family—or are they friends?—regardless, they are here together—we are here together—I mean, they pose for selfies and a group shot. I point my camera at them to measure their collective heat and register their delight. Here I am some kind of instrument.

Thousands of messages to the dead are all still burning up in the air.

A minute passes, and then another.

It's getting colder. The infrared tells me the air around us is 55 degrees, and I see that my corner of the crowd is suddenly dancing. Through the lens I watch their heat signatures sway, and so I sway a little too. How could I not? When I move the camera fast, the bodies blur into one whole mass of undifferentiated heat. When I keep it still we separate, and even if I can't make out our faces, I can tell who we are.

Notes and Acknowledgments

Some of these essays have appeared elsewhere, often in substantially different forms:

— "American Renaissance," in the *Los Angeles Review of Books*
— "Exchange Rate," in the *Gettysburg Review*
— "The Exhibit Will Be So Marked," "The Sadnesses of March,"
   and "Uncharitable Thoughts on Dokken," in the *Normal School*
— "Facing the Monolith," in *Ecotone*
— "I in River" in *Passages North*, reprinted in *Ground | Water*,
   edited by Ellen McMahon, Ander Monson, and Beth Weinstein
— "Long Live the Jart, Heavy and Pointed and Gleaming," in *Defunct*
— "My Monument," in *True Story*
— "Remainder," in *Territory*

"The Exhibit Will Be So Marked" also appeared in *The Best American Essays 2015*, edited by Cheryl Strayed, and was reprinted in *The Normal School First Ten Years* anthology.

If you'd like to watch the video mentioned in "Five-Star Review of a Safeway," find it here: https://www.youtube.com/watch?v=D4rbuaA3nhg.

Thanks to those who read and talked about and contributed to parts of this book, especially Megan Campbell. Thanks to our many March Xness co-conspirators. Thanks to: Ellen McMahon and Beth Weinstein; Terry Monson and Paula Jacobs, for parenting, support, material, and fact-checking and gap-filling in "Remainder"; Pam Simon; Rob Young; Matt Vadnais; Daniel Sullivan; Mary-Frances O'Connor; Evan Kindley; Jon Reinhardt and Clint McCall; Rachel Rubin; Paul Weir; Paul Hurh;

234 Jake Adam York; Rebecca Lindenberg and Craig Arnold; Nicole Walker; Steven Church; Cheryl Strayed; Alicia Holmes; Robbee and Andy Robinson; and Christopher Schaberg. To Jacqueline Ko and Katie Dublinski for their shepherding of this book to light. To Manuel Muñoz and Aurelie Sheehan, fellow travelers and readers of this work. And to Athena, the boss: Rednex forever!

ANDER MONSON is the author of eight books: four of nonfiction (*Neck Deep and Other Predicaments*, *Vanishing Point*, *Letter to a Future Lover*, and *I Will Take the Answer*), two poetry collections (*Vacationland* and *The Available World*), and two books of fiction (*Other Electricities* and *The Gnome Stories*). A finalist for the New York Public Library Young Lions Award (for *Other Electricities*) and a National Book Critics Circle in criticism (for *Vanishing Point*), he is also a recipient of a number of other prizes: a Howard Foundation Fellowship, the Graywolf Press Nonfiction Prize, the Annie Dillard Award for Nonfiction, the Great Lakes Colleges New Writers Award in Nonfiction, and a Guggenheim Fellowship. He edits the magazine *DIAGRAM* (thediagram.com), the New Michigan Press, *Essay Daily* (essaydaily.org), and a series of yearly literary/music tournaments: March Sadness (2016), March Fadness (2017), March Shredness (2018), March Vladness (2019), and March Badness (2020).

The text of *I Will Take the Answer* is set in Clerface. Book design by Ann Sudmeier. Composition by Bookmobile Design and Digital Publisher Services, Minneapolis, Minnesota. Manufactured by Sheridan on acid-free, 30 percent postconsumer wastepaper.